THE TEACHER'S GIFT

THE TEACHER'S GIFT:

Discovering and Using your
CORE GIFT to Inspire and Heal

Bruce Anderson

ISLAND PRESS
VASHON ISLAND, WASHINGTON

Comments and inquiries regarding this book may be sent to the author at www.communityactivators.com

ISBN-10: 0-9773877-0-4
ISBN-13: 978-0-9773877-0-0
Library of Congress Control Number: 2005909257

Published by:
Island Press
28321 Vashon Highway S.W.
Vashon, Washington 98070

Book Layout and Design:
Natfly Productions

Cover Art:
DRG94253 #259 Heart Tree, 1996
(gold leaf, oil and varnish on canvas)
by Lane, Tony (b.1949) Private Collection.
Dreamtime Gallery, London

Back Cover Photo:
Martin Koenig

More information about CORE GIFTS and other related topics may be obtained by visiting www.communityactivators.com

Bruce Anderson is available for seminars and speaking engagements through www.communityactivators.com or by contacting Community Activators at (206) 463-3666.

This book is available for purchase at www.communityactivators.com and also through bookstores, Amazon.com and Barnesandnoble.com. You may also order it directly, 24 hours a day, by calling 1-800-594-8766.

Body text font: Berkeley Oldstyle Book, 11 pt.

This book is dedicated to my children, Bria and Izak.
Your father spent much of his life unaware of his gifts.
May you discover yours early, find unexpected delight,
and prosper through giving them.

ACKNOWLEDGMENTS

A book about giving gifts, if it does nothing else, should acknowledge the gifts which made the book possible. Over the past twenty years, seven teachers appeared in my life—in exactly the right order and with precise timing—to offer me guidance about core gifts and their usefulness.

John O'Brien and *Connie Lyle-O'Brien* introduced me to the foundational concepts of valued and devalued citizens, and the severity of devastation that occurs in a person's life when they are not given an opportunity to contribute and be seen as worthy by others.

Mary McGovern, just about the time I thought these ideas could be contained within logical theory, re-ignited my spiritual life in the hallway of a convent and caused me to both widen and deepen my understanding.

Tom Mosgaller was the first person in my life to call me a leader. He saw something in me that I could not see in myself, and encouraged me forward when I was evaluating whether or not to walk away from these ideas because of the internal and external turmoil they were causing in my life.

John McKnight, at a time I thought gifts were only about personal development, instructed me about reciprocity—communities are best designed using gift exchange as the basic commodity, and individuals become citizens only when they have received a welcoming from their community for their gifts.

Parker Palmer came next into my life to help me blend ideas about gifts within the immense and beautiful context of welcoming, and also to help me more fully understand how essential both gifts and welcoming are to the act of teaching and encouraging others forward.

Michael Meade, neighbor, mentor, and friend. He added layer upon layer to my understanding by opening up the world of old stories, wisdom, and cultural traditions about gifts and welcoming. He also appeared as a powerful model of someone who has put these ideas together and to good use in the world. He caused me, for better and for worse, to take a stand. This book is one of the many results of his influence.

To my wife and working partner, Gina Anderson. Most of what I have discovered about gifts has been while teaching alongside you or as a result of your encouragement, and I am certain this has not been accidental. Our gifts are conspiring to push us further down our path.

I continue to extend gratitude to the five teachers who gathered to create the dialogue that appears in this book. They took a risk—many of them not knowing each other—to share their lives and love for the craft of teaching in a way that expanded the ideas in this book. They are Brian Anderson, Chris Heimrel, Catherine Johnson, Renae Taylor, and Roger Taylor.

In addition: Dottie Adams, John Allen, Orland Bishop, Roger Brobst, Chris Carter, Joyce Duran, Bobbi Emel, Charles Hopkins, Joy Eason Hopkins, David Pitonyak, Pat Puckett, Jack Kornfield, Dee Lemonds, Vince Mandela, Robert Moody, Beth Mount, Malidoma Somé, and Lee Valenta. Also, the courageous staff at seven publicly-funded mental health centers in California and Washington who helped me expand my vision by pioneering the idea of giftedness with the most discarded citizens in their neighborhoods—those carrying the labels of mental illness and homelessness: In California, the Village, a program of the Mental Health Association of Los Angeles; Kern County Mental Health in Bakersfield; Home Center in Fresno; Stanislaus County Behavioral Health and Recovery Services and the Telecare program in Modesto; and Contra Costa County Mental Health in Martinez. In Washington, the Clark County Youth House and Youth Commission in Vancouver.

TABLE OF CONTENTS

The Interior Life of the Teacher

The Teacher-Student Relationship

V. YOUR TURN: FINDING YOUR CORE GIFT

INTRODUCTION

There is a crack in everything.
That's how the light gets in.

LEONARD COHEN[1]

Do you know what your core gift is? If you do, according to cultures from all over the world, you have access to a powerful tool to increase both your success and satisfaction as a teacher. This book is written for any person who is in a position to guide others, including teachers, mentors, and other helping professionals working with both young and old in all kinds of environments including traditional classrooms, community centers and neighborhoods, corporate training rooms, social service centers, therapy offices, and spiritual settings. Its purpose is to answer three primary questions about core gifts from the vantage point of teaching:

What is a core gift?
How can I identify my core gift?
How can knowing and using my core gift help me to be a better teacher?

Relying on a multicultural foundation, this book explores and brings to life the old idea that each human being has a distinct and primary pur-

---

1. Cohen, Leonard. *Anthem*, from *The Future*. Sony/ATV Music Publishing Canada. 1992

pose to his or her life. When we have precisely named this purpose, we can act more powerfully in our daily life. Far from being limiting or holding us to doing one thing, your core gift can be used to strengthen your ability to make decisions and act powerfully in all aspects of your life. In addition to your core gift helping you know more about what to do, you can also become more aware of what not to do, which can save you from going down roads you are not meant to travel. More than simply a vague and "interesting, but not practical" idea, core gifts have been used for centuries by individuals all over the world to find purposeful life, navigate difficult times, and locate deep joy and peacefulness. This book is specifically tailored to the ways teachers can use their core gifts to increase their satisfaction and skills while teaching.

Two years ago, I was relaxing in a sauna with a teacher of mine telling him a story about a moment I learned something significant about the power of core gifts. When I got done with the story, he looked up from the beads of sweat forming on his legs and said, "You have to write that down." I knew in the moment that he was right, but had little confidence I could write something others would want to read.

During high school, I was proud of having gotten away with two things—avoiding physical education classes because of a serious multi-year illness, and having the unexpected good fortune of receiving a passing grade in English my senior year, though I did little to earn it. Forty years later, I am fully realizing the fallout from both of those choices. Throughout my life, I never once dreamed of being a "writer." I struggle writing a page for hours when I suspect others would have long ago finished and gone on. I admire my friends who write "for a living," and have always suspected they possessed intelligence far greater than mine.

I can tell you this from repeated personal experience—all the incompetence you possess, whether it is real or imagined, cannot stand up to the compelling urge to give your core gift once you realize what you must do. I am quite certain it is no accident, but instead an act of supreme grace, that our core gifts are not as concerned with competency as much as commitment. People, young and old, are often calmed and find renewed confidence when I remind them that "you don't have to be good at giving your gift." Your core gift instructs you in what you must do, and understands that over time you will get good at it. Your core gift has its eye on something much larger than whether or not you are competent in a given moment in your life—it is calling you to go in a specific direction. It has the patience to wait for you to find the path, and generously rewards those who do. Later on in this book it says:

> "...Each of us has a specific thing we are supposed to be doing. When we rise up, after bending down and picking up our load, we find ourselves pointed towards the path that reveals our place in the world—where we can give our core gift, find the trouble we were meant to encounter, and where opportunities to heal from suffering lie waiting for our arrival."

Teaching is just one of the many ways that your core gift shows up in your life. Once you know your core gift, you will be able to see how you keep coming back to it for help, both inside and outside your life as a teacher. You will think back to younger years and see how powerful its influence has been in your life. You may laugh or you may cry as you reflect back and realize how giving this gift too much or too little has gotten you into much of the trouble you have found in your life. Most of all, I hope after reading this book you will look forward to, and actively welcome, your core gift as it follows you into your later life, whatever path you choose.

If any part of the integrity of teaching requires us to model that which we believe in, then reawakening our commitment to gifts, and providing a living example of the power of gifts in our own teaching style, is one step we can take to shift the tide back towards a richer and more useful definition of giftedness. It is unlikely that educational and social service systems will reclaim a fuller meaning of giftedness with students until teachers can speak with clarity about their own core gifts, use them purposefully when they teach, and discuss the impact with other teachers and students. We are the place to begin.

How this book is organized

If the core gift idea is new to you, or you are unsure how a core gift is different from your other abilities, this book will help you make those distinctions. The first part of the book defines the differences between skills, talents, gifts, and core gifts, and gives a brief history of the gift idea—how it was used in older times and how it disappeared from modern life. The first part of the book also connects the ideas of teaching, gifts, and mentoring, by describing a powerful learning phenomenon called "second-level learning" which results when teachers are aware of and use their core gift while teaching.

The middle part of the book describes six benefits that can result when teachers pursue and use the core gift idea. The benefits are described in detail, and are accompanied by reflection questions to help teachers more fully understand how core gifts can influence their individual teaching style. Each benefit is also followed by a dialogue with five teachers who describe how that benefit relates to their life as a teacher. Representatives from elementary and high school, college, social service environments where teaching and mentoring are actively encouraged, and corporate training are included.

If you want to identify your core gift for the first time, or already know the general nature of your core gift but want to more accurately describe or understand it, the last section of the book includes a comprehensive method. Included in the explanation of the process are tips to help make it go smoothly, as well as specific examples of common pitfalls in core gift identification and how others have overcome them. The process includes instructions for developing a powerful core gift statement, making it easy for you to use and others to understand.

I. LOST AND FOUND: GIVING GIFTS A FOOTHOLD IN OUR LIVES

---

1. A TEACHER FINDS TROUBLE

I am grateful that, as I have gotten older, saying I am a teacher has become easier and more comfortable to say. The ease does not come from having settled into a profession I have mastered, but from one of the grand permissions that comes with age if we allow it—the blending of what you have done, and what you still intend to do, into a larger framework which does not use time or competency as its primary measurements of success. Rather, the measurement of success and the comfort comes from having answered, at least partially, the fundamental question we all have: "Who am I?" I know that I am a teacher—past, present, and future. It is as basic a fact about me as the color of my thinning hair.

My first employment as a teacher came as the result of what I thought was a mean-spirited whim on the part of the professor in charge of connecting graduating college seniors with potential teaching jobs. His observation of me as a student teacher in a local high school had been sufficient for him to decide that it would be best to exile me to the most remote school possible where I could do the least damage to the fewest students. He connected me with the superintendent of a village school district in a remote part of Alaska where, after a fifteen-minute phone interview, I was hired to teach high school. At the time, I thought the short interview was an indicator of my powerful interviewing skills. I later came to believe that I was the only applicant.

In the beginning, life as a schoolteacher in Alaska was everything I hoped it would be. I was in a classroom teaching subjects I loved to a handful of friendly and agreeable students; the townspeople were welcoming; and I was able to go out fishing each day after school. How could it get any better? It didn't. I can't say exactly when things started to go wrong, but go wrong they did. There were no disasters in the classroom, no cataclysmic events that plummeted me to despair. There was a fate much worse waiting for me—a persistent, sinking feeling in my gut telling me that, slowly but surely, the students were moving away from me and the subjects I was teaching. After one year I quit, convinced I was ill equipped to be a teacher. As I walked out of the classroom on the last day I didn't look back, and no one encouraged me to stay.

What I needed more than anything else that first year was another teacher who could help me discover more of who I was by helping me figure out why my teaching methods weren't working. Rather than trying to regain my confidence by running from trouble, I needed someone to nudge me further into the depths of my difficulty, asking me questions such as "How is this situation like other difficult times you have encountered? What is the opportunity for learning and healing facing you now? How can you use your skills, talents, and gifts to navigate in this situation?" However, full of pride and not wanting the principal to know just how badly it was going, I struggled to be successful by hunkering down and trying not to be noticed. Looking back, I can clearly see the four strategies I began to use as the students became more and more distant from me. I used these strategies interchangeably and, as my efforts got more desperate, I seemed to switch between them by the hour. I offer them in this story for two reasons. First, I have discovered they are more commonly used in the profession of teaching than we, as teachers, may want to admit. Second, I have found these strategies are the ones I still fall back on when I have forgotten who I am, failed to rely on my talents and core gift, and wavered from my commitment to being an authentic teacher.

My first strategy was to remind myself that I had organized the curriculum in such a concise and logical way that any student could learn it. The hours spent reviewing and selecting materials, the repeated evenings spent deciding which activities would be just right in order to propel the students into an activated state of learning and comprehension—it had all been worth it. The learning design was unmistakably brilliant. Far from being beneficial to the students, using this strategy was entirely self-serving because it allowed me to blame the students for any lack of comprehension or motivation.

Since it was the students' fault if they weren't learning, it was logical and permissible to move immediately to my second strategy—go over the material repeatedly, using the same format, until the students demonstrated comprehension. More is better, and there was certainly nothing wrong with repeating information to students who were either not listening or just needed to be nudged one more time. While this strategy worked on occasion, I could feel the students drifting away through various combinations of boredom, shame, and anger.

When the one-two punch of these strategies didn't work, I became more desperate. Strategy three was to think of teachers I had known and respected, and try and "teach like them." Faced with a difficult classroom situation, I would quickly scan my memory and come up with a teaching technique I had seen another teacher use. I cannot remember a single instance when this strategy worked for me. Although I could recall the outward behavior of the teacher who I was mimicking, I had no idea why he or she had chosen the strategy, how to prepare to use it, or what to do as a next step if it didn't work. Using their strategy left me hopelessly adrift with no idea of how to get my feet back on the ground. In those moments I remember being acutely aware and unnerved by one thing: I had no idea who I really was.

Strategy four was my final and fallback position. When I could think of nothing else, I would appeal to the student as if we were friends. This buddy system of learning, which relied on false befriending through joking and cajoling, was the last step in losing any authority I ever had. My most vivid memory of using this strategy is of a student much larger than myself, who now had my permission to see us as simply friends, throwing me down to the ground and washing my face in the snow and then encouraging other students to climb on top of me. It was the final humiliating blow to my dream of being a teacher. This happened in the spring, and I spent the rest of the year waiting for the last day of school.

Believing I was a trained professional and obviously in an environment where no one appreciated my skills or the importance of getting a good education, I began to look outwards, to the school and the community, to find all the reasons for my failure as a teacher. I did not do the one thing, the only thing, that could have benefited both the students and myself—look within myself for the reasons why I was failing. As embarrassing and laughably unaware as it now sounds, because I had graduated from college and was a certified teacher, it never occurred to me that the problem could be me. The power of my degree had bestowed within me a false authority that shielded me from recognizing how far I was from being in a position of genuine authority as a teacher.

I stayed in that community for almost ten years after I quit teaching—building houses, serving a stint as the mayor, getting married, and finally becoming a commercial fisherman. When my wife tired of very small town life, we moved to a larger city in Alaska. Wanting to volunteer some time, I visited a local social service agency to see if I could help out. After several months, in a string of events that now seem anything but accidental, I became the director of the agency.

I was highly passionate about my new job which, looking back, should have been more curious to me than it was, considering that I had never worked for a social service agency, had no training as a manager, and had no specific knowledge about how to work with the clientele who used our services. Full of enthusiasm, I never questioned the root of it. After about six months on the job, I began to notice that I was tired all the time at work. Exhausted, my enthusiasm waned further with each new day. I started to have trouble sleeping and often found myself in the embarrassing position of falling asleep at my desk without realizing I was doing so. I went to the local physician, who could find nothing wrong with me. He advised me to make a trip to Seattle where I could get more sophisticated testing. I flew to Seattle on three separate occasions, but the specialists were unable to find anything wrong. One of them, having exhausted all the physical possibilities, suggested as I was walking out the door of his office that some of my symptoms could be "from an emotional problem." He advised me to see a psychiatrist or therapist. I remember looking at him and laughing as he made this suggestion, being certain I had no problems that could warrant the need for a psychiatrist. This was the next pivotal time in my life, after my failure as a teacher, that I had the opportunity to look within myself for the answer. Once again, I chose to look the other way. But as my health worsened, and with no other options in sight, I made an appointment to visit the local therapist.

Just halfway into my first visit he helped me understand that my symptoms of extreme tiredness were related to the split position I had put myself in at my new job. On one hand, I was managing an agency that was helping people who were at serious life crossroads to learn more about who they were and gain the courage to make significant changes. I, on the other hand, was insistent that the reason I could be doing this helping work was that my life was put together quite well and I needed no help. This, of course, was a carefully crafted bluff, which took the therapist less than another ten minutes to deconstruct with me. Shell-shocked by this new awareness, I made a mental note to cease and desist making disparaging remarks about the therapeutic profession. By the end of that first visit I understood that my tiredness was the outward result of an inner turbulence coming to the surface that refused to be quieted. A voice inside me was asking, "When are you going to spend time with you?" With each new story I heard about a person our organization helped, this inner voice got louder and more insistent. My body's solution was simply to go to sleep, hoping the voice would be gone when I awoke.

As it turns out, the waking up has involved more than greeting the sunshine of a new day. I have spent the twenty or so years since that visit to the therapist reminding myself, at each turn in the road, that the place to look is within. I am still surprised by how frequently I try to look the other way. On both occasions where I failed to look inward, as a teacher and an agency director, the question that would have been helpful to ask was, and still is, "Who am I?" By "Who am I?" I mean making a genuine appraisal of my current situation by asking and answering three questions. First, how is this current situation connected to other difficult times I have faced? Second, what am I here to learn in this newest example of that recurring thread? Third, how can my core gift and my talents be used to navigate through this situation and how are they standing in the way? An adequate answer to these three questions would have provided me the footing to depend on when I was on unstable ground.

For me, as I face each new challenge at this point in my life, answering the three "Who am I?" questions requires having the courage to cross ground that offers the opportunity to further reveal my gifts and wounds. I know it is ground worth crossing, if only because my pride keeps shouting at me to stop.

2. HELP FROM TWO DIRECTIONS

Which way to look?

There is a story, found in many different cultures with slight variations, about the struggles a young man goes through to prove he is worthy of a woman's hand in marriage. In this variation, a young man wants to marry the King's daughter and, along with it, become a landholder in the village. He goes to meet with the King, who tells the young man that, of course, he can marry his daughter—provided he can endure an entire night on top of the mountain next to the village. The young man is thinking this will be no problem and heads for the door to prepare. Just as he is about to exit, the King says he has neglected to tell him a few of the rules he must abide by. Stopping in his tracks, the young man turns back towards the King and gets the following instruction: "First, you must remove your clothes at the bottom of the mountain, and remain naked the entire night. Second, although the temperature will be freezing, you will not be allowed to build a fire. And last, your mentor will not be allowed to follow you up the mountain and help. If you abide by all of these rules and make it through the night, you will be able to have my daughter's hand in marriage." The young man is slightly shaken by the addition of these rules, but the power of young love blinds him to the difficulty he is about to face. As he goes out the door, he passes his mentor who wishes him well and disappears into the distance.

The young man hikes to the base of the mountain, removes his clothes, and begins to climb. He reaches the top of the mountain and waits for the darkness. Soon, the blackness of night is upon him, and the air becomes penetratingly cold. To his surprise and dismay, wild animals come from the surrounding darkness and begin making fierce noises as they circle him. His body begins to shiver from the freezing air as he turns and turns in a circle trying to make out the shapes of the animals in the blackness surrounding him. In the middle of the night, just when he is about to give up, the young man looks with despair off in the distance and sees a small light, burning brightly, on the top of a neighboring mountain. He knows there are no villages in that direction, and it is unlikely a person would be foolish enough to be hunting in this kind of cold weather. Then it comes to him—this must be a fire that has been started by his mentor. Following the rules exactly, the mentor has not gone up the mountain with the boy. Instead, he has gone up a neighboring mountain and is sending a message to the young man. Throughout the night, the young man stays focused on this light as a source of comfort, courage, and hope. Although the mentor is a mountain away, the young man feels he is no longer alone. This light is the reason he is able to make it through the night and descend the mountain in the morning and eventually get the blessing of the King.

We have all used a light to get through a difficult time in our lives. As our troubles mount, we begin to look all around us for help in easing the pain or solving the problem. The story's light from the nearby mountain represents the direction we often look for help, from a source outside of ourselves. Whether it is the comforting words of a friend, the advice of a co-worker, or the counsel of a helping professional, there are many sources of light available to us. The story is a reminder of the powerful nature of this kind of helping light. But the story is also instructing us, at a deeper level, about a different kind of light—the light that shines within us. Although the mentor set the fire, the fire represents more than the knowledge that the mentor is encouraging the young man to make it through the night. The fire is a reminder to the young man that there is a purpose to his life, a light, that is worth paying attention to and living through the night for. Although in the story this light is far away on the neighboring mountain, it is also possible to think of this light as being far away inside a person. The light represents a vision—a dream we have that is bigger than our current circumstances and is calling to us. It is the light in this kind of distance, the reminder of a purposeful path, which can provide both the knowledge about which direction to move and the courage to take the first steps. This interior light reminds us of our core gift and direction just as the mentor did—not as specific instruction how to live but rather a carefully placed light that causes the student to look that way. It is a reminder to us, during the times when we are most prone to get distracted by fear, hesitance, or muddled thinking, that there is a specific direction which is calling us. There is a next step on the path.

As teachers, we will undoubtedly encounter difficult times, whether because of uncertainty of our commitment to the call of teaching, a difficult student who tests our will and intention, or simply being too tired to think of facing another day. If you did not encounter difficulty today, it is likely you will tomorrow. Although they do not feel like it at the time, these are points of renewal, both small and large, being offered to us as teachers. Most times, these offerings are made during times when suffering has entered our life. We can decide to attempt to avoid or tolerate the pain, or we can decide to look for a pathway through it. If we choose to look for the path forward, which light will we use to help us on our way? The light beamed in our direction by our allies and friends can pull us through these times, but may not always be there. The light that burns within each of us illuminating our core gift, should we choose to look inward, is always available to us. There it is, in just the right spot, giving us a gentle and sometimes not so gentle reminder that there is a fundamental question being asked underneath any trouble we encounter: "Who am I?" It is in the remembering of who we are that our genuine authority can emerge, helping us find the answers to our next steps.

Authentic teaching is teaching which springs from the very core of the teacher. It is teaching which originates from a place of authority that is not based in technique, nor is it the result of simply being a teacher in an environment where there are students. Parker Palmer, in *The Courage to Teach*[2], writes, "Good teaching cannot be reduced to technique. Good teaching comes from the identity and integrity of the teacher. Good teachers have a strong sense of personal identity that infuses their work." Speaking on the other side of this same coin in another of his books, *The Active Life*[3], he

---

2. Palmer, Parker. *The Courage to Teach*. Jossey-Bass. San Fransisco, Ca. 1998. Page 10
3. Palmer, Parker. *The Active Life: A Spirituality of Work, Creativity, and Caring*. Jossey-Bass. San Francisco, Ca. 1990. Page 71

says "...one reason that we sometimes have bad teaching in our schools, teaching that does not touch and transform students, is that teachers are sometimes paralyzed by unexamined fears... If such teachers understood themselves and their fears better, the result might be teaching that comes from within the teachers' self knowledge and that makes learning into a live encounter once more."

Authentic teaching then, relies on the interior authority of the teacher—it declares that each teacher's uniqueness is an essential ingredient for creating an authentic learning environment. This feeds the dream and hope of every teacher—their presence in the lives of students matters.

Looking over my shoulder

Reflecting back on my first year as a teacher, I am not sure that my uniqueness served the learning needs of the students. To be more blunt, I am not sure I mattered much. This awareness spurs me towards questions which engage me in a profound way related to my current and future capabilities as a teacher. What if I had known my core gift and been willing to engage in reflection about how it was both helping and hindering me? Would I have been able to do something other than flee the situation?

At that time, I thought I was quitting teaching because it was the right thing to do. I had convinced myself that I was simply not cut out for the profession. Even though I wanted to be a teacher most of my younger years, even after excelling in college, even after being completely drawn in by the act of helping others learn, even after seeing the look of satisfaction on my parents' faces when I told them I was going to Alaska to teach—in the face of all that I still ditched my dream. At one level, using the evidence of my failures in the classroom, it was the easiest decision I ever made. At another level, I knew I was giving up because it was the easiest thing to do. There were lots of other adventures to be had in that remote Alaskan town, and all of them appeared to be substantially more rewarding than the hole I had dug for myself as a teacher. Perhaps fish, I decided, would not be nearly so difficult as students. I bought a fishing boat only to discover that fish can be considerably more elusive than students. They rarely show up on time, and seemed to find little pleasure in my company. I remember thinking of my mother who, whenever I struggled as a young child, would tell me that life would get easier as I got older. I look back on her comment as a genuine attempt to comfort and console, but also as a not-quite-accurate appraisal of older life.

The wisdom of hindsight tells me that I quit teaching because I didn't have the courage to face the difficulty that would undoubtedly result from an honest appraisal of my situation. How would my experience as a first year teacher have been different if I had known and intentionally acted based on knowledge of my core gift? I have no desire to go back and change the course of my life, but the hindsight provided by age instructs me about how to approach the future. Later in this book, there are chapters that describe the six primary benefits available to teachers who know and use their core gift as part of their teaching strategy:

1. Teachers have an increased level of courage to face difficulties arising in the classroom and surrounding teaching environment.
2. Teachers have a source to continually recharge their energy and hopefulness.
3. Teachers contribute to their own healing and willingness to be compassionate with others.
4. Teachers, by knowing students' gifts, have access to specific strategies to welcome them into the classroom and decrease non-desirable behaviors.
5. Teachers place themselves in a position to be welcomed and respected for who they are rather than for their temporary positional authority.
6. Teachers have an increased ability to recognize and effectively use mentoring/second-level learning moments.

Looking at the list, I can immediately see that at least four of the benefits could have been useful to me during that difficult period in my life.

Being welcomed and respected for who I am. Because I had no other reference point for understanding my authority as a teacher, I relied on my positional authority—I know more than you about the subjects I am teaching and I am standing in the front of the classroom and you are seated in front of me—as the primary source of my power. This combination of superior knowledge and positional authority provided me what I thought would be a solid base for my presence in the classroom. When the students became disinterested in the subject matter and began to see me as someone about their age who was vulnerable to being manipulated, my authority quickly eroded. Every move I made was a futile attempt to regain an authority that they had already decided I would never have. Feeling alone in my struggle at the time, I have since learned that this is the essential nightmare of many beginning teachers.

Being aware of and using my gift could have given me a different base of authority. Rather than seeing myself as being "one up" on the students, both in terms of power and knowledge, I could have approached the students on the basis of the ideas that we were all interested in learning about. By dropping my defensive control posture and talking honestly about the roots of my passion for the topic—how I saw it connected to my gift and how it was serving the purpose of my life—the students could have seen me as a whole person. They could have seen me as someone who, like them, is struggling to make meaning out of everyday life. Once the power struggle is dissipated, a vacuum is created. The students, rather than framing me as someone to conquer, would have needed to find a different purpose for being in the classroom. This shift allows the student to have a larger imagination of the possibilities within the learning environment. Now that I am no longer focused on conquering my opponent, why am I here? What other benefits might there be for me in this environment?

Making students aware of your gift and how it is tied to the subjects being learned also establishes that you are not in the classroom solely to serve other people. You are also there for yourself. This sets up the possibility, which students can immediately feel at an intuitive level, that you are a learner—and you might learn something from them. Now, rather than offering comments and actions designed to disrupt the power balance between teacher and student, the students' contributions become shaped by their current imagination and struggles with the learning topic. One of the great satisfactions of being a learner comes during the moments when you realize you are teaching the teacher. It is as I had hoped—students and teachers in a learning community together, worthy of each other's regard and respect.

Using my gift as a source for recharging my energy and hopefulness. Having fallen into disrepair because of my teaching strategies, I could no longer see the point in continuing. Feeling hopeless, I decided to quit. At the time, my inability to envision a future in which I was a successful teacher had undermined my hopefulness. Hope finds its origins in the belief that a person might be successful as they travel towards a vision, which, to them, is worthy. If I had known my core gift, and recognized the importance of following the threads of that gift through difficult times, I would have been more committed to continuing. Energy is restored, at least in part, by the idea that you are on the path you are supposed to be on.

Another source for recharging my energy could have been the recognition that the difficulty I had found was a significant opportunity for me to learn something about my gift. The detours and difficulties, as painful as they are, are a necessary and rewarding part of the path. How is this current difficulty serving me? With no idea of a larger purpose to the suffering I was experiencing, there was no need to continue. I was only looking for relief.

I left that classroom, believing that the pain was over. What did I do afterwards? I went right out and discovered a new way to get myself into exactly the same kind of trouble in a social service agency! Our psyche, and our core gift, have a way of orienting us towards that which we need to learn. It can be a significant source of hope when a person recognizes the difference between purposeless and purposeful suffering. The trouble we have found may be more than just another difficulty to face down and solve so we can feel good once again. The search for pleasure, and the running from suffering, become less urgent when I remember that there can be deep rewards from intentionally moving towards what is difficult in my life.

Knowing and utilizing students' gifts as a teaching strategy and source of classroom vitality. Not aware of my own gift, or even the idea of gifts, I had no incentive to identify and use the students' gifts as a way of enlivening the learning environment. If I had been attuned to each student, and had been able to discern his or her gifts, I would have had a powerful strategy at my disposal to engage the students. I would have been able to ask each student questions which were tailored to his or her specific talents and core gift, thereby increasing their motivation to learn. Rather than trying to control and maintain order through my position, I would have been able to create and maintain students' engagement based on their genuine interest in being in the classroom. The more I spend time as a teacher, the more I see the immense possibility in this idea.

Remembering my core gift as a source for healing. Gifts, because they are so central to who we are, are often at the root of difficult times we encounter. Unaware of my gift, I blundered through my first year as a teacher, allowing the situation to worsen without useful clues about how to improve it. Not only would knowing my gift have given me more motivation to stick around and figure out my difficulty, it would have given me significant clues about how to problem-solve the situation. Given that my gift is encouraging people to use their imagination to create a new hopefulness, it might have been more curious to me that I had stopped looking for new ideas myself, and had decided the problem was with the students and the community. Where was my interest in new ideas? Where was my fascination with the ideas that were dangerous and part of uncharted territory in my own experience? Where was my hope? Faced with difficulty today, and knowing my core gift, I naturally gravitate towards solutions that don't fit my preconceived assumptions and that often test the limits of my courage. I showed none of this curiosity, and none of this courage, during my struggles as a first year teacher. Looking in the wrong direction—outside of myself—for the source of my troubles, I ran fast and furiously ahead in my life only to find out later that I was running towards the exact same kind of trouble.

3. OLD AND NEW GIFTEDNESS

Why didn't I, as a result of my upbringing and professional training, have the language and practices of gifts to lean into when I found myself in trouble? Over time, schools, social service systems, and the larger communities we all live in have adopted a narrow definition of gifted—it is now used primarily to identify a person who has an extraordinary ability in a certain area. Most of us, when thinking about gifted programs in schools, imagine a room full of students who far outpace other students. Gifted students are at the opposite end of the spectrum from those students assigned to special education who, along with students in standard classrooms, are identified as not being gifted. By using the word gift to define differences in capability, we have turned our attention away from an older and more useful definition of gifted—one which was common to cultures around the world and used to honor and unite community citizens rather than divide and categorize them.

The word gift was originally used to describe the primary contribution a person was bringing to his or her community. A person's gift was most often named as a single general theme or direction, within which the person found specific and practical contributions to make to his or her community. For instance, a person with a gift for healing may be a doctor or spiritual advisor; a person with a gift for seeing how the pieces of things fit together may be a home builder or a manager of projects; a person with a gift for helping others expand their imagination may be a teacher, artist or a mediator; and a person with a gift for working with nature may be a farmer, well digger, or expert in the use of medicinal plants.

Gifts, using this older definition, are not only directed at vocations, but also threaded throughout all aspects of a person's life. For instance, consider John, a person with a gift for working with nature. As a young child, no matter what the weather, he always wanted to be outside playing in the woods. He was the kid who "hated school," but came alive when he found out about the subjects of biology, nature, and science. When it was time to find employment after high school he got a job driving a bulldozer clearing land, but became disenchanted with the noise and exhaust. He went to the local community college to study horticulture and landscaping. After graduating, he got a job working for a landscape design company, but soon quit because there was little opportunity for him to get his hands in the dirt. He married, bought a house, and although the house desperately needed painting, the first weekend he began to improve the yard. Over time, he built a quiet spot with a small fountain in the corner of his yard as a place where he could go to find silence and solitude when he had questions that needed time to think through. Retired after a successful career owning a landscaping company, he began to volunteer his time in front of the grocery store on weekends as a "plant doctor" for the local gardeners club. His final wish? —to be buried and return his body to the earth as a gift for what it had given him. Although John's life was varied and he was pulled in many directions, time and time again he kept finding ways to orient himself to nature. And when he did, he felt on solid ground, both literally and in a way that he described as "feeling satisfied...like I'm doing what I'm supposed to be doing."

Although they are mostly lost traditions in modern cultures today, communities around the world had carefully designed practices for each community member to define, declare, and be honored for their gift, continuously learn about it through mentoring from others with a similar gift, and find opportunities to give it which benefited the community. In this way, each person had a fundamental purpose to their life and communities had a construct by which to declare and utilize the contributions of each citizen.

How did the idea of gifts disappear from the dominant culture in this country? It is possible to track at least four shifts. First, as the earth was colonized by different groups traveling from their homeland to conquer other parts of the world, the patterns and traditions of the conquered peoples slowly dissipated or were driven underground. Local cultural traditions for identifying each person's core gift, which usually happened during the phases of youth initiation, were lost to the conqueror's rules and customs. The natural rhythms of community life, which revolved around a delicate and intertwining balance of nature, spirit, and the gifts of community members, were distorted and interrupted by this forced introduction of other cultures. Furthermore, the common act of taking substantial resources from local peoples and shipping them back to the homeland of the conquerors left a void that made community sustainability difficult. If the trees were robbed for lumber, there was no longer a need for the gifts of a wood craftsman. If the invading culture demanded adherence to their spiritual practices, there was no longer a need for community members with spiritual gifts. No longer able or allowed to depend on the balance of gifts amongst each other, community members were put in a position to adopt the invader's culture.

Second, in the language of industrialized nations, cash economies, and mass production, citizens began to be identified primarily as producers of goods rather than givers of gifts. Individuals became another tool in the chain of events necessary to produce and market products. Like equipment, production laborers became assets when functioning smoothly, and problems to fix when not working properly. In addition, these same producers of goods became seen as consumers of goods. Industrialized economies, depending on the purchase and consumption of goods for their survival, see citizens as the mechanism that both instigates and completes the production/consumption cycle. The giving of gifts is an unnecessary component within this ever-growing framework for how economies and communities function.

Third, as the language of gifts was replaced by the language of production and consumption, civilizations began to reduce the number of citizens identified as gifted, generally reserving the designation for community members seen as having extraordinary ability. Sadly, we began to refer to these few gifted individuals as "geniuses," although the original intention of both the word gift and genius was similar—to describe a capacity which rested, not just in a few, but also in every person. One of the results of this global shift from "gifted" to "producers of goods" has been to allow a generalized permission to see individuals who are part of social service systems as takers and non-producers, therefore having little value to the community and certainly not gifted.

Fourth, science and logic became the model for understanding in the industrial age, decreasing our commitment to using spiritual explanations for "why things are as they are." Within this new framework, Newton's idea that everything can be broken down into separate parts and analyzed pushed us towards the idea that humans are like machines. In the machine age, what you can't yet fully understand is simply a matter for further scientific research. Also within the industrial age, Darwin's "survival of the fittest" idea came along. Genetics interacts with environment to determine the evolution of a species. It can all be explained by the science of genes and environment. This idea, again, pushed us towards a view of humans that is scientific and logical rather than spiritually oriented. Thus, the blank slate, or tabula rasa, idea took further hold. Humans start as a blank or erased slate at birth and are filled up by experience. If you want to explain a human, simply tell the story of their birth, and all subsequent stories up until their most current action, and you have a complete description of who they are. The dangerous underpinning to this idea is that you start at "zero," a blank slate. The idea of gifts provides a contradictory view—humans do not start out as a blank slate. Each person is given a gift from spirit, and this gift is present at the beginning of life. This transition from gifted to blank slate puts humans in the position of believing they have to earn all of their capacity through hard work and skill building, removes the spiritual component to capacity, and gives us permission to see community members who have not-yet-discovered or hidden gifts as "empty" and not useful to our community.

These four cultural patterns, along with others, have put us in a position of having to reclaim the idea of gifts. Because we no longer have youth initiation practices as a primary and traditional venue for the gift discovery process, we are left with having to use radical measures to adapt this essential idea and give it a foothold back in the culture. Where do we start? Education and social service systems, because they are working with community members who are trying to learn more about themselves and develop skills that lead towards community contribution, are natural places to reclaim the idea of gifts. However, by promoting the exceptional ability definition of gifted, educators and other helping professionals have become a partner in the modern cultural tradition of labeling and dividing

citizens. When we believe there are have-nots—those without much to offer and who are a burden to us—we have forgotten the most basic premise
of gifts: every person has something to contribute.

Forgetting this has caused extraordinary damage to our collective culture's willingness and ability to welcome every person and find a place for
their contribution. We have changed our focus from believing everyone
has something to contribute towards a culture which is becoming increasingly concerned with the questions, "Who's not doing enough?," "Who
is taking advantage of me?" and "Who is ahead of me and who is behind
me?" These three questions take us away from our heart and point us in-
wards towards the selfish and needy parts of ourselves that seek fulfillment
through believing that others are less than we are. However, when we are
certain of our core gift and have been welcomed for it, we can feel a wholeness inside ourselves and an acceptance from others that makes us less interested in becoming one of the haves by pointing out the unstable ground
that others are standing on. Knowing our core gift draws us towards a
more compassionate approach to others, where we find the stranger on
our doorstep not dangerous, but a gift waiting to be understood, valued,
and included.

A director of social service programs in a large county in Washington
State told me recently that he was shocked to learn that roughly a third of
the school-age children in his county were placed in specialized programs
of some kind: gifted, developmental disability, psychiatric disability, learning disabled, after school detention, probation, pregnant mothers, high
risk for school dropout, and remedial topics, just to name a few. Although
these programs are always created with an intention to offer an environment and curriculum which increase learning success rates, it may be that
the more powerful outcome for gifted and ungifted students alike is the
feeling of being unwelcome with their peers in the general school community. Is this education at the expense of a division that creates isolation
and alienation—firmly embedding the idea of haves and have-nots in the
minds of children eagerly trying to find acceptance and love? I remember reading a research study done with hundreds of elementary students
about their fears. The number one fear of students in that age group was
the death or loss of a parent. The number two fear was being put in special education. This is a powerful reminder of students' yearning to be
included in and valued by the general school community.

Currently, with the emphasis more towards measuring students against a standard than on bringing out each student's individual gifts, we are in the midst of a massive national effort in the United States to institutionalize standardized testing. In social services, the unprecedented need for money, housing, food, and employment often mask the underlying intensity of a person's need for healing and identification of their worth and value to themselves and others. Both of these modern institutional focuses take us yet one step further away from a common culture that values and promotes the unique gifts of each unique student.

What will it take to reinvigorate and utilize the original meaning of giftedness within the routines and rituals of schools and other helping professions? First, a clear remembering of the idea in all its beauty and richness so we can once again be drawn towards committing ourselves to its practices. Second, it will be necessary for individual teachers and helping professionals to identify their gifts and be able to talk fluently about how the idea is useful, both in their own lives and as part of their teaching and helping strategies. And third, for those of us in positions of influence as teachers, mentors, and helping professionals, to actively help others identify and more fully use their gifts as a primary tool for moving forward in the world. The next chapter begins the focus in these three areas.

II. UNDERSTANDING THE LIGHT IN THE DISTANCE

4. WHAT IS A CORE GIFT?

When we go back to reclaim older, and more useful, meanings of gift, there are many forks in the road. What is a gift? Does a person have one gift or many gifts? Do gifts, in any way, describe an extraordinary capability? Where do gifts come from? Depending on which cultural, psychological, or spiritual interpretation you use, there are wide-ranging answers to these questions. Gifts are variously described as the contributions a person makes, capacities given from spirit to a person, the outcome of a situation in a person's life, contributions we are obligated to give, the descriptor of a path we are meant to follow, and as the reciprocal affirmation of love between spirit and humans. In oral and written story, gifts are often referenced within several contexts in the same story.

For the purposes of this book, and for specific reasons related to understanding gifts within the context of helping and healing work, I have chosen to use a framework which says humans have many skills, talents, and gifts, and there is one specific gift in each person which is their core gift.

I am calling it the core gift because it is the central and innermost contribution a person desires to make (gift) to the world. And also core gift because the old roots of the word *core* can be traced to both the words courage and heart. *Your core gift, then, is the central and innermost contribution that will require both courage and heart for you to bring to the world.* Within this paradigm, a person's core gift does not necessarily have an extraordinary level of capacity, in terms of being "better than another person at it", as an essential component. The remainder of this chapter describes the "one core gift" paradigm I have chosen and the reasoning behind the choice.

That I have chosen a specific orientation to gifts does not preclude other variations and uses. It would be a mistake to further the damage that has been done to the word by its current limited usage in the world of industrialized nations and, in particular, social services and education. My enthusiasm for the idea of gifts, at least partially, lies in its expansiveness and mystery. My intent is to explore one path of meaning in the hope of reclaiming some of its beauty and richness.

A word of caution: If you are a teacher, your core gift is not "being a teacher." This statement confuses many teachers, particularly if they have made a deep commitment to the craft of helping others learn and see it as the primary purpose of their life. This book helps to clarify one of the most misunderstood aspects of core gifts. I often hear teachers claim their core gift is teaching. In the same vein, social service employees often claim their core gift is "helping others." Good teaching and good social work involve using many different skills, talents, and gifts which, when taken as a whole, result in good work being done. But core gifts are more specific, and have a precise nature to them. There is one very specific ability within the act of teaching to which you are drawn more than all the rest. That ability is your core gift. It could be helping others to expand their imagination. Maybe it is creating a welcoming and safe place for people to learn. Perhaps it is helping others to put a logical sequence to complex ideas. Or could it be helping people to discover the truth? The possibilities are many, and the idea of core gifts instructs us that each teacher is attracted to and insatiably curious about one particular attribute within the practice of being a teacher. Do you know what that specific attribute is for you?

Four levels of capacity

One way to categorize capacity in humans, beyond instinctual response, divides our actions into four types—skills, talents, gifts, and a core gift. Each action that I make in the world, whether it is internal (thinking) or external (swinging an axe), can be placed in one of these four categories.

A capacity that, for myself, I place in one category will often be in another category for another person. For instance, for me, driving a car is a skill. For others, driving a car is a talent. For me, discerning the emotional truth in a situation is part of my core gift. For others, discerning the emotional truth is a skill used as a necessary part of compassionate listening. We determine in which category a capacity rests by considering our experience in learning and giving it. Starting with skill and working our way towards our core gift, each level builds on the capacity in the level preceding it.

Skills

The most common and prolific of all our abilities, our skills are in use throughout the course of our daily life. A skill is defined as:

1. A thinking process or action which you had to learn how to do. More than instinct, the capacity did not erupt out of spontaneous combustion. The learning may have taken a few seconds or a few years to accomplish, but there was learning necessary for competency to occur.

2. The desire to perform the skill comes from the necessity to get through life, not from a deep sense of joyfulness or fulfillment. You may get deep satisfaction during performance or upon completion of the task, but the original desire rests in a simple necessity to get through the tasks necessary to complete the day as you have planned it (or not planned it).

Talents

Talents are the second level of capacity. Talents are fewer in number, and can be defined by the following attributes:

1. Like skills, you learn how to perform a talent. All action, beyond simple instinct, requires some level of learning.

2. You have a natural ability or knack for it. You notice that it was, unlike some of your skills, easy for you to learn and you felt a sense of joy and fullness during the learning process. Some people say they feel like they were "born to do this." If you were learning it with other people, you may have noticed you picked it up faster than the others. During the learning, you noticed it "made sense" to you. Unlike some of your skills that required repeated attempts to be proficient at, your talents seemed to come easily, even if they took extensive time to learn.

3. The desire to perform a talent comes from an intrinsic sense of joy and fulfillment. When we see the opportunity to give a talent, we feel a sense of urgency and attraction towards the opportunity. Although it may not be easy to do, we don't see it as a burden. While talents can often be necessary to give in order for us to get through our daily life, they are different than skills in that they produce a feeling of joy and satisfaction that is beyond the feeling of simply "being successful at it and getting it done."

Gifts

Gifts are the third level of capacity. Our gifts contain the same attributes as our talents, but have one additional feature which puts them in the gift category.

1. A gift is a talent which has been initiated or further developed in order to get through a difficult life experience. Because you have had to develop this ability in the midst of a suffering event, you place a particular importance on it and connect it to your own healing. In future circumstances where you believe this gift could be useful to you or others, you feel compelled to give it.

Core Gift

A core gift is the fourth level of capacity. Each of us has only one. Like our gifts, our core gift has all the attributes of our talents. A core gift is distinguished from other gifts by one attribute:

1. A core gift is the talent which has been initiated or further developed as a result of your *most difficult* life experience. It is, in a very precise way, the healing force and antidote to however your psyche[4] has framed the most serious suffering you have known. In many cases, this gift is what we wish we could have gotten from others—or been able to give to ourselves—during this difficult

---

4. In this discussion, the orientation to psyche is spiritual—the wound is intentionally designed by Spirit to produce an elevated motivation in the person to discover and give their core gift. The construct for a different orientation to psyche—the mind being the center of thought—can also be used by saying the mind has made a list of all the suffering a person has experienced, has prioritized that list, and put one item on top. Using either orientation, the end point is the same—one wound has been determined to have an elevated focus above others.

time. This suffering may have been a one–time occurrence, or may be the result of repeated experiences. For most of us, the initial event happens during our youth, and there is a recurring thread of this same suffering that continues to appear throughout our life, almost as if it is there to remind us of, strengthen, and urge us to give our core gift. Like your other gifts, when faced with a difficult situation—even though afraid—you are still compelled from a deep place within you to act.

The precision of suffering and gifts

This last component of the core gift, that it is the healing force to our largest suffering, is the characteristic that supports the idea that there is only one core gift in each of us. Because our psyche has framed one primary suffering, we have developed one primary solution as the counterbalance and antidote to it. This does not mean that we have experienced only one difficult life experience—we should be so lucky! It simply means each of us can identify one kind of suffering which we have placed in an elevated status to all the other difficulties we have faced.

If you can imagine your psyche making a list of all the difficulties you have faced in your life and then prioritizing that list, the one at the top of the list has been the most difficult. In the language of gifts, this suffering is called "the wound," and the resulting paradigm is referred to as "one gift, one wound." Because the relationship between our core gift and our wound is the only distinction between our core gift and our other gifts, it bears some examples and further explanation.

The most important characteristic to pay attention to when defining your primary suffering is that your psyche has framed your situation in a very particular way and developed one primary healing antidote or solution. By your psyche framing your suffering, I mean this: In this situation, there was a part of the experience that was more difficult for you than other parts. Your psyche identified this difficulty, and responded by naming it as the primary source of pain. Others who experience what appears—on the surface—to be the same kind of difficulty may frame their suffering in a different kind of way, which results in a different conclusion about what would get rid of the pain. This is a critical distinction, because it is the mechanism that causes the precise nature of the attraction towards a person's core gift.

For instance, consider Mary, who grew up in a home with parents who were alcoholics and fought constantly. She would sit in her bedroom, listening to them fighting, and hope for the day when her parents would make peace with each other. Because they were alcoholics, they were undependable at many times, and Mary learned to fend for herself, believing she could only depend on herself. The chaos was rampant. Mary adjusted to the messiness of life in her family by keeping her room extraordinarily tidy. For Mary, only one thing really mattered—she just wanted her parents to be peaceful and stop fighting.

Now, consider Tom. Tom grew up in a family very similar to Mary's. His parents were alcoholics and fought constantly. Tom would sit in his room and listen to them fight, wishing for the day when the yelling would stop. They were undependable and seemed uninterested in Tom. As a result, Tom had to make decisions for himself. He found solace in his room, which he kept extraordinarily tidy—his desk was spotless and the clothes in his drawers were lined up in neat piles. On the surface, Tom's life in his family was remarkably similar to Mary's. Both children experienced fighting, undependable parents, and chaos. However, Tom's psyche responded differently than Mary's. For Tom, there was only one thing he really yearned for—someone he could depend on and trust to be there for him when he needed help.

Mary's psyche framed the largest difficulty in her life as a lack of peace. Tom framed the largest difficulty, within the same kind of environment, as having no one he could depend on and trust. Once your psyche names the most extreme component of the suffering for you, it identifies the solution—what you believed would stop the hurt. This is the core gift you desire to bring to yourself, and also to the world. As I said earlier, your core gift is the healing force to your primary suffering. For Mary, then, her core gift is helping herself and others find peace. Tom's core gift is being someone who others can depend on and trust, no matter what.

Because our core gift surfaces in opposition to our largest suffering, it becomes a central focus in our life. Unable to make this solution happen during the initial stages of the original suffering event(s), we carry the longing for and the desire to give it for the rest of our lives. Consciously or not, we are called to attention in our own life, and in others' lives, when we detect that giving this core gift may be useful. Since we believe it would have been the pathway out of pain in our earlier life, we carry it with us as a primary solution to many of the difficult situations we face later on. In this way, it can be seen as a thread that weaves its way throughout our life, coming back to help us out when we need it. Our core gift also has a dark side. Because of the compelling nature within the core gift to be given, much of the trouble we find in our lives can also be tracked back to situations where giving our core gift creates difficulty for ourselves or others as a result of the way we give it.

Compensation and the origination of gifts and wounds

Compensation, a psychological theory which claims that the woundings of a person result in his or her desire to compensate by making the opposite effort later in life, is commonly used as a way to understand the pathology of behavior. We do this now because of something that happened to us in the past. My house was always messy when I was growing up, so now everything is always spotlessly clean. My Dad changed jobs and was out of work a lot, which caused our family to not be able to buy things we needed. Now I am sticking with a solid career and my kids get a stack of presents at Christmas that would cause Santa to blanch. Compensation is the principle of cause and effect exacting its obligation to the suffering parts of our lives. Whether we are compensating for the suffering we witnessed in our parents, hurt inflicted upon us by others, or self-inflicted wounds, the compensation we make is aimed at the elimination of the original feelings we had during that time in our lives. In the preceding paragraphs, compensation is described as one of the distinguishing and formative roots of a person's core gift.

James Hillman, in *The Soul's Code*, leaves no room for his readers to mistake his disdain for the idea of compensation as a complete explanation for the giving of gifts and good acts of humans. Saying that compensation is a theory "so degrading to inspiration it deserves the derision I am giving it", he sets about to have it "torched and discarded." Identifying psychologist Alfred Adler as having universalized the idea of compensation, Hillman says,

"According to Adlerian theory, challenges of illness, birth defects, poverty, or other untoward circumstances in youth provide the stimulus for all higher achievements. Each person—in less spectacular fashion than the eminent and extraordinary—compensates for weaknesses with strengths, transforming inabilities into empowerment and control. The human mind is basically constituted to think in the constructs of strength/weakness, superior/inferior, striving to stay on top."[5]

What would cause such a fierce response to the idea of compensation? It doesn't appear to me that Hillman rejects the idea that people make reactions based on prior events. What I am certain about is that he is opposed to the idea that a person's gifts originate in those reactions. He raises a critical point in understanding the source of gifts. If we accept that compensation is the seed of our gifts, then "We are each alone on the planet, without an angel, subject to our hereditary flesh and all the oppressor's wrongs of family and circumstances, which only the willpower of a 'strong ego' can overcome."[6]

I share Hillman's dislike for the assumption that our gifts are merely the product of our suffering. This belief continues to prop up the mistaken notion that we are nothing more than the result of the experiences we have after birth. Identifying our gifts as simply a reaction to our woundings removes the mystery of larger purpose from our lives—whenever we have done some good in the world, it is simply because something hurtful happened to us previously. Under this assumption of cause and effect, there need not be any discussion of spiritual paths, and yearnings for initiations that teach us the great lessons become unnecessary fluff in a life which has such certain predictability. The beauty and mystery in who we are is discarded and replaced by the simple equation of this causes that. To live under this belief reduces us to a level of understanding humans within the same logic-based underpinnings we use to understand the machines we use to drive to work and make our food. Looking into any child's eyes should tell us there is more to a life than this.

There is a darker side, even yet, to placing the origination of gifts solely within the construct of compensations. These reactions to our suffering can then be labeled as unhealthy responses—a diversion from our true nature and genuine self. Karen Horney, Founder of the American Institute for Psychoanalysis, describes the reaction to our primary wounding as re-

---

5. Hillman, James. *The Souls Code: In Search of Character and Calling.* Warner Books. New York, N.Y. 1996. Page 24

6. Hillman, James. *The Souls Code: In Search of Character and Calling.* Page 26.

sulting in the formation of a "comprehensive neurotic solution"[7] which is a diversion from self-realization. She further labels these behaviors in the categories of vindictive triumph, compulsive nature, neurotic ambition, search for glory, and the need for perfection. The goal in self-realization, she says, is to outgrow these responses and be liberated from them.

Now we no longer have the gift of the person being seen as coming from their true nature, and given out of the generosity of their spirit, but rather as an unhealthy behavior and deformation of their character which is a diversion from the person's genuine path. Horney, while in the midst of this explanation of compensation, acknowledges there is a self within us that is the real self, that "central, inner force, common to all human beings and yet unique in each, which is the deep source of growth."[8] It appears to me that she believes, in order to find this central inner force, we must eradicate our neurotic solutions. Could it be that the two—our real self and our reactions to our woundings—are from the same source and, when we eliminate our "neurotic solutions", we eliminate an essential and useful part of our true nature? Is it possible that, rather than eliminating those behaviors she labels as unhealthy and neurotic, we should instead see them as sources of strength and wisdom, and actively find ways for their contribution to be seen and valued by ourselves and those around us? In the language of gifts, these questions are worth pursuing. While they do not have easy or absolutely clear answers for many of us, they certainly reveal the mystery, possibility, and richness of our gifts and wounds.

What, then, is the source of gifts?

The focus of this book is not to offer a significant overview of the many cultural and spiritual belief systems about the origination of gifts. Rather, it is attempting to widen the imagination of the usefulness of gifts for those of us who believe there is such a thing as a gift. While being mindful of recognizing and understanding our compensations and behaviors which do not serve the world in a healthy way, there is another focus, equally important, which will take us to a larger imagination of who we are. This focus is centered, not in the recognition and reduction of destructive behaviors, but in a nurturing of our greatness.

---

7. Horney, Karen. *Neurosis and Human Growth: The struggle for self-realization.* W.W. Norton & Company. New York, N.Y. 1950. Page 23.

8. Horney, Karen. *Neurosis and Human Growth.* Page 17

Vincent Harding, one of the contributors to a book advocating the integration of education and spirituality, referring to those who have spoken before him in the book, says:

"Then Joan said something else, as she talked about how hard it is to develop holistic, integrated education. 'We have really underestimated who we are,' she said. And of course, before long, the Dalai Lama was singing the same song: 'We don't know who we are.' And Huston Smith was saying the same thing: 'We've got to become acquainted with ourselves.' Not just with the shadows that we so often seem to specialize in—though not making believe that they aren't there—but becoming acquainted with the great light that is us, in us, through us. To nurture this light, develop it, value it.

So where do we go from here? To get to know ourselves a bit more, especially, most especially, our beauty."[9]

Where do gifts, so essentially a part of this beauty, come from? Although I have heard many answers to that question, the vast majority of those answers begin to speak, almost immediately, of spirit. The belief in gifts, when an imagination larger than genetics and evolution is used, goes directly to the great mysteries—that in which we have faith—and the grace of these potent forces. The certainty with which a person describes the origination of gifts depends on the certainty of their faith.

Although gifts and wounds can be triggered in each other's presence, neither is devised by the other. Both have already been planted within a larger whole, the mysterious seed which contains our entire life, and both become visible to ourselves and others within the circumstances we encounter along our path. That gifts and wounds are useful to each other is, as far as I am concerned, undisputable. Without both, weaving in and out of each other's way along the same path, we lose our ability to navigate meaningfully in the world. Learning about and giving our gift provides us with the focus to follow the road we are meant to be on. By giving our gift, we realign our wounds from purposeless to purposeful suffering. The remembering of our suffering causes us to stand at attention at future forks in the road, alert to the injustice and the failures that can result from not

---

9. Glazer, Stephen, ed. *The Heart of Learning: Spirituality in Education.* Jeremy P. Tarcher/Putnam. New York, N.Y. 1999. Page 235

following a calling in a way that brings beauty to the world. This memory of suffering also provides the unsubtle reminder that serves as roots for the courage we muster to give our gifts in a world full of both opportunity and danger.

Making your list, checking it twice

It might be helpful to you, in order to take the "four capacities" (skills, talents, gifts, and core gift) idea from the theoretical into the practical realm, to take a few minutes to make some of these distinctions in your life. Here is one way to do it:

On a sheet of paper, list at least 15 things you are willing to say you are "good at." An easy way to do this is to break your life into different "pieces," and come up with a few items in each piece of your life that you are good at. It is helpful to be as specific as you can. For instance, instead of saying you are good at being a friend, pick out the quality in being a friend that you are particularly good at. Is it making enough time for the relationship? Is it listening when a friend needs to talk? Is it sticking by that person, even when they are having a hard time? Is it being willing to go through a conflict and not abandon the person? Using another category as an example, rather than saying you are good at cooking, what parts of cooking are you good at? Is it in thinking of creative ways to combine ingredients? Is it in the presentation of the food? Is it creating a hospitable environment for people to gather and share food?

Typical divisions people have used to make their list include:
At my job
In the kitchen
In the yard
Maintaining a household
When I was growing up
When I'm being creative
In my relationships with friends
In my spiritual life
In school
Things I appreciate about myself
With my life partner
With my children
Hobbies, special interests

After you have developed a list of at least 15 things, first put an "S" next to the items that are skills, and a "T" next to the items that are talents. To do this, refer back to the definitions above for skills and talents and go down your list item by item. When you are done, you will have identified every item on your list as either a skill or a talent.

If you have difficulty labeling any item, the main determiner is whether or not the primary desire to do the listed item comes from a simple need to get through daily life or whether the desire to do the task springs from a sense of joy and passion. If the primary desire comes from the need to get through the day, it is a skill. If the primary desire comes from a sense of joy and intrinsic satisfaction, it is a talent. Only you know which of those is true for you. If there is a little of both, decide which is more true for you. This is not a task to labor over…and you might be unsure of how to label some of the items on your list. Don't sweat it. Put a question mark next to items which you are unsure how to label. The purpose of making this list is to begin to see how skills and talents differ, and to provide the framework to see how to distinguish our gifts and core gift.

Next, look at the items you have identified as your talents. As I said earlier, your gifts and your core gift are actually talents which you can connect to suffering events in your life. Look over your talents and see if you can pick any out that you developed as a result of difficult life experiences. Mark them with a "G". Most readers, particularly those who have not had a prior opportunity to carefully consider the distinctions between skills, talents, gifts, and core gift, will find it very difficult to identify their core gift at this point. During our Core Gift Identification workshops, it has been our experience that very few participants, without going through the entire process, can pick their core gift from the list they have created. If you are one of those unsure readers, it might be comforting to know that Part Five in this book is devoted to helping you pinpoint your core gift by providing you with four different techniques for core gift identification. If you were able to identify your core gift from the list you just created, Part Five will affirm your choice, help you to develop a more precise definition, and increase your understanding of the various dimensions and capabilities you have within your core gift.

In our workshops, participants at this point are eager to get on with discovering their core gift, I think because they can see the possibilities for understanding, richness, healing, and contribution which lie within whatever their core gift is. How could so many of us not know, and, by not knowing, not have access to the power of our core gift? How could we have gotten, in so many cultures, to the point of this not being a central idea in the raising of our children? By its definition, our core gift is one of the primary driving forces in each of our lives. Most of us have developed the urgency to give our core gift as a result of enormously difficult times in our lives—we have come out the other side with a strength we feel compelled to bring to the world. Far more than simply making "lemonade out of lemons," our core gift is a well-point of capacity that we bring in an effort to heal ourselves and others.

5. DIMENSIONS OF THE GIFT

The gift idea is present in cultures and faith traditions around the world. Although the stories and examples differ slightly in the meaning and usage of gifts, there are similarities threaded between many cultures. Since there isn't one common definition, we can look at some of the generally acknowledged attributes to get a wider imagination we can use to understand the nature of gifts and their usefulness. This keeps us out of the trap of having one culture's interpretation be the "right one," and allows each of us to develop a definition of gifts that serves our needs within the culture in which we live.

Your gifts are part of your genuine authority.
The word authority was carefully chosen to include in this book because its defining Greek roots, *authentikos*, go back to *acting from one's essence, springing from an original source*, and *genuine, of undisputed origin*. Many of the language roots for the word gift are in the very same vein. The Hebrew is related to *gareen*, which means the *seed*. The Latin word *genius*, is the *distinctive character of a person* and *the guiding spirit*. And finally, the Greek *daemon* refers to the *inner or attendant spirit*. Many of the old definitions related to authority and gifts are hinged together by the idea that

there exists, inside each person, a distinct seed or gift. Across cultures, there are at least two common threads to the words used to describe this central source of authority in a person. First, the gift is itself a gift from spirit, and the person is then obligated to re-gift this capacity to his/her community. The idea implies that the essential capacity is already in the person at birth, waiting to be discerned and attended to. Second, many of the words tied to gift have their roots in heat, flame, fire, or spark. The gift can be described as the central source of fire in us, which can be used to both illuminate and invigorate our soul and provide the intensity and inspiration necessary for change. *Genuine* authority, which rests in knowing and acting on the seed gifts and capacities we possess, may be a necessary first step to being able to know what paths to take in life and what choices to make.

We live in a country that has, in many ways, forgotten these older ideas defining genuine authority, although we quickly and lavishly reward other kinds of efforts that we often mistake for genuine authority and power. We elect citizens to office and award them the right to represent us (positional power), we—particularly those of us involved in teaching—positively regard individuals who attend schooling and learn skills (power of concentration), we admire individuals of high character and dedication to a cause (power of purity), or we may closely follow the life of famous musicians or others who seem "larger than life" (power of charisma). James Hillman, in his book *Kinds of Power*,[10] describes these and seventeen other kinds of power. We have all witnessed power used in the service of ego and self-aggrandizement, oftentimes by individuals without a clear and present understanding of the fundamental motives driving their actions. The results can be devastating to the recipients.

Because "gift" is so closely associated with positive attributes in a person, we tend to assume that it is always given in a helpful and life-affirming way. But this is not always true. Trouble occurs when we forget that our gifts are powerful, but neutral, capacities in us—they can be used for good or for harm. A young person with a core gift for leadership may choose to be a gang leader. He may also choose to be a spokesman for a city youth commission. The core gift being used is the same in both situations, but the choice the young person makes about how to use this genuine au-

---

10. Hillman, James. *Kinds of Power*. Doubleday. New York, N.Y. 1995.

thority contributes to either building healthy community and relational capacity or undermining it. I have heard it said that one of the definitions of character is whether we choose to use our gifts for good or for harm.

Of the power of genuine authority, Hillman says, "We belong to each other, and the recognition by others of the qualities that each person embodies is as basic to human awareness as is the recognition of cries and songs among birds and smells among mammals. Authority may be intrinsic, but it is not really there until given confirmation by the world."[11] When we give our gift, it is always in the context of community. After all, the use of the word gift in this sense is accurate because it describes what we are freely giving to the other. All kinds of power can be useful, provided they are serving something larger—the essential gift the person is bringing to the world.

Your core gift is large, and worthy of a lifetime's work.

If you identify your core gift and core wound, and you can get it all mopped up, healed, and taken care of within a month, a year, or two years, it's not your core gift. Well, that's not quite accurate. It may indeed be your core gift and core wound, and you are not giving it nearly the attention it deserves. Your core gift has a quality in it that says, "I'm going to be around for the rest of your life. Get used to me, get to know me, and be curious about all the ways in which I will bring both deep joy and serious trouble into your life." The benefit of the core gift is that it serves your whole life, and is more than just useful during one period of time.

Most cultures believe that gifts are given to humans by however that culture defines spirit. Gifts are seeded and present at your birth, and with you until your death. The promise in the idea of gifts being around during your whole life is twofold. First, from having the opportunity to repeatedly give your core gift, you build a craft, which creates a larger possibility for using your core gift in many different situations and serving the world in wiser ways. Second, each time you give your core gift you act to heal your own wounds. The more you give your core gift, the more you heal your wounds. Over time, your wound consumes you less and becomes lighter as your core gift takes a more dominant role in your life.

---

11. Hillman, James. *Kinds of Power.* Page 162

Your core gift is a calling and a vocation.

The typical definition of a vocation is "a strong feeling of being destined or called to undertake a particular type of work." Joseph Campbell, in his interviews with Bill Moyers,[12] refers again and again to the possibilities inherent in responding to the call by locating and using your gifts. If you are on the right path, he says, "...invisible hands will help you along the way." His reference is an unmistakable connection to one of the Latin roots of gift, *gignere*, which is translated as *"the spirit watching over a person from birth."* When we have found trouble, or trouble has found us, and we have chosen to look within for the pathway, we can go back to the roots of our most central authority by focusing on our core gift. We will find it, seated right next to our suffering, waiting to be used to bring understanding, healing, and instruction about the path we are on. In these moments when we look within, invisible hands offer us visible evidence that we are not alone on the path.

In many frameworks for how gifts are understood within culture, the idea is that you were chosen by spirit to do this work. This takes the inspiration, dedication, and interest in the work to a level that is extraordinary compared to other kinds of work we are engaged in. Carl Jung says, regarding vocation, "The fact that many a man who goes his own way ends in ruin means nothing to one who has a vocation. He must obey his own law, as if it were a daemon whispering to him of new and wonderful paths. Anyone with a vocation hears the voice of the inner man: he is called."[13]

The idea that core gifts are a calling produces another possibility—that gift giving is a practice. By practice, I mean that the act of giving your gift is, in itself, a spiritual act. Like meditation, prayer, or other acts of engaging with spirit, giving your gift is a method to both connect to and further deepen your understanding of your relationship with spirit. The idea of practice also holds the possibility that there are various ways to engage and that the practice might change during the course of your life.

Related to core gifts, this means that, although you retain the same core gift during the course of your life, you may alter many times the way you give it. For instance, a teenager with a gift for making peace may

---

12. Bill Moyers interview of Joseph Campbell in 1988, audio recording entitled: *Joseph Campbell and The Power of Myth*. Winstar Productions.

13. Jung, Carl. *The Development of Personality*. Princeton University Press. New York, N.Y. 1973. CW 17, pars. 299f.

make repeated attempts to be a peacemaker amongst arguing friends. In midlife, this same person may become a professional mediator, judge, or law enforcement officer. After retirement, this same person may focus on developing a more peaceful approach to life by developing a meditation practice. In all three stages of the person's life, the core gift of peace-making found a way to become a focus of both learning and intention.

Because of the compelling urge to give your core gift, it is likely a person will respond to the call in his or her professional life. It has been well documented that this is particularly true for people employed in helping professions. The common term, wounded healer, erupts from this idea. The consequences of giving your core gift, without the balancing and healing recognition of its relationship to your suffering, can have disastrous results in the unaware social service employee. James Hollis, talking about compensation and helping professionals says, "It can both constitute one's vocational calling and at the same time be the chief source of stress and burn-out as the primal wounds are evoked over and over again, unceasingly pulling the caregiver back into the place of wounding to suffer it anew."[14]

Your core gift is active, simple to identify, and trying to be seen.

Because of our modern culture's tendency to believe that the essential nature of our spirit and our trouble is deeply secreted within our psyche, and, if we are in serious trouble may require a therapist to unravel, we may naturally assume that our core gift is difficult to discover and figure out how to put to use. Gratefully, for ourselves and for our communities, our core gifts are not as deeply buried as many assume.

Parker Palmer, in *The Active Life*, makes the case that core gifts may be difficult to discern for many reasons, including the notions that we are incompetent without training, we have poor self-images of ourselves, or the belief that we have to earn everything which has value. But, he says, there is often a more basic reason why core gifts are so difficult to discern: "...the most subtle barrier to the discernment of our native gifts is in the gifts themselves. They are so central to us, so integral to who we are, that we take them for granted and are often utterly unaware of the mastery they give us."[15]

---

14. Hollis, James. *Creating a life: Finding your individual path.* Inner City Books. Toronto, ON. 2001. Page 73-74

15. Palmer, Parker. *The Active Life: A Spirituality of Work, Creativity, and Caring.* p. 64

In working with therapists as they learn how to help others discern their core gifts, I have been told many times that the talent which is so useful during therapeutic conversation is the very talent that makes it difficult for therapists to help others discern their core gift. In an odd twist, in working with all different kinds of professionals, therapists seem to have the most difficulty mastering the skills of core gift identification. Upon mastery, however, they become very adept at the task.

What is the initial barrier to learning the process of core gift identification? What I have noticed is this—the therapist's analytical ability often is the barrier to their client's core gift discovery process. One of the finely crafted talents good therapists possess is the ability to help a person pick a spot in their life, and then ask a set of carefully worded and successively deeper questions. Each question builds on, and goes another layer deeper into, helping the person unravel and understand that part of their life. Depth is the key here, and it is the very thing that contradicts core gift discovery. Core gifts are on the surface. They are trying to be actively seen and are in use in obvious ways in the person's life. Going deep clouds the obvious, and makes the person's core gift more difficult to detect.

Saying that our core gifts are simple and on the surface does not mean that core gifts lack substance. Nietzsche reminds us that, "For whatever is his own is well concealed from the owner; and of all treasures, it is our own that we dig up last: thus the spirit of gravity orders it."[16] Your core gift has a complexity and weight to it that keeps the self-aware person on his or her toes. Most of the trouble you will encounter on your path will, in some way, awaken and be interwoven with your core gift. There is learning and opportunity available throughout the course of a whole life related to understanding and giving this gift.

Your core gift is a primary relationship between you and your community.

Chris Heimerl, who participates later in this book in the teacher's dialogue, says "Communities can sustain themselves in a meager way with the absence of gifts, but communities thrive with the presence of gifts." The gifts of every citizen are essential to create a whole community and,

---

16. Nietzsche, Frederick. *Thus Spake Zarathustra*. Translated by Walter Kaufmann. Penguin Books. New York, N.Y. 1954. Page 198

if we acted on this idea, we would devote more serious effort to the creation of inclusive communities. The citizens now at the edges, whether due to hiding from suffering, ethnicity, disability, age, or any of the other "isms," would be welcomed. They would not be welcomed out of an act of charity—from the vantage point of citizens who are seen as "less than me"—but rather from the wisdom of gifts, which instructs us that genuine community is built around the idea of gift exchange. Every person, regardless of surface appearance, has a gift to offer.

It also says that it is in the exchange of these gifts that the foundation for community sustainability is built. We are able to sustain ourselves because we value each other's gifts. We care for one another because we know that when one of us is in a position of not being seen for and able to give our gift, our community is not whole. We also know that if one person's gift is not welcomed, that person feels exiled and our community has a member who is imprisoned by non-participation.

Further, it is even more than knowing the person has a core gift—it is understanding that the person's presence in my life is a gift to me. To accept this gift from the other, I must move towards them eagerly and welcome them into my life with hospitality. As I heard Parker Palmer say, "I must believe I need the stranger as much as the stranger needs me." There is not, in my opinion, a more powerful case for the necessity of community building.

Having worked in the social service profession for a number of years, I can give you a direct example: My belief is that the largest obstacle to social service recipients being successful is the belief system of the social service worker. This statement will, I am sure, not endear me to those in helping professions who see the essential issue they are facing as the incapability and current life condition of the person they are helping. But, to me, it most certainly is not the "lack of capacity" of the person, nor is it a lack of funding or services, as so many believe. Fortunately, the answers are not that simple.

If it was just about getting a person some training for a job, money for food, or help with finding a place to live, the lines at social services offices would have long ago shortened considerably. If we really believed that the cure to homelessness, disability, or poverty could be solved by more resources and more money, I believe we would have found the money long ago. But we know money will not, in the end, be the lasting solution. Could it be that we know our darkest fear, the fear that causes us to not face and seriously engage in solutions to these problems, is true—the problems of the stranger on our doorstep are the problems of all of us, and will not go away simply by offering resources and then turning them away?

The root of our fear, I believe, is that we see in the stranger our own vulnerability, our own sorrow, and our own desperate loneliness. Unwilling to face these unwanted feelings and the trouble they will most surely bring into our lives, we keep turning away from ourselves and, in a desperate attempt to not be personally engaged, keep blaming the stranger. Our collective bluff is that we hope, by focusing on the messenger, we will not have to listen to the larger message.

For genuine help to occur and sustain itself, communities must look beyond the surface-level messages being brought by the person asking for help. Messages such as "I am hungry," "I have no place to live," and "I need a job," as important as they are to attend to, are not the primary message. The more urgent and more lifesaving messages—for all of us—that the stranger is laying as a gift at our doorstep are: "How am I like you? How is my suffering like your suffering? In what ways do both of us know the feeling of being unwelcome for who we are and the gifts we have to offer?"

Time and time again I have witnessed that, when social service workers act in ways that are less directed towards preparing an "incapacitated" person for community re-entry and focus more on developing existing places in the community to actively reach out and welcome the gifts of these citizens, remarkable things begin to happen. Social services, long focused on a "getting a person ready" model of service, have neglected the most powerful solution to the issue of being excluded—and requesting social services help—the belief that each person has a gift to offer.

The most revolutionary and important work for social service agencies in current times is to remind communities that each person has a gift and to encourage them to act on it. As Palmer helps us remember, we must believe at the very core of our being that we need the stranger as much as the stranger needs us.

Your core gift is an essential ingredient in your cultural assimilation within your family and community.

A person being prepared to join any group, using a cultural assimilation model, is given three kinds of instruction. By cultural assimilation, I mean being instructed in the underlying and visible patterns that allow a person to be successful and included within a group. Much of this assimilation depends on the person understanding the customary beliefs of the group upon which individual and group decisions are made. This instruction, when combined with participating in the daily routines and rituals of the community, result in a person being culturally bound to the group.

The first kind of instruction necessary is for the person to understand how he/she is supposed to understand and use spirit. This includes learning "what spirit is," as well as the group and individual practices used to interact with spirit. The second kind of instruction is how a person is supposed to relate to what is "outside of him/herself," namely other persons and the rest of the natural world. What is my relationship to other humans, animals, and the natural world around me? What is my obligation to the external world? How can the external world be useful to me? The third kind of instruction is how the person is supposed to define who they are. How do I think about "self-hood"? Beyond flesh and blood, who am I? What is my true nature and character?

The idea of the core gift is a necessary and inherent part in all three kinds of instruction. In the first kind of instruction, spiritual, the core gift itself is a gift from spirit. If it weren't for the grace of spirit, we would not have gifts at all. All gifts are gifts from spirit, and we are simply re-gifting what we have been given. To give our gifts requires an active and ongoing relationship with spirit—for both further understanding and to heal our own suffering through surrender.

In the second kind of instruction, how to interact with others and the natural world, our core gift is one of the primary methods by which we relate to what is outside of us. Our core gift opens a pathway for us to bring our spirituality from an interior relationship with spirit to an external relationship in the world. Our core gifts are, in an exact way, an expression of spirit and of our intention to bring love to the world. Our life is oriented, when we are aware of our gift, towards walking on a path that intersects with those in need of our gift, others with similar gifts who can instruct and mentor us, and towards finding the trouble awaiting us.

In the third kind of instruction, how to think about who we are, our core gift forms an essential foundation to our description of who we are. When we think about our capacity, our core gifts are one essential element. Because our core gift is connected to our suffering, without a core gift we would simply be bringing our skills and talents to a world without the intrinsic motivation to help heal others and ourselves.

6. GIFTS AND HEALING: LOVING YOUR LIMP

It's difficult to get very far into the idea of gifts, regardless of the cultural or spiritual interpretation you use, without running into the idea of wounds and suffering. Gifts and wounds have a symbiotic relationship and, for healing to occur, are necessary to be seen as complementary forces serving each other. The idea of healing, or making whole, involves understanding your suffering and resulting wounds and seeing how they are both helping and hindering you in following your life's path. Within this understanding, there is hope that the suffering will be transformed into a vital and life-giving force. William Stafford, in his poem *Consolations*, says:

> "No good thing is easy." They told us that,
> while we dug our fingers into the stones
> and looked beseechingly into their eyes.
> They say the hurt is good for you. It makes
> what comes later a gift all the more
> precious in your bleeding hands.[17]

17. Stafford, William. *The Way It Is.* Grey Wolf Press. St. Paul, MN. 1998. Page 244

This chapter breaks down the steps in one typical Western healing model and describes how a person's core gift can be used to both understand and contribute to the healing process. This chapter is not an attempt to fully explore the wide variety of healing methods and conceptual frameworks available. It is only to provide the reader with an overview of how knowing and giving your core gift fits within, and is useful to, one typical healing process.

A simple and common paradigm for healing involves five stages or steps.[18] They are 1) discovering and telling the truth of your story of suffering; 2) naming the unhealthy behavior that developed in you as a response to your suffering; 3) developing a compassionate understanding of yourself, others, and circumstances; 4) forgiveness; and 5) giving your core gift. Most healing paradigms involve the first four steps or stages, but do not include giving the core gift as the final act in healing. It is critical to include the step of giving your core gift because an essential "healing moment" comes at the point of giving the core gift—for it is in the moment when you act in direct opposition to the suffering you have known that hope is restored. Up until you act, you are still trapped within the paradigm of suffering because you are not certain it can be different. The moment of action is when your psyche offers a rebuttal to your suffering, saying, "This is how love happens. I am offering the world my core gift—the capacity triggered by my suffering—as a testament to my intention to move forward in my life."

The steps detailed below are not necessarily linear, and the process can involve cycling back and forth between the steps for many years. The five steps are:

1. *Discovering and telling the truth of your story.* This involves, sometimes with the help of another person, mining the depths of the situation that caused you harm and telling your version of the true story. It is important to recognize that it is your truth, and may not include all of the facts and may be different than another involved person's truth. The telling of the story allows the acknowledgment of and release of at least the initial layers of anger, guilt, shame, and sorrow. Further release will come as you

---

18. Modern therapeutic practices generally engage in the first four stages described above, and often include cognitive reframing and resulting behavioral changes. As helpful as this may be, it does not give the person one of the primary benefits of the gift paradigm—connecting the suffering to the development of a powerful capacity and the subsequent healing that comes from being acknowledged for this capacity.

continue to decide to unravel layers of the story and acknowledge the suffering you have experienced.

2. *Naming the unhealthy behavior(s) that developed in you in response to the suffering event.* Most of us develop a reaction to our suffering that causes us to be afraid of, hide from, or lash out at the world in a particular way. Oftentimes, our response is to be angry with ourselves and others, or to accept an unhealthy level of responsibility for the event. Other times it may involve disengaging from the world by becoming fearful of and avoiding certain situations that are a normal part of being alive. This healing step involves developing an understanding of the behaviors that developed in you resulting from the suffering, which are keeping you from fully engaging in the world. Do you respond angrily towards others in situations, which, even in a small way, resemble the suffering event? Are you unnecessarily distrusting of others? Do you feel and act less competent than you are? Do you not speak up when you know doing so would be healthy?

There are countless iterations of the ways we hide from or engage unhealthily with the world, and seeing the threads of our behavior is a necessary step because it allows us to name the behavior we can change. Understanding these behaviors is necessary because they are a continued threat to our health. Most times, these behaviors are unconsciously acted out by us, and take intentional reflection to discover and describe. Because they are rooted in the methods we used to protect ourselves from the suffering we have known, they are often heavily defended by our psyche.

For instance, in the previous story of Mary, we saw that she hid out in her bedroom. It is very likely that in Mary's adult life she hides out when faced with conflict. To give her core gift of peacemaking, Mary will have to name this hiding behavior and work towards changing it. Hiding out is not the best and brightest skill to bring to conflict resolution! This step of accurately naming the behavior is critical because it helps us to recognize our core gift, which, remember, is in some way the opposing force to the behavior we have developed.

The wounds relationship with the core gift is the source of our urgency to give our gift. If we did not know this suffering, we would not have nearly the motivation we have to give our gift. Giving our gift is literally our effort to not have others suffer in the way we have suffered.

3. *Developing a compassionate understanding.* Developing a compassionate understanding involves understanding the story of "how that could have come to this"—in the person(s) who caused you harm, and/or in

yourself for your own wrongdoings. Developing a compassionate understanding can be a necessary task to do in one or more of three different domains—for others, for ourselves, and for the circumstances in which our suffering occurred.

Related to others, this may mean you have to develop a compassionate understanding for how the events in another person's life could have led them to justify acting towards you in a way that caused you suffering. What happened to them that allowed them to believe they had the permission to act towards you in that way? You also may have to develop a compassionate understanding for yourself. What were the events in your life that led to you act towards yourself in a way that was hurtful? What were the events in your life that led to you giving another person permission to act towards you in that way? In both cases, with yourself and others, it is important not to confuse compassionate understanding with justice. Developing a compassionate understanding does not include saying what they did was justified or "right." Compassionate understanding simply means you can see how the events in your life, or their life, led to the point where the suffering event occurred.

The third kind of compassionate understanding that is sometimes necessary is related to circumstances. This is usually when a suffering event happens to you that is not intentional— for instance, a car crash, or other kind of accident in which the involved person(s) did not intentionally act in a way which resulted in your suffering. Another example would be the onset of a disability, either at birth or later in life. Achieving compassionate understanding can involve different variations of understanding ourselves, others, and circumstances.

You can tell when you are reaching a state of compassionate understanding, because there is a softening in the way you think about yourself and/or the other person or circumstances. Oftentimes, this feeling of softening can be noticed in the center of your body. In the moment of understanding you have a feeling of being able to breathe deeply—oftentimes your breath will sigh, as if expelling the dwindling vestiges of anger. This softening can also be accompanied by a feeling of genuine sadness for the other and seeing how you may have been the most convenient target for them lashing out at the world as a result of their own suffering.

4. *Forgiveness*. This step has three parts. First, forgiveness is accomplished, in part, as a natural result of moving through the first three steps. The capacity to forgive develops within us and surfaces as a by–product

of our effort to understand our story and our unhealthy behaviors, and develop a compassionate understanding. You realize one day that you are ready to forgive. You can't force forgiveness, and it will not happen until your psyche is ready. Forgiveness is necessary in order to move on with your life. James Hollis, in his book *Creating a Life*, says, "when we see a person still nursing a wound, years after the fact, still blaming another for their life, years after the fact, still embittered by injustice, years after the fact, we see not only someone who is stuck, but one who has never fully picked up responsibility for his or her life."[19]

Forgiveness does not mean deciding what happened was right or will be forgotten—rather it means you are willing to make a step over the line and move forward in the world. If it involved something another person did to you, forgiveness involves deciding you are not going to carry the weight of this person's suffering as your burden. If the suffering was something you did to yourself, forgiveness involves the decision that you are willing to not have this situation frame who you are for the rest of your life. You make an agreement with yourself to see this event, both for yourself and the other person, within the context of your whole life.

Second, once you recognize you are in a state of forgiveness, there is the possibility of surrender and release. The act of forgiveness involves the release of the weight you have been carrying to something larger than yourself. In many cultures and faith traditions, the act of forgiveness requires the releasing of the suffering to spirit—giving the pain to something greater than you. Surrender, the willingness to release your suffering to a source larger than yourself, is an essential task within forgiveness because it allows the space once filled by the emotions of anger, shame, and guilt to be replaced by the healthy emotions of love, compassion, and joy. It is important to remember that, for most of us, there are many small moments of surrender rather than one earth-shaking event.

Third, forgiveness involves deciding to step over the line and get on with your life. No longer carrying the suffering as an oppressive weight on your back, you have the ability to straighten up, look forward, and begin to act differently. Forgiveness requires a decision to act, whether that action is to think differently, feel differently, or behave differently towards yourself or others. A ritualized moment—whether it is lighting a candle, stepping through a doorway, saying a prayer, or conscious breathing in

---

19. Hollis, James. *Creating a Life.* Page 98

and out—is often helpful in acknowledging this step of forgiveness. As you return later to your suffering to release further levels of hurt, repeating the same kind of ritualized act acknowledges that you, once again, are releasing this further layer and moving on in the world. The comfort you receive from this ritualized moment is, in itself, a moment of healing and grace in your life.

To not forgive is self-serving in the short run because it allows permission to continue the unhealthy behaviors. Self-pity, arrogance, unhealthy habits or addictions, anger, intolerance, and hiding are given permission to act themselves out as long as the decision to forgive has not been made. These unhealthy behaviors are self-serving because they provide a protective shield from seeing and acknowledging the truth of your suffering and facing the resulting pain.

The result of forgiveness is an opening of the gate to the future—a future in which there are larger possibilities waiting for your consideration. The act of forgiveness creates the space to imagine a future that is not choked off by our limps, but nourished by the strength we have built through our suffering.

5. *Identifying and giving your core gift.* Giving your core gift is the final act in healing. It is the literal act of stepping over the line you have agreed to cross by the act of forgiveness. It is the pronouncement that you are, once again, engaging in the world and bringing it your gift and your love. It is a statement that you are intentionally acting in a way that is the opposing force to the hurt you have known. It is as if you are saying, "This is how we ought to be treating each other."

Giving your core gift is also a statement that you believe your life is worth living, and you are not going to be stopped in your tracks by the difficulties you have known—it is a visible sign that you have hope and faith in the future. The giving of your core gift is essential for healing because internal understanding is not enough to complete the act of healing. Action is required in the external world. Giving your core gift is making a statement that we heal, in part, in the context of community.[20] I heard

---

20. This has implications for the role of therapists, counselors, and other healing practitioners because it mandates that helping a person know their story, develop compassionate understanding, and forgive—steps which are the assumed role of many therapists—is only part of the task of healing. The therapist also has the obligation to help the person understand their core gift and help locate ways for the person to give that core gift in the

Malidoma Somé[21], an elder in the Dagara tribe from Burkina Faso, West Africa, say, "A person should never suffer or celebrate alone." Just as we heal by giving our gift, the community heals through receiving it. There is cause for celebrating together. What has been missing is now received, and the community is more complete.

Understanding your limp

Giving our core gifts often requires courage. Why? Because our gifts are connected to our suffering, and hold the possibility of renewed difficulty and of remembering the original story of wounding. Our attention is heightened to this possible danger. Raising courage, when giving gifts, requires going within ourselves. This is because most resistance to act is not the result of an external force, but can be traced to an internal message we are listening to. Oftentimes, this internal voice has given us this message many times. It has become the mantra for inaction in our life. It has, as the old stories say, become our limp. The voice of this limp was born in the suffering event(s) which we have named as our primary suffering.

For most of us, at the moment we are choosing whether or not to give our gift, a small afraid voice within us begins its chant, reminding us of all the reasons not to act. This voice from our psyche, always there to be a cheerleader for our survival, begins to create its list of reasons why we shouldn't do this courageous thing. The closer we get to acting, the louder and more insistent the messages become. These messages can be a good thing when they protect us from acting when it is foolish to do so. In fact, this message inside you kept you safe and protected you from hurt when you were younger. Because of this, it is a message you will not ignore when you hear its voice coming up, once again, to do its job.

Most of the time in our adult life, however, these messages serve to try and stop us from taking an action which would take us more fully into the world and provide the opportunity to give our core gifts and heal our wounds. The psyche, which is the source of this message, has the goal of avoiding suffering. Period. It does not evaluate whether or not the suffer-

---

context of community life. This involves more than simple cognitive reframing and resulting action; it involves helping the client understand the suffering event in terms of the core gift paradigm and the resulting action as a conscious healing act.

21. Somé has written several books directly related to understanding core gifts and their relationship to suffering and healing. One example is *The Healing Wisdom of Africa*, Putnam Publishers, New York, NY, 1998.

ing has the possibility of being helpful in our lives. The loudness of the message is the same whether we are facing imminent death from a foolish act or preparing to act in a way that heals a wound from our past.

For most of us, there is one primary message we learned from our woundings during youth which comes back to do its duty in every courageous situation we will face until the day we die. Its basic message is, "This is what happened to you when you tried this before. It didn't feel that good, did it? I'm warning you, don't try it again." Examples of these core courage-stopping messages are:

> Someone will be disappointed in me.
> Those people won't like me if I do this.
> I'm not smart enough.
> I'm not good enough to deserve this.
> I always fail, so why try.
> I haven't earned the right to have this.
> I don't have enough time.
> Somebody else could do it better than me.

Chris Heimerl, mentioned previously in this book, has spent the majority of his life helping people with severe and persistent disabilities be a part of community life. I showed him this list of limping messages, and he said, "Everything on the list can be traced back to one thing. How, in this situation, am I not going to be enough?" His question helps to put the frame on identifying your core limping voice. When you are faced with a difficult situation, what is the usual way that you feel you are not enough? Within the answer to that question is the voice of your "limp."

Susan is a bright, motivated woman in her forties who, on the surface, seems unstoppable. With two young children, she decided to get divorced from an abusive husband. Her main concern during the divorce was that her parents would be disappointed in her for not being successful at marriage. She went on and graduated from college despite being a single mother. Through that struggle, the message she had to overcome was that her kids would be disappointed in her because she was not able to be around them as much as they wanted. In order to stay healthy during all the studying, Susan began to run laps at the college. She loved it so much that she tried out and got a place on the cross-country running team. After each time her team lost, Susan would sit silently on the bench in the locker room, feeling a deep sense of disappointment in herself. She believed that if she could have run just a little bit faster her team might have won. Although she was offered a promotion at her job, she turned it down because it would require extensive travel away from her family. Her primary worry was that her boss would be disappointed in her for not being eager enough to rise up the company ladder. Throughout Susan's life, whenever she is in a situation which will require courage to act, the internal message that rises up to stop her is the same: "someone will be disappointed in me...I'd better just leave things as they are."

What is the primary message that comes up in you when you are facing a difficult situation? For most of us, there is a favorite. It wants to be seen as our friend because it has helped us to avoid so much suffering in the past. In truth, this message is not our friend—it is the torn ligament that is the source of our limp. It is the voice that has kept us from fully participating in many situations. It is the voice that has excused us from facing our wounds. It is the voice that has kept us from giving our gifts fully and engaging in the world. This message is the friend, not of our true nature and our capacity, but of the part of us that desires to hide from the world by excusing us from engagement with ourselves and others by reminding us that the world doesn't always go our way.

The essence of courage is the willingness to fairly evaluate risk and have the character to act based on that evaluation. Our limp does not desire to fairly evaluate risk or calculate the rewards that could come from action, it is simply present to protect us from all suffering. The voice of our limp is quiet at the beginning, gently reminding us that there may be some danger in the action we are thinking about. It has no need to speak up forcefully at the beginning, for action is not on the immediate horizon. But the closer we get to taking action, being on the ledge, the louder the voice gets. The message is always the same, but the repetitions and the loudness of the voice increase. The message reaches its peak of intensity right at the point before a decision is made—one final hurrah to try and stop the action. Once the action starts, the voice does not slowly go away, it completely disappears at that moment. It senses that it is of no use now, and settles into the dark cracks of the psyche waiting for its next call to duty.

The power of the limp is that it blindsides us. It seems to come out of nowhere. We are already wondering whether we should act in this situation and, all of a sudden, this powerful reminder erupts, almost like spontaneous combustion, out of the depths. The scales, already delicately balanced, are often tipped towards retreat when we hear this limping voice giving us the standard warning we are so used to hearing. Its familiarity gives us a comfort; we settle into the feelings of relief we have had in the past when our limp saved us from pain.

In order to reduce the power of the limp, it is helpful to remember, before taking action, that this message will likely crop up. Its power of surprise is reduced, and its status is no longer elevated. We remember that our limp is not the whole story of who we are. From this position the limp is evaluated, not from the power of its dramatic entry, but from its place amongst all the other criteria we have available to us to evaluate whether or not to act. When it does crop up, you can say to yourself, "Oh, this is what's supposed to happen right now. I'm supposed to hear this message, and it's going to try and stop me. Its goal is to block me from action, and my job is to put this message into the basket with all the other things I am using to evaluate this situation. It will not, on its own, stop me from acting."

Questions that can help a person identify and understand their limping voice:

1. What negative messages usually rise up inside you to stop you from moving forward? What is the most common one, your limping voice?
2. How is your gift related to your limping voice?
3. What benefit do you get by letting your limp determine your response?
4. How can facing your limp, not letting it control your action this time, help heal your limp?
5. What action would be exactly opposite of your limp?
6. How can facing your limp help you to be more fully in relationships with others?
7. How does your limp give you power and strength?

III. CORE GIFTS AND SECOND-LEVEL LEARNING

7. THREE DIMENSIONS OF TEACHING

What is it that fundamentally attracts students towards a teacher? All teachers have wondered about this, if only to satisfy their own need to feel welcome and secure by conjuring up remembrances about successful interactions with students. Beyond self-assurance, however, teachers have the opportunity to substantially increase their capacity to teach by reflecting and acting on this question.

Is comprehensive knowledge of the topic what primarily attracts students to a teacher? To answer this question, you only have to ask yourself to remember the teachers you have known who were well versed in the topics they were teaching. Were you drawn to the topics primarily as a result of the teacher's exhaustive knowledge? Probably not; we have all been inspired by teachers, both inside and outside of classroom situations, who were barely prepared to teach the subjects they were assigned. We have also been in learning situations with teachers who had extensive knowledge in the topic area, but we had little interest in listening to or learning from them.

Is being lively, energetic, and enthused what fundamentally attracts students? Surely this is not a fundamental necessity, for I have been fully engaged in topics with teachers who were, simply put, dreadfully monotonous and physically unenthusiastic in their approach to students. Standing behind a podium, speaking in a voice that could calm the dead, they droned on between the classroom bells, seemingly unaware of the students' presence in the classroom. Those teachers had something, however, that drew me towards them and caused me to have an increased interest in the topic.

Is the fundamental draw related to being welcoming and creating a hospitable classroom environment? It must also be beyond welcoming and friendliness, for I have been woefully uninterested in the topics of some teachers who were certainly hospitable and approachable. I have also been drawn strongly to teachers who, far from being hospitable, created classroom environments that were almost antagonistic. I kept coming back for more.

If the primary draw is not caused by comprehensive subject knowledge, being lively and energetic, or creating a welcoming environment, then what is it that attracts students towards a teacher? The answer can be found by separating out the dimensions of teaching.

Simply put, there are three dimensions to teaching. The first is the *content* being offered. What information about the topic, and resulting understanding, is the teacher focusing on? The second dimension is the *method(s)* the teacher uses to deliver the content. Whether it is lecture, discussion, activities to bring out artistic expression, or encouraging silent reflection, the methods are carefully designed to increase the desire to learn and maximize the comprehension level of the student. As teachers, we learn a variety of methodologies during our professional training and subsequent experience which prepare us to systematically choose a topic, outline the content, identify learning objectives and develop activities that lead to those objectives. As Palmer says, these skills of content and method are a part of teaching, but do not encompass the whole description of what it means to be an authentic teacher. The third dimension, the *style* of the teacher, provides the avenue through which the student's primary attraction towards a teacher occurs.

Not coincidentally, style also provides the fundamental mechanism through which both authentic teaching and the teacher's core gift emerge. By style, I mean the physical, emotional, and spiritual presence of the teacher in the classroom. Certainly, a teacher's decisions about content and method are a necessary part of successful teaching. When left to themselves, however, content and method are devoid of the glue that initiates and sustains learning. The style of the teacher offers the invitation for learning that transcends mere memorization of facts and concepts. The style of the teacher is determined by his or her answer to two questions: "Who am I?," and "What do I want the students to know about me?"

All teachers are continually answering these two questions while they are teaching. Whether it is conscious or not, a teacher's behavior is largely driven by their answers. For example, a teacher during the course of a day decides: Will I share a story from my own life? Will I make statements that reveal my own mistakes and pathways of learning related to this topic? What range of emotions am I willing to share while teaching, and what level of intensity of those emotions am I willing to share? If I am telling a story and I feel a tear coming to my eye, should I fight it back or let it come? How will I decide? Should I let my own feelings of frustration or anger be known when it is part of my understanding of a topic? How should I dress, and why? What are the daily rituals I will use to begin and end a classroom session? Why are those rituals important to me? Should I share my unanswered questions related to this topic of learning? Will I tell them why I haven't been able to get those questions answered? There are many opportunities to reveal who you are in the context of a learning environment, and each revelation provides important clues—clues that provide information a student needs to initiate learning that goes far beyond the surface-level facts being ingested in response to the content and methods being used.

The Desire for Second-Level Learning

Why is this third dimension of style the critical component to attracting students? Because the student is trying, in the context of the subject matter being taught, to do two tasks. First, to digest facts that lead to being competent in the subject. We learn to draw straight lines. We learn how to put together sentences. We learn to add numbers. We learn how World War II began.

The second task of the learner is to understand how new information and competency in a topic serve the larger assignment all humans are engaged with—further unraveling and understanding their basic orientation to the world in order to decipher the path forward. Who am I, and how is learning this going to be helpful to me? Until the student has the opportunity to complete, at least in part, this second level of learning, the content of the subject is simply floating in the mind of the learner, looking for a place to land.

Teachers can play a pivotal role in encouraging this second level of learning, provided they answer the "Who am I, and what do I want the students to know about me within the context of this learning environment?" questions in a way that triggers and encourages this deeper introspection in a student. Students are eager to understand why the teacher is attracted to this subject and how it has been helpful to them. Why does the teacher get so excited about mechanical drawing? What part of making lines on paper has been worth committing a career towards? What is so fascinating about writing a well-constructed paragraph? What part of writing keeps you up at night from excitement? In both of these examples, the student is seeking to learn how the teacher's basic orientation to the world has shifted from knowledge about this topic.

Learning how the subject has become integral in the teacher's life provides a glimpse into the passion the teacher has for the topic. This desire in the student to see the passion of the teacher, in whatever form it takes, is really part of the student's own desire to love the topic. The first step is often the student's unspoken, or loudly spoken, challenge to the teacher—tell me how this has been useful to you, so I can believe this is a road worth going down! When teachers take this courageous step and reveal their own unique yearning and passion for the topic, the student's own yearning for the topic can begin to find its roots because an unspoken permission has been granted. Because the teacher has revealed the unique roots of their passion for the topic, the student now has permission to seek their own authentic source of desire for the topic. This is mentoring in one of its truest forms: the teacher, by example, being a springboard for the student to look inside for their own authentic path to learning.

8. YOUR CORE GIFT IS LOOKING FOR TEACHERS

Think back to the teachers who have had a significant influence in your life. What was it, more than anything else, that attracted you towards them? Whatever that attraction was, it is likely that you will also say it was the primary thing you learned from them, regardless of the topic matter they were addressing. I also suspect that your answer to that question, rather than naming something about the teaching content, will instead name an essential quality in the style of each teacher. And perhaps, if you have not reflected on this question before, you will be surprised as you become aware of just how influential that teacher was in shaping your style.

When I think back to the teachers who have had a profound influence on me, they have been spaced throughout my life and easily come to mind. I have picked out a few of them who represent a wide span of learning topics. One of my earliest memories is of Mr. Steven Giovannini, the gruff and stern drafting teacher in junior high. I shuddered as I got in the line of students in front of his desk who were waiting as he reviewed each student's crude drawings of circles and cubes. When it was my turn, I am certain he purposefully spoke loud enough for all the class to hear, pointing out the flaws in my drawings while circling them with great sweeps of his large red pencil. Almost always, though, he would begin to smile and then scribble an almost illegible "A" or "B" on the top corner of my drawing as he sent me away. He had this same routine with all the students—beginning gruff and ending with a sweet kindness. Because of Mr. Giovannini, I will never forget that sometimes I am gruff and not kind, but there is a deep obligation to show kindness as a parting gesture. I can still see his face turning from a scowl into a smile, as if I am standing in front of him this moment. Forty years later, this is what I remember most.

Gordon Isaacson taught me most everything I know about operating a commercial fishing boat, yet what I learned most from him had nothing to do with lines, hooks, diesel engines, or weathering storms. It came from witnessing his deep devotion, for the more than thirty years I have known him, to a day's work. You get up and you go do it. Every day. Some days are going to be better than others, but you agree—before you know how it's going to turn out—to put on your raingear and head out the cabin door. Because of Gordon, I came to understand the sheer beauty in simply putting in another day, irrespective of the outcome. Oftentimes now, when my work is done, I will stop quietly for a moment wherever I am and feel the deep joy coming from the simple recognition that I have put in another day. In those moments, Gordon often comes into my memory, standing on the deck of his boat gazing at the sea with a devoted eye.

John McKnight, the sage community organizer and teacher, captured me with his ability to tell a carefully crafted teaching story, embedded with powerful levels of compassion, humor, and rage for injustice in the world, as if he had just thought of it all a moment ago. Drawn in at first by his sweet tone and humble presence, listeners to John's stories are then catapulted into an arena of reflection that often results in a deep commitment to change. Although his years of teaching and street experience have filled his mind with facts and irrefutable arguments that could convince even the most entrenched disbeliever, John always chooses to tell a simple story which takes the focus off himself and relies on the wisdom in the listener's bones to come up with the truth. Because of John, I will never forget to use and tell stories as the fundamental tool to navigate the world both inside myself and with others.

John O'Brien is a teacher in the disability movement. Almost twenty years ago, while I was managing the social service agency I referred to earlier, I received from him a fundamental orientation to disability issues. To this day, what I learned from John is still radically progressive and serves as a foundation for my conceptual understanding of and work related to community organizing. But that is not the most influential learning I received from him. It is this: He stands up in front of a room of people, no matter the size, and listens silently for a half hour or an hour to a rapid-fire barrage of different viewpoints. It is like a fireworks display, with each viewpoint and idea exploding as if it was the only one worth looking at. Then, when the participants in the room have exhausted their dialogue, he proceeds to reflect back to the group the exact key phrases everyone has said, while simultaneously converging all these details into a resulting pattern which clearly outlines the next focus for learning the group is headed for.

This technique, which relies on the cumulative wisdom of a group rather than John's vast expertise, results in the group feeling both deeply acknowledged and capable of taking the next steps. To watch John in action is one of the most concise examples of empowerment I have ever witnessed. I do not know exactly how he does this, but I know what I have learned from watching him carefully. Listening—not just regular listening but a relentless and deep desire to hear and understand—has much to do with this ability. I remember John often, but most powerfully at times when I am in trouble or confused as a leader and recognize it is because I am talking rather than listening.

I remember the first time I heard of Parker Palmer, a teacher and activist who writes about, amongst other things, education. I was at a lively party following the closing of a conference. There was a TV in the corner of the room, and on it was playing a video of Parker giving a speech. Amidst all the laughter and loudness, I sat alone and silent, completely focused on this videotape. It was as if he was speaking to me directly. To this day, I don't know why the videotape was playing, or who put it on and then left the room.

I have learned many things from Parker, in conversation with him and through his writings. Because of his influence, I have an increased understanding of and respect for the usefulness of silence, see my own struggles as universal and similar to those I am in a helping relationship with, and am more willing to discern my genuine motives from the motives I would prefer to publicly declare. But what stands out—what I most remember— is his devotion to and unflinching respect for the question. His commitment to asking non-manipulative questions, within a non-rushed context of hospitality and generosity, encourages introspection and truth telling which can have remarkable outcomes.

I recall sitting with him while we were taking turns asking another person a series of questions. I was immediately aware of our different questioning styles. I used my usual style of asking a question with a reasonable pace, listening carefully to the response, acknowledging the response, and then moving to the next question. My style could be referred to as respectful, focused, and efficient. I thought it was going quite well. When it was Parker's turn, however, he asked the question with a voice and a pace that slowed the world down and provided an opening for deeper introspection. Then he sat comfortably while the question was hanging unanswered in the room, giving no signals that he wanted an answer anytime soon. Once the question had been answered, he let that answer sit in the room for what seemed to me to be an awkward length of time before uttering a soft "hmm" or "aha" and then moving on to the next question.

I noticed that the responses he got from using this questioning style had a beauty to them that was not so apparent in the answers to my questions. By beauty, I mean the answers were deeper and more carefully thought through; there was a poetic and rhythmic quality to the sentences the person spoke when answering; and the person presented a self-confidence that was not self-aggrandizing but rather from a recognition that a simple but elegant truth about himself had been revealed. I will never forget that day.

I met Michael Meade, teacher, mythologist, and storyteller, while he was leading weeklong "at risk" youth events at remote camps with a renegade cadre of risk-taking teachers, activists, spiritual advisors, and representatives from indigenous cultures. He has planted seeds of what feels like insatiable curiosity in me about how welcoming works in communities, particularly between the haves and have-nots, the usefulness of the core gift idea, and the value of using old stories to increase our understanding of modern dilemmas.

But underneath all that there has been something even more significant about his influence—the clear instruction that it was about time for me to figure out the weight I am supposed to carry, and get on with carrying it. By weight, I mean the genuine authority and resulting responsibility I am supposed to bring to the individual or community of people I am involved with. In the introduction to *Thus Spake Zarathustra*, Friedrich Nietzsche writes, "When you are a camel, you bend down and get a load."[22]

---

22. Nietzsche, Friedrich. *Thus Spake Zarathustra*. Random House. 1995 Page 193.

Because of Michael, I have been unable to avoid le
of us has a specific thing we are supposed to be doing. \
after bending down and picking up our load, we find (
towards the path that reveals our place in the world—where we ᴄᴀⁿ ᵍ···
our gift, find the trouble we were meant to encounter, and where opportunities to heal from suffering lie waiting for our arrival. Because of Michael's
explanation, and observing him as a courageous and living example, I
have been more willing to figure out the weight I am supposed to carry
in different situations and not shy away from it. Most times, it seems I am
making painfully slow progress in this direction.

My formal interaction with all six of these teachers, both inside and
outside a classroom environment, was organized around a framework of
learning more about a particular subject area. The subjects I was learning
about were mechanical drawing, commercial fishing, community organizing techniques, the craft of teaching, disability issues, and the power of
myth and ritual in working with youth.

While I learned many things about these topics from being in the
presence of these six teachers, the most influential things were the importance of showing kindness and hospitality as a parting gesture, the beauty
inherent in a hard day's work, the importance of using stories rather than
facts, the desire to learn to listen, the power of the hospitable question,
and the importance of carrying your own weight. Each of these represents the completion of the second level of learning within those topics
for me—there was a significant way in which my basic orientation to the
world was altered, my own yearnings for the topic were clarified, and my
path in life was confirmed.

Choosing Not To Hide

The primary learning I received from each of these six teachers share
one thing in common: they rose to the surface not directly from the subject
matter, but out of their massive presence in the style of the teacher. Why
were these the things, more than anything else, I learned from these teachers? Why did I respond so purposefully to the style of the teacher rather
than the topic content and activities? What caused my psyche to read that
particular attribute, in that particular teacher, as the most critical piece of
learning? My answer is twofold.

First, the teacher chose not to hide that powerful attribute of their
style from me. Why do I frame it as choosing not to hide, rather than as

making a choice to reveal? Because the first inclination in humans is to protect that which is tender, and we do this by trying to hide the very attributes which reveal our soft underbelly. When a teacher chooses, through their style, not to hide part of their passion for the subject, they give a glimpse into their emotions, attractions towards certain ideas and styles, and clues that point towards some of the difficulty they have discovered on their path. All genuine paths involve encountering the opportunity to understand and give gifts and to struggle with wounds. These teachers, by making the choice not to hide those parts of themselves, provided an opportunity for the natural generosity of their core gift to come to the surface and be seen. As Palmer says: "Each time I walk into a classroom, I can choose the place within myself from which my teaching will come, just as I can choose the place within my students toward which my teaching will be aimed."[23] Each time a teacher makes this choice, they provide a glimpse into the weight they have bent down, picked up, and are carrying on the path.

One of the oldest, and to me most elegant, ideas about mentoring is that it is the gift in a person speaking directly to the gift in another person. It is as if our gifts know what to do, if only the intellect, ego, pride, and fear in the student and mentor will step aside for a moment and let our gifts have their conversation with each other.

The teacher's passion and yearning for the topic, evident in this powerful attribute of their style, is an alive and visible link to the teacher's core gift. Why is this? Like the student, the lens that the teacher is using to see the usefulness of the topic is embedded in their gift. The teacher's gift, like the student's, is trying to make sense out of the relationship between the topic and the purpose and direction of the person's life. How can I weave this learning into the main thread of my life? How is this connected to my core gift and my wounds?

When both the teacher and the student are in the active position of further integrating the meaning of the learning topic into their own lives, there is an opening for each other's gifts to be in a conversation that enlivens, inspires, and consoles.

The second reason I focused on those particular elements in the style of the teacher is that my own core gift purposefully chose to notice those

---

23. Palmer, Parker. *The Courage To Teach.* Jossey-Bass. San Francisco, CA. 1998. Page 57.

things, more than anything else, about the teacher at a time when it was trying to discern and integrate those elements into its style. The elements of the teacher's style are presented to every student in the room, but I noticed certain elements that were directed at the learning I was ready for. It is the simple truth of the old saying, "when the student is ready, the teacher appears" playing out in each of our lives. There was a readiness, disposition, and attraction towards the learning being offered by the teacher. The seed in me, already planted, sensed an opportunity for nurturing and growth.

It is possible that, if I had met each of these teachers at a different point in my life, I might have been attracted to a different element of their style or not have been attracted to them at all. It is also possible that I was perfectly prepared to meet those teachers at exactly the right moment. More than a question about luck versus fate, the timing of encounters between teachers and students is part of the deepest mystery surrounding relationships and gifts. Why do we encounter those on the path who can instruct us, if we choose to pay attention? Why do they keep showing up? It is, at least partially, because they are walking on either the same path or are on a path that has intersected ours. If we are purposeful about the path we are on, it is likely we will encounter these teachers. One after another, they will show up in the midst of the fog, making their offerings to us if we will only slow down and look in their direction.

Our core gift is guiding us and looking out for both danger and opportunity. On the path, it senses the opportunity in others with similar gifts, regardless of their personality traits, story, or physical appearance. The invisible hands that Campbell referred to keep shepherding us towards the people who cause us to learn more about our gifts. As we see the light in the other, we are given the opportunity to see more of the light in ourselves.

In order for the second level of learning to take place within the student, the teacher must decide to reveal the authentic roots of their own yearning and desire for the topic. This sets off a chain of events which results in second-level learning—the student seeking their own source of desire for the topic, integrating the learning into their life's path, and building the capacity of their own core gift. The opportunity for this second level of learning I received from each teacher would not have been possible if the teacher had not been willing to answer the "What do I want the students to know about me?" question in a way that revealed these essential elements of their style. In each case, they could have chosen a more limited range of revealing—by choosing different instructional styles—which would have diminished or eliminated the possibility for me to engage in a deeper level of learning.

If courage involves acting in the face of fear, then certainly these teachers are courageous. Facing the fear resulting from revealing parts of themselves which were tender and which were threaded back to their own yearnings and desire for the topic, they chose to reveal those elements of their style in a way that allowed the second level of learning in a student to take place. Authentic teaching requires continually making the decision to face this fear. By facing these fears and revealing authentic elements of their style, the teachers I described were modeling the difficult decision of whether or not to respond to the small afraid voice inside that holds us back, or to respond to the larger calling within asking us to bring ourselves fully into the world. The teacher-student relationship is full of opportunities, on both sides, to face this fork in the road.

9. EXPANDING GIFTS: ASKING SECOND-LEVEL LEARNING QUESTIONS

Infants depend on adults for their survival. In addition to food, shelter, and safety, their survival as whole and healthy humans also depends on receiving nurturing for their emotional and spiritual life. As these young people grow up and begin to learn that life will have struggles in it, they continue to depend on others for help. The primary focus of the help changes from physical needs to another kind of help: answering and asking questions that help the young person establish their individuality and their place with others in the world.

Questions from the student to the teacher

The idea of second-level learning has within it the possibility of teachers being able to help the student with this task. By revealing how the topic has helped them to find their place in the world, the teacher is encouraging the student to use the teacher's example as a provocation to do the same. Oftentimes, the student's observation of the teacher results in questions which are asked by the student to further clarify the second-level learning that the student is trying to achieve. When looking towards teachers and mentors for help, there are three distinct kinds of questions students ask.

The first kind of question can be labeled as a suffering question.

This question type rises out of the student when they encounter confusion, pain, and difficulty that causes them to want to stop moving forward. At a recent conference on mentoring I attended, a young helping professional, trying to deal with the aftermath of a failed grant project, asked the older members of the group, "If you make something with your heart, and it gets broken, what do you do?" She wanted to know how you keep going in life when your heart has been broken. Suffering questions can result from a broken heart, but can also arise from feelings of anger towards oneself or others ("How can I stop being so mad at John for what he has done to me?"); feelings of failure ("Why should I go on...I made such a huge mistake the last time I tried?"); being afraid to take the next step ("How can I call her when I feel so scared of what she might say?"); confusion regarding a relationship with another ("What if John won't talk to me after I do this?"); spiritual confusion ("How do you know if you are doing the right thing?"); or an attachment to an idea that is no longer serving you well ("How do you give up something that used to be really important to you?").

Although the question(s) can erupt out of either a single event or a string of occurrences, the answer the student is looking for is the same: "Given the struggles you have faced, why did you decide to keep going forward?" It is a plea for help with establishing seeds of hope.

The task of the mentor/teacher is twofold when encountering a suffering question. First, to listen to the story of the person. More than just casual listening, the teacher must listen in a way that the person is certain he/she has been heard—that one other person in the world knows the specifics of what is happening to him or her. This requires a listening stance that is undeniably attentive, and usually involves acknowledgement, whether verbal or physical, that the story has been heard. The purpose of establishing that the person has been heard is to embed the idea in the person that they are not completely alone in the world.

Secondly, the teacher must declare what they have learned about negotiating their path when they were inclined to stop because of difficulties they encountered. The stories of difficulty should include examples of where they found hope, but also include stories about what did not work. The successes are important to share, because they give the student examples of how the older teacher established hope, and also provide practical problem-solving information that may help the person negotiate their own path. But the stories of failure and resulting feelings of hopelessness may be even more important to share. *For, as contradictory as it sounds, it is often in sharing the stories of our failures that the seeds of hope are planted in the student.* To see that the older person, in spite of spectacular failures and feelings of hopelessness, has made it through to this point in their life gives the student hope that they might make it too.

When a teacher declares their own life has mattered, they are also saying that the difficult times they have faced have been worth going through. It has not just been suffering for the sake of suffering. Within a story of failure is the message that the failure has been in the service of a life that has been, as the student said, amazing.

The second type of question is an integration question.

The student asks this kind of question to establish how and what the teacher has achieved as "second-level" learning within the subject matter. How has the mentor/elder/teacher integrated the subject matter and made it meaningful on his/her path? Students ask integration questions as a way to kick-start their own process of finding passion for the topic and meaningful integration of the information into their life path. This type of question rises out of the student at the point of trying to integrate into their own life a style they have seen in the gift of the teacher.

For instance, if the student notices that the teacher is good at asking questions, and the student is trying to develop their own questioning style, they may ask the teacher, "How do you ask a question in a way that the person doesn't get afraid?" Another example might be, "What do you do when someone gets mad when you ask him or her a question?" Or, "What is a good question to ask somebody who is really stuck?" If the student notices that part of the teacher's style is to stick up for the underdog, to never give up on somebody, the student might ask, "If you are sticking by somebody, and your friends stop talking to you, what do you do?" Or, "What do you do if you find out somebody you are sticking up for has lied to you?" Integration questions are asked by the student in order to assist them in building their own craft related to the style element they are attracted to in the teacher.

The third kind of question is an expansion question.

Expansion questions are designed by the student to stretch their understanding of the topic and also to expand the teacher's imagination about the usefulness of certain dimensions of the subject matter. In this question type, the student is asking the mentor to comment on an idea that the student has related to the topic. While the student's question and the teacher's response may be a rehashing of commonplace knowledge, it is also true that the student's question often opens up both the teacher and student to a new and expanded understanding of the subject matter.

In both cases, what is important for the student is not whether the idea is "new" in the field, but rather that it is new to the student and is serving the function of expanding their capacity in a certain area at the exact time when that expansion will serve the second level of learning. One of the dimensions of the student/teacher relationship is that the student is supposed to stretch their investigation of the subject matter into areas that the teacher has not explored. Sobonfu Somé, in her book *Falling Out Of Grace*, reminds teachers that, "Questions that followers bring to their leaders lead them to new places, where they find answers they didn't have before."[24]

Why has the teacher not explored certain areas? There are at least three reasons. First, and most provocative, is that the teacher has been afraid to explore the areas because of his/her own suffering. Oftentimes, the areas of the subject matter that rub most deeply against the wounds of the teacher are the last areas that the teacher chooses to explore. After all, why submit to the pain when there are warm, safe, and inviting areas of the topic still left to explore? However, what is pain for one person to learn about is often matter of fact and not emotionally laden to another person. The student, whether due to naiveté, intention, or sheer courage, is in the role of prodding the teacher to venture into areas which open up chasms of hurt and suffering. A tangent in this area worth considering by the reflective teacher is whether or not they have ever put a student off by responding harshly or made a student suffer in another way in an attempt to avoid the suffering the student has brought to the surface by asking an expansion question.

The second reason the teacher may not have investigated certain areas of the topic may be due to a lack of interest in that area. The third and simplest reason may be due to a lack of time. Regardless of the reason for

---

24. Somé, Sobonfu. *Falling Out Of Grace*. North Bay Books. El Sobrante, CA. 2003. Page 85.

the teacher's lack of knowledge, the student's questions serve to expand the core gift of the teacher. The essential beauty in this transaction of information exchange is that it is core gifts helping other core gifts.

The expansion question serves another purpose in the teacher/student relationship—it reminds the teacher of his or her own gaps in understanding of the topic. What does the student know that the teacher has not yet considered? The wise teacher responds to the student's question with a humble acknowledgment that their own knowledge of the topic has not staked a claim in this area of the student's interest. This approach contradicts the positional authority of the teacher that traditionally has served to elevate the status of the teacher to expert, and the student as novice. It reminds us that we are all learners, regardless of our expertise in the topic area, and that the positional authority of the teacher is balanced by their lack of knowledge in certain areas of the topic. The teacher who feigns expertise as a way of maintaining authority and dominance in the teacher/student relationship is working in direct opposition to the truth of core gifts; individuals with similar core gifts have expertise in different areas of that gift.

It may be one of the great unspoken truths about the student/teacher relationship that both sides come with the desire to have acknowledgement from the other of their basic value in the other's life. Am I worth it or not? When teachers respond to the call of teaching by revealing their own passion for the topic, and are clear about both their core gift and their struggles, they encourage a learning environment where genuine self-worth, on both sides, can be acknowledged. Worthy students, with worthy questions, are willing to overcome their initial fears and ask the questions that matter. Teachers, responding from a position of genuine authority, can teach in a way that opens students to the second level of learning.

What fundamentally attracts students to teachers is the opportunity to engage in the second level of learning. To create safety, feel encouragement, and receive wisdom in this endeavor, the student is looking for a knowing in the teacher that is beyond his or her surface appearance, beyond content, and beyond classroom activities. Quite literally, what students may be looking for and responding to is the radiance, the light, in the teacher beyond the surface-level information being presented. The outward form of the light, or what the light is emitting, is the core gift of the teacher being seen in a palpable form by the student. As in the mentoring story told earlier, it may be that this light is the fire from the other mountain—the light the student needs to find the path forward.

Questions from the teacher to the student

The light, the wisdom in second-level learning the student is seeking, has two forms for discovery. The first, which I just explained, is initiated by questions from the student directed to the teacher. In the second form, the teacher has the opportunity to initiate or further provoke second-level learning by asking the student questions. Oftentimes, a student who is not engaged in the learning topic will become engaged when the teacher asks the right question. The "right" question is a carefully designed question that intrigues the student and propels him or her into a thinking pattern that results in second-level learning.

Once the process of second-level learning is initiated, the student is compelled by a combination of curiosity, pleasure, and the desire for healing wounds to complete the cycle of learning and make meaning. Frequently, more questions are asked in return. Questions by the teacher, whether they are attempts to provoke a lethargic or stuck student or pointed in the direction of a student who is inspired and alive, result in a learner who has an internal motivation to discover how the subject at hand can be integrated into their life.

Asking questions without prescribing direction.

As an underpinning to asking questions, the teacher must always be aware of one rule which, although it seems obvious, is very difficult for most of us when we are involved in this type of engagement—asking a question which is actually a question. A genuine question is a question that is asked from a place inside the teacher which does not assume to know what the answer "should" be. A genuine question is literally a question asked to provoke the imagination of the student and expand the understanding of the issue and increase the variety of options prior to making a choice.

One way to understand this obligation in the teacher is to see the difference between asking a question designed to have the student consider the difference between "this or that" (Do you want to drive to work or walk?) and a much better question, which forces the student to make a list of all the possible choices (What are all the different ways you could get to work?). In the first question, the teacher has put the frame on the issue and limited the solutions. In the second type of question, the student puts the frame on the issue and is forced to create a list of multiple options. This is a critical skill in questioning, because it is tied to the obligation of the teacher not to tell the student what to do (that's not teaching, it's simply being directive), but rather to shine a light in a specific, but general, direction and have the student decipher the pathway there. It goes back to the story told earlier in this book about the mentor who goes to the neighboring mountain and builds a fire. The fire is fueling the young person's imagination by saying, "Hey, look over here. What do you see?"

Although most of us are very skilled at recognizing the uneasy feeling we get in the pit of our stomach when someone is trying to manipulate us into doing what they want us to do or believe what they want us to believe, it is also true that most of us are equally skilled at masking that same desire in ourselves when we are trying to control the beliefs or actions of another.

Questions are wake-up calls.

Questions asked by the teacher are designed to shine a light on the disparity between the person's current level of understanding or action, and the possibility of a much larger vision. The question is sometimes phrased in such a way that it is heard by the student as a challenge, thus raising the desire of the student to "prove the teacher wrong." I heard a story a while back that illustrates the power of this kind of question.

A young man, who has a serious disability, was working at a mental health center as a custodian as part of a job-training program. Although he seemed dissatisfied with this job, he was unwilling to take the leap to go back to school or to look for a better job. He had settled into the uncomfortable comfort of non-action. The man telling me this story was an employee at the mental health center, and had noticed this young man's disillusionment with his impending career as a custodian. One day, in passing, the older man said, "Do you plan on mopping floors for the rest of your life?" The young man uttered an unrepeatable phrase that clearly outlined his intention to not spend the rest of his work years in close proximity to a mop bucket. The wake-up call question had hit its mark! The purpose of the question, to point out the disparity between a dream and a person's current life, had been accomplished.

In this story, the young custodian was compelled to seek out the vocational counselor at the mental health center to inquire about going back to school. A simple question, said in passing in a hallway, altered the direction of that young man's life.

Wake-up call questions do not have to be nearly so dramatic as the question asked of this young person. Any question which helps a student to recognize and feel the disparity between their current thinking/life and a compelling vision of the future is a "wake-up" call. *The question does not have to clarify what the gap is, but merely open the student to recognize there is indeed a gap.* This is an important clarification because, for the teacher to point out both the current situation and vision would assume that the teacher knew the direction the student should go. Although this may be true in some cases, the power in the wake-up call happens in the moment the student recognizes the gap. This creates an eagerness to learn something that the student believes will narrow the gap between their current situation and a larger vision of who they want to be.

How are wake-up calls connected to gifts?

There is an additional opportunity with wake-up call questions that can be mined if you know the student's core gift. In this case, the wake-up call is purposefully designed to force the student to recognize whether or not they are remembering and utilizing their core gift in this situation. This type of question is used in a situation where the teacher notices the student not using their core gift, and also in a situation where the teacher believes the student may be in trouble because they are using their core gift too much or unwisely.

Because core gifts desire attention, the student will, when asked a question related to their core gift, feel compelled to stop in his/her tracks and consider this question. Oftentimes, the teacher can simply ask, "If your core gift was in charge right now, what would it do?" Many other types of questions can be asked, all related to the person recognizing the gap between their current action/beliefs and action/beliefs that would likely be taken if the person integrated a healthy giving of their core gift.

For instance, if the teacher knows the student's core gift is related to being welcoming to others, and it appears that the student is showing some kind of hostility towards another person, the teacher might ask, "How is your core gift of hospitality being used in this situation?" If the teacher notices that a student's core gift for putting structure and order to things is not being used by a student, the teacher might ask, "How could your core gift of organizing things help you in this situation?" In reverse, if the teacher believes a student's core gift is getting in the way because it is too much of a focus in the situation, a wake-up call question can also be asked to highlight this possibility. If the student has a core gift for showing compassion, and he/she has gotten inappropriately enmeshed in another person's life, the teacher might ask, "In what ways is your core gift for compassion affecting you now?" A teacher who notices a student with a core gift for justice being used to excess might ask a student, "With a core gift for justice, how do you pick the battles to engage in and the ones to let go of?" or "How do you decide whether or not you are treating yourself fairly while you are engaged with a justice issue for others?"

Wake-up call questions related to gift usage, when used with good timing, will usually cause either a dramatic deepening of engagement or a shift in direction. I still vividly remember a time, ten years ago, when I was discussing my thoughts and feelings about a teacher with Tom Mosgaller, another teacher of mine. In the process of describing all the wonderful things I had learned from the teacher related to my core gift, I also mentioned to Tom what I thought was a major fault in that teacher's personality. It was a behavior in the teacher that clearly was in opposition to his stated beliefs and teachings. As I belabored the point, pointing out with great detail the chink in this teacher's armor, Tom listened quietly. When I was done, he turned to face me directly and asked, "I have noticed something in you, Bruce, which I am seeing you do once again. Why do you feel the need to tear down the very people who have been most influential in your life?" The question took my breath away. I felt the immediate need to defend my conversation, and began to once again point out the obvious faults within this teacher. Tom listened to me once again, and did not make any response.

We sat quietly for a time, and I could feel my emotions coming to the surface. Finally, I just quietly said, "I don't know." That was the end of our conversation, but it was not the end of my thinking about that moment. Tom had wisely planted a seed that gnawed away at me for several years. There were three things he did that demonstrated his knowledge of how second-level learning works. First, when I began to defend myself, he didn't feel the need to "prove me wrong." He let me have my say a second time, and depended on the power within his question to do the work. Second, he asked me an honest question, which did not have an assumption of the answer in it. And third, he was patient.

As it turned out, I didn't learn the answer to his question for more than five years, and he didn't hound me for the answer. He knew me well enough to know that part of my core gift is related to discerning the emotional truth in situations, and he knew that his question would cause me to recognize the disparity between my conversation and my core gift. The wake-up call question was targeted correctly to a place deep within my psyche, and would not go away until it had been answered.

I never forgot Tom's question. Whenever I thought of him, the question he had asked me came to the forefront in my memory, usually accompanied by a deep sense of exposure, embarrassment, and guilt. Tom, in many ways, began to represent that question. Then I heard an old story, told by Michael Meade, which helped me to understand why I had been so eager to tear down this teacher. The story had within it the understanding that at some point the student must differentiate him or herself from the teacher. This is a critical step in order for the student to maintain their individuality and not just become a clone of the teacher. It is also critical because the student can then explore areas that the teacher has not explored. In this way, the core gift, ideas, and styles of both the teacher and the student become richer.

When the student recognizes this need to "leave the teacher," he or she will usually cause a fight to erupt between the teacher and student as a way of causing permission for the leaving to occur. In some cases, wise teachers, who see the need for the student to begin the separation process, will instigate a conflict. If my memory serves me right, in the story I heard Michael tell, a fight erupts and the student actually kills the teacher as the final step in leaving.

Sitting in a roomful of young and old people, listening to him tell this story, my mind immediately went to the conversation I had with Tom years before. In that moment, I understood that my effort to point out the faults in the teacher had been an attempt to begin the separation process the story was teaching me about. After all, if the teacher was not perfect, I would not have the obligation to "become just like him." Bring on the list of faults! Each one granted me further permission to go out into the world and make my own mistakes and find the pathway for my own unique style. I had located my permission to leave. This was a powerful, personal example for me of a perfectly targeted question, and a lesson in the psyche's deep need to answer questions that point out the disparity between a person's current action and the person's larger vision of who they want to be. In that awakening, my gift had taken another step down its path.

IV. FOR THE TEACHER: SIX BENEFITS OF THE GIFT

Introduction to the Benefits

Not long ago, a teacher said to me, "Most books I read about teaching talk about the philosophy of teaching, but don't tell you what to do differently when you get to work at eight in the morning and are faced with students. Or they have impractical solutions that I can't do in my classroom—I sometimes wonder if the author understands what a real classroom is like." In another town, a social service person working with homeless youth said, "I go to these trainings where they teach their techniques for working with youth. They must be working with different kinds of kids than I see every day...the ideas they have are so unrealistic."

What does it take to do things differently at eight in the morning in your classroom or social service office? That depends on whether or not you want to do things differently based on your current thinking, or based on an expanded imagination of what the "problem" you are addressing is and therefore the variety of solutions facing you. If you act out of your current assumptions, any change you make will come from simply ideating—coming up with more ideas—based on the frame you have used in the past to describe the issue. There is a natural tendency in most of us, based in our desire for a quick solution due to the fast pace and pressures of our workday, to respond based on our tried and true (or not so true, but we're going with it anyway!) assumptions. We don't have to spend the time reorganizing our thinking. We simply need to come up with untried ideas and act on them.

On the other hand, if you change your assumptions, you automatically create the possibility of ideating a completely different list of solutions to choose from. More than fifteen years ago, I participated in an intensive seminar about different models for creative processes at the Center For Studies In Creativity in Buffalo, New York. What I remember most, after all these years, is this: In a vast majority of cases, the final choice a person makes from a list of brainstormed items is one of the last five ideas put on the list. The explanation for this phenomenon is that the person has already thought of—and probably tried—most of the easy things that everyone else will think of at the start of the brainstorming session. It's not until the ideas get out there on the edge that the person will become inspired by seeing something on the list they have never considered. Humans facing difficult situations have a natural inclination to become enlivened and inspired when a novel idea comes into their life—there is a feeling of renewed or expanded hope. Things might really be better, or at least different, after all. For most of us, the idea of core gifts is one of those ideas that comes at the end of the brainstormed list. It's not one of the first ideas we would come up with, but seeing it on the list causes many teachers to choose it as a solution because they sense hope, inspiration, and possibility in the idea. Are you inspired by the idea of core gifts?

This next section asks you, as a teacher, to expand the basic framework of assumptions you use while teaching. Listed below, there are six primary benefits to understanding and using your core gift. Any one of them can cause a substantial change in how a teacher thinks, feels, and acts while teaching. The primary benefits are:

1. Teachers have an increased level of courage to face difficulties arising in the classroom and surrounding teaching environment.
2. Teachers contribute to their own healing and have increased compassion for others.
3. Teachers have a source to continually recharge their energy and hopefulness.
4. Teachers, by knowing students' gifts, have access to specific strategies to welcome them and decrease non-desirable behaviors.
5. Teachers place themselves in a position to be welcomed and to establish genuine rather than positional authority.
6. Teachers have an increased ability to recognize and effectively use mentoring/second-level learning moments.

The benefits are connected by several overarching threads. First, being aware of how your core gift influences your life, and using the expanded strategies available to the "core gift aware" teacher will increase your ability to effectively teach. Second, within all of the benefits, it is possible to use your core gift as one of the paths for you to find healing in your life. Core gifts, because they are tied to core wounds, provide opportunity for the teacher to mend a broken heart. Third, teaching with your core gift in your back pocket will increase your ability to fend off some of the deadening effects of working within the often-institutional environments of schools and social services.

Each of the six benefits sections includes 1) an overview of how learning about and using your gift can enhance your teaching, 2) a list of questions designed to inspire reflection about how this benefit relates to your own gift and teaching style, and 3) a dialogue with five teachers representing different kinds of learning environments. Let's meet the dialogue participants.

Meeting the Dialogue Participants

I am a working teacher who has found the idea of core gifts to be tremendously useful in both my teaching and non-teaching life. Would others find the ideas and strategies interesting and useful? I decided to satisfy my curiosity by inviting five teachers, from different kinds of teaching environments, to dialogue with each other. The conversation they had was divided into the six benefit areas and has been added to the end of each benefit section as a way to expand this book's imagination and usefulness.

What were the criteria for selecting participants? First, I looked for teachers who had exhibited, according to others, that rare combination of subject matter depth of expertise coupled with a gentle but commanding presence that drew people in and got them engaged. Second, I wanted teachers who were willing to share stories from their own life that were compelling and could be used as a platform for the dialogue. Third, I wanted teachers who had demonstrated an ability to take the balcony view—to see how their own teaching style and life intersected with the larger ideas about gifts being talked about in the book. And last, all of the teachers I chose have demonstrated courage in the face of adversity, whether from personal or professional life challenges.

I want to thank each of the dialogue participants for their thoughtful contribution, and for the unique style each of them brought to the discussion. While I expected the dialogue to be very useful, I did not expect it to be as far ranging and provocative as it turned out to be. The idea of gifts was brought to life and viewed from vantage points that I had never considered.

Below are brief sentences naming the teachers and their teaching positions. Next, I have excerpted the parts of the dialogue where each one of them names their core gift and briefly discusses it, as a way for you to begin to get to know each of them.

Brian Anderson
High school English teacher and curriculum specialist
Bothell, Washington

Chris Heimerl
Developmental and Behavioral Health Specialist
Albuquerque, New Mexico

Catherine Johnson
Core Faculty, Leadership Institute of Seattle (L.I.O.S)
Kenmore, Washington

Renae Taylor
Elementary school teacher
Hagerman, Idaho

Roger Taylor, Principal
Roger Taylor & Associates
Leadership and Organization Consulting
Vashon, Washington

Teacher's Dialogue
Beginning Dialogue: What are your gifts?

Bruce: Thank you for agreeing to spend time together talking about core gifts. All of you have been through the core gift identification process, so I'm going to ask you to say your core gift as one of the ways for readers to get to know a little about who you are. Who will start?

Chris: O.K., I'll go. Bruce introduced me to the gift idea a few years ago and, as his learning has evolved, so has mine. I recently did the core gift process again, and ended up pretty close to where I was a few years ago. *My gift is creating openings where belonging occurs. I rely on forgiveness and love to be open to patterns that create possibilities for change.* Somehow, my gift sums up what I think I've learned in forty years or so. Most of us are not as alone as we think we are, and most of us are more alone than we'd like to be. This whole business about creating space where people belong is really important to me. I can see how it comes out of my wound. It's clear to me why you are all here, but what contribution am I bringing? That's not so clear to me. But that's the wound side talking. I do know that—however I have led my life and however I have created my work—it has been around this sort of stuff fundamentally.

Roger: The way I've thought about that, related to myself, is that we teach what we need to learn. We give to other people, usually unconsciously, what we need from them—the mirror image of the gift and the wound is what we are all about. I'm a fellow traveler with Bruce on the path of working with the gift and wound layer.

Cath: I'll share my gift. The gift statement I created as part of Bruce's gift identification process was tough to own, just because of the language I came up with. I've tried to shift it around and come up with language that appealed to me, but every time I do I say to myself, "No, this really is the one." I have to live with my own shadow. That's part of fully understanding and living your gift. *My gift is to ease suffering. I do this by bringing compassion, encouragement, clarity and appreciation of beauty to challenging situations.*

Brian: One of the nice things about hearing other people say their gifts is that I recognize "That isn't my gift, and that could never be my gift." Cath, I was trying to imagine what kind of person could possibly have that gift. It's so alien to me that I'm trying to imagine myself even saying it out loud. And I'm sure that when I read my gift, other people will have a similar experience to what I am having right now. What's important about that for me is that it is the nature of gifts that we each have our own. In that sense, I can see how people could really appreciate each other's gifts. If that's your gift, Cath, you must have a lot to offer me, because I have absolutely no talents in that area. That's one of the good things about gifts that I can see.

Cath: I'm hanging on your every word. Now I have to know what your gift is. Would you tell me? I'd love to have that same experience you are talking about.

Brian: *My gift is to see and act on the truth in the world. I do this by self-understanding, keeping commitments, and by having a sense of shared and common humanity.*

Chris: The interesting thing to me is that everything Brian just said, I had somewhere on my list of things while I was working on finding my core gift. But I ended up with a very different core gift than he did. I talked a lot about integrity and commitment, and a lot about truth...I had a whole pile of truth information. But I ended up with something different at the end.

Roger: It is interesting how there is one thing on each of our lists that, in the end, had priority over everything else.

Chris: My experience with hearing other people's gifts is I'm thinking, "I want that one. Why can't I have that one? Who gives out these things, anyway? Where was I when that one was handed out?"

Brian: For me, when I hear others say their gift, I wonder why they would want that gift.

Roger: That's probably because you know that, when you get the gift, you also get the wound. And you have an idea of what their wound is.

(Group laughter)

Chris: I'm glad the core gift process doesn't ask you to make a "wound statement"!

Renae: But it clearly comes out in the process of finding your gift.

Brian: But I never thought about that. It just sounded so appealing and nice to have a gift, I never thought about the flip side of it at the time I was doing the process.

Cath: Brian, after hearing your gift I would be very drawn to know more about your life. I can see how working with you would be a wonderful opportunity for me. I could imagine, in encountering you, that we could rub each other the wrong way. The truth teller and the compassionate one meet. Me, wanting to hear everyone's story, and you wanting just to tell the truth and get to the point! So I might miss, or not appreciate, who you are.

Chris: I can see Brian rolling his eyes while you are trying to hear someone's story.

Cath: It seems like this idea would be such an incredible joining up opportunity for a group. I'm thinking what it would be like for a group of teachers, or the students in a classroom, to start by knowing each other's gifts. It would give me so much to work with while I am up front as a teacher…things that most of the time I end up discovering by a lot of trial and error.

Chris: I came into this discussion really disagreeing with Bruce's statement that knowing and acknowledging each other's gift is critical to wholeness and community. I was thinking, "Nah, I just think it's acknowledging that we have gifts that's important—we don't necessarily need to know what they are." But through the course of this conversation I have become convinced that, yes, we need to know what they are. It creates a richness and the possibility for relationship.

Roger: I'll share my gift. *My core gift is holding the whole that contains polarities. I do this by listening for and honoring hidden intentions, power, vulnerability, and courage and coordinating contributions.*

Chris: I want that gift.

Roger: It's so satisfying to hear other people's gifts. It's interesting, it's sometimes validating, but sometimes I think to myself, "I wonder if I have some of that one in me?" There is this list of things to choose from, and there is something that resonates as more important and, for me personally, it's taken a while for me to get at that.

Renae: I did the gift process with Bruce's wife Gina, and we are in much the same space related to some interests we have. So when I speak to her, I speak to her in terms of that connection. That's what I try to do in relationships. Because of that, some of the language in my gift statement is related to how she and I speak together and what we share, and I need to rethink that, in terms of what I really feel and what the right language is.

Roger: Are you saying that, with Gina, you access a certain part of yourself, and you are going to go back and integrate that with your whole self?

Renae: Yes, that's what I need to do. *My core gift is opening to spirit and healing others hearts through our combined truth. I practice this gift by opening* *to spiritual resources as my teacher, seeking the truth in others and holding my own truth, capturing the essence of others who need relationships, and loving others with understanding, forgiveness and sacrifice.*

Chris: Thanks, Renae. I'm wondering, did any of you get strong reactions when you were talking with other people about your core gift?

Brian: Well, as I said, my gift is about speaking the truth. When I read my gift statement to my wife, she said, "You mean YOUR truth?" And I said, "No, THE truth". Then she said, "Do you mean A truth?" And I said, "No, THE truth." Then she wanted to know if truth was capitalized. I said it was. (He laughs) When I got done talking with her, my gift was so diminished. I had no gift. I wanted somebody else's gift at that point.

Chris: I called my wife Sandy today, and told her I was working on my core gift statement. She said, "I'm really looking forward to hearing it." I told her I could read it to her on the phone, but she said, "No, I'd really like to go out somewhere together where there are no distractions." I think she wants a public place, where I can't escape, to inform me about how it isn't my gift and dismantle it right in front of my eyes! *(Laughter)*

Roger: She could have asked you for a copy of it a week before so she had time to completely review it and prepare what to say.

Chris: I got a little preview of what it will be like when I showed it to someone else who said, "You know what, this is absolutely perfect, but if I were going to make just a few changes to your gift…" *(Laughter)* I thought, this is just what it's going to be like to talk with Sandy.

Bruce: All right, everyone's had a chance to describe their gift. Again, I want to thank you for coming. Let's move on to the benefits and begin the discussion.

End.

(Note: The dialogue resumes beginning at the end of Benefit One.)

THE INTERIOR LIFE OF A TEACHER:
BENEFITS ONE, TWO, AND THREE

10. BENEFIT ONE: INCREASED COURAGE TO FACE DIFFICULT SITUATIONS

What causes courage to erupt in a person? Regardless of whether courage compels you to stand up and be counted in a way that causes others to notice and comment on your bravery, or you act quietly and invisibly, what will drive you to stop thinking and act? Although it may seem superfluous and not-quite-the-point in the moment, grounding yourself by remembering your core gift can cause courage to erupt with surprising levels of intensity. Why is this?

You are more likely to act when you can see a direct link between the purpose of your life and the action that needs to be taken.

When courage is required, there is always risk. And few people will take a risk without a firm tie to a value and principle that is meaningful to them. Remembering your gift, and seeing how it can be used in the situation, can cause you to become motivated to act. Because you see your gift as one of the primary driving forces in your life, you feel compelled to give it, even when there is danger involved.

When you give your gift, you are protecting your integrity and acting in a way that you are willing to be seen. Your commitment to act, even when there is a high level of danger involved, increases because you are doing what you believe you are supposed to do. This certainty does not reduce fear, but it compels you to act in spite of your fear.

Regardless of my judgments, a person in an alley taking a life-threatening risk by shooting heroin is operating under a value/principle that is meaningful to him or her. It may be "My life is going to hurt less if I get high," or "No one really cares about me, so I can do whatever I want with my life," but this person has definable goals they are using for making the decision to take the drug. What if the person knew their gift and decided to act out of that understanding rather than continuing their addictive thinking patterns? This is the power within the gift. It has the capacity to compel you towards action that is grounded in the contribution you can make to the world rather than the harm you also have the capacity to offer. When gifts are involved, action is involved.

You become less willing to be pushed around by others.

If you don't have a solid idea about who you are, people will make of you what they want to. If the ground you are standing on in a conflicted situation is unstable, others can sense your tentativeness and move in to make your ground into their ground, drawing you into their way of thinking or acting which may or may not be who you really are. By remembering your gift, you have at least one solid idea to ground yourself in during a conflicted situation.

The courage you muster erupts, not out of a false sense of bravado and ego, but from the roots of who you really are. This provides a solid base for you in the situation that reduces the likelihood of being easily swayed by the strong emotions or ideas of others. When you offer your gift, you are making a statement that you are grounding yourself in the situation through identifying the contribution you intend to make. You may be on the fence related to the final outcome or decision within the situation, but you are not aimlessly floating and offering yourself for manipulation to those around you. You know who you are.

You feel worthy enough to act.

Many times, we choose not to act because we do not feel "good enough." These feelings of not being good enough come in two forms. First, that we are not skilled enough to be successful in the situation we are facing. Remembering your core gift grounds you in the fact that you do have some skills to use in this situation. Because your core gift is one of the primary problem-solving tools you have at your disposal, you can immediately begin to use it to your advantage in engaging in the situation. The situation may need more skills and talents from you than just your core gift, but getting started by giving your gift will propel you into initial engagement.

You know how it goes—getting started is often most of the battle. I frequently remember this in my own life. As I have said, my core gift is to help people use their imagination to find a new hopefulness, even when it is risky to do so. Whenever I need to muster courage in a situation, I try to remember my gift and begin my engagement by requiring myself to come up with a few ideas to offer the situation that are novel to myself and the others involved. This gets me started down the path of engagement and provides comfort by engaging me in a way that feels familiar and safe.

Similarly, a person with a gift for compassion might feel confident to initially engage by first asking him- or herself who needs compassion in the situation and approaching them and offering their gift. A person with a gift for logic and order could get the courage to engage in a situation by creating a list of logical steps to solve the problem. Every person's gift can be used in some way to enter a difficult situation, and can provide an initial sense of comfort and safety in what may feel like a storm of conflict, indecision, and hopelessness. You can depend on your gift.

The second reason we may not feel good enough to act is that we believe we do not deserve a positive outcome to the situation. We have already decided—because of weaknesses in who we are, mistakes we have made, or our impression that the other person(s) involved are better than we are—it is payback time. We are going to lose this one. Framing this as a "you win and I lose" situation creates the possibility for us to be the loser, which is the result we desire from the situation. When this kind of hopelessness overcomes us—I'm going to lose because I deserve to—it is because we have forgotten that there is a difference between being unworthy and being incompetent. They are not the same. It may be true that I am not skilled enough to successfully navigate this situation, but that does not mean I am not worthy enough to engage.

The baseline question being answered when I decide whether I am worthy is: "Am I deserving of life?" When I retreat, I am answering that my death—whether it is a small or large part of me—is what I deserve. Remember the examples in Chapter Six of core courage-stopping messages that come from your limp?

Someone will be disappointed in me.
Those people won't like me if I do this.
I'm not smart enough.
I'm not good enough to deserve this.
I always fail, so why try.
I haven't earned the right to have this.
I don't have enough time.
Somebody else can do it better than me.

When we do not act out of courage, it is often because the voice of our limp has overtaken our willingness to engage fully with the world. We have retreated into the comfort of being less than who we are. What advantage does this retreat bring us? Judith Simmer-Brown reveals what is often my hidden desire when I heed my limping voice and choose not to act in a situation requiring courage.

> "One of the Tibetan teachings that probably puts the most surprising sort of twist on understanding the feeling of unworthiness comes from Shantideva. He says that not feeling worthy carries a kind of discouragement, which can then be used as an excuse for laziness. One thing is to look at the causes of low self-esteem; another thing is to see how we might use it as an excuse for not doing things. For example, one might think, "I don't feel like I am worthy of that good job, so I will not take it."[25]

When we remember and choose to use our gift, we decide that we are worthy. To remember my gift in my lowest moments, when I feel no courage, no self-worth, and no vision for a future in which I am fully alive, is a seed of hope. It is a point of worthiness from which I cannot escape without deceiving myself into believing I am less than I am. Amongst the clutter of my imperfect existence, I know there is a part of me that is worthy. I may give my gift in an incompetent way, but that does not detract from the truth: By saying my gift is worthy, I am saying that I am worthy. They are one and the same. Courage erupts from this remembering.

---

25. Mitchell, Donald W. and Wiseman, James O.S.B. eds. *Transforming Suffering*. Doubleday. New York, N.Y. 2003. Page 109.

You see the actions of others within the context of their gifts and wounds—they are not just out to get you.

Well, they may indeed be out to get you, but you don't see it coming from a desire that is genuinely directed at you. You represent something to them that has triggered their wounds or caused them to want to give their gift. Their action has brought conflict into your relationship with them. It also might have caused you to act out of your gifts and your wounds and escalate the conflict. Remembering your gift helps make the distinction between "not liking the behavior of the person" versus "not liking the person." This is one of the foundations for love—"I can act in ways that displease you, but you will not abandon me." When we are able to separate out a person's hurtful actions from their desire to hurt us, we become more willing to be in relationship. In this case, courage rises as a direct result of feeling less threatened by another's actions.

You see the current situation as part of a larger path in your life. It's worth engaging in order to stay on the path.

Remembering and giving your gift puts you in the position of standing on a certain path. This path is most often the larger direction of your life— the path you have chosen to be on in order to fulfill your dreams and find the trouble you were meant to encounter. Courage rises in you primarily because you become more willing to endure suffering when you believe the path is serious and connected to the direction you have decided to go. I'd better act, even if it hurts, or I'm going to get sidetracked.

Parker Palmer talks about the decision we can make which is to "live divided no more."[26] Part of this decision is to acknowledge that I am who I am, and my actions must be congruent with this awareness as much of the time as I am able to remain alert. Hiding becomes less of an option, because the suffering that results from not being authentic becomes unbearable. On the other side, the suffering we experience when we are on our path is balanced by the deep satisfaction of having acted out of our genuine self.

---

26. Palmer, Parker. *The Courage to Teach.* Page 167

Benefit One

Questions for teachers:

1. What person or situation is pushing you around? What is the source of your willingness to be pushed?
2. When courage rises up in you, is there a common seed—a thought, value, memory—which usually initiates the courage?
3. How can you use your gift at times when courage is required?
4. How is your gift a source of comfort in courage-demanding situations?
5. Have you ever confused being unworthy with being incompetent in your own life? Can you tell us a story about that situation?
6. Thinking back in your life, can you think of a person who seemed determined to bring difficulty into your life? How could their gift have contributed to this determination on their part?

Teacher's Dialogue
Benefit One: Increased Courage to Face Difficult Situations

Cath: Benefit One is about how gifts can increase the level of courage to face difficulties in the classroom or surrounding school environment. Does anyone have a story?

Brian: I like the Nietzsche quote in Bruce's book, "When you are a camel, you bend down and pick up a load." It reminded me of something from *Paradise Lost* when someone says, "Who can advise, may speak." I think that's how you recognize what your gift is. There was a time last year when our staff was having problems, and at one critical point in the discussion, I had a really strong sensation of, "Now it's your chance to say this." My reaction was, "Oh, shit, I don't want to say that." Then there was a big, long, pause. I looked around the room and realized there was no one else in the room who was aware of this and could say it. I was certain I was the only one. It's not bragging or my ego, it was the truth at that time. So I stood up and said it. It made a huge difference. I realized there are knowing moments when you know what your gift is and you have a choice—and you have to make a choice—to give it or not. The dread, initially, comes from reopening the wound. But in doing it, you get stronger. And so, in that sense, I do know my gift. And I've gotten to know it better by giving it, and it does heal.

Cath: You are speaking to something I've wanted to pay attention to. When do I truly feel called to act or speak, and when am I doing it because it's expected? There is a difference. I know something about those moments when "I'm the one who is being called," and it's a different thing.

Renae: If, however, your gift is there and it's being exercised, then the strength of that calling is not so much because it comes more naturally to you. Sometimes you are feeling confident and you do it. Other times I feel it coming and I ask myself, "Was that necessary? Why did I do that?" For me, the pain comes out in all the wondering about if I did it right. When you do have a voice that speaks from your gift, confidence builds in giving it, but you still have to deal with the pain.

Brian: I can remember the attendant thoughts right before I decided to speak up. They were that "the person you are would say that. And if you don't say that, you're not the person you are. You are actually giving up your identity. You will no longer be a genuine person if you don't speak right now. You will disappear if you don't say this, and you will have to live with that." And that's some of the dread, also. It felt like a crucifixion kind of thing, "Why was I given this gift, God?" I don't want this. I have a talent for this, but I don't want it! It's like you want to run away from your own cross. It's a funny kind of irony—"Oh boy, I'm going to suffer again for this! This is going to make me bleed, but it's a talent I have."

Renae: Isn't that also what your students want from you, Brian?

Brian: Yes.

Roger: For me, part of the danger—based on my own wound—is fusing the giving of my gift with my desire to influence others. The more I want to be influential by attaching this thing I'm going to say to having a certain effect, the more problematic it gets. Versus giving it with no attachment to the outcome. I'm much more satisfied when someone comes up to me afterwards and says "Hey, thanks for saying that" than I am the times when no one notices that I've said it. But, the truth is, it may have been just as much of a contribution to the outcome. But sometimes I can get into managing the desire to be influential. I need to separate that from just giving the gift.

Bruce: This goes back to the language of gifts. One of the problems with understanding gifts is that we have associated a meaning with the word that can confuse us during gift-giving moments. Most of us think about our gifts as wonderful, and full of beauty and goodness. But what if the gift is actually a completely neutral capacity within us, waiting to be used? I heard Michael Meade, a teacher of mine, say it's your character that determines whether you do good or harm with your gift. That fork in the road seems to be what you are speaking about, Roger.

Brian: Either way, there is a calling to it. That's how you know, for better or worse, there is a gift there.

Chris: There is a line from a Bruce Cockburn song, "When you know, in a moment, that it is your time, you walk with the power of a thousand generations." When you absolutely know this is what you are supposed to be doing, you have tremendous power.

Renae: When you know your gift, that's true.

Brian: This idea of gifts gives me such a different perspective. I am thinking of another situation where I'm realizing that I did give my gift, but nobody else did. Looking back at it, that was my frustration. I was the only one who spoke up, and there was dead silence for weeks after that. Cath, there was no-one who had your gift of easing suffering that stood up and said, "How can we do this in a compassionate way. How can we eliminate this suffering?" Since that's not my gift, I couldn't do that. I did give my gift of trying to tell the truth. I know we have people on our staff with gifts of compassion, but nobody gave that gift.

Renae: Brian, if you were in those situations with teachers and you knew each other's gifts—and you asked each other to give their gifts—I believe the whole situation could be reoriented. It would change the whole culture.

Cath: Gifts is a much more appreciative approach. You are getting people to bring to the situation a contribution to what's not working. It's generative rather than destructive.

Bruce: Yes, it is. Brian's example highlights the fact that it's not enough simply to believe in gifts. You have to know each other's gifts and be willing to ask for them to be given.

Brian: If I would have known how this works, I could have done something about it. I could have asked.

Chris: What did you get from giving your gift?

Brian: I got a lot of secret emails, "thank you's" after the fact, and private comments. And, you know what, I hated every one of them. What I should have done was say, "Thank you for your comments, but next time would you also give your gift, too?" That's something that would legitimately work. I never thought of doing that. I could expect them to give their gift. I could have expected people to do things differently

Cath: There is a simple energetic about this. Actually having the conversation with people about gifts and saying, "I need your help in this. Will you do your part?" Thanks for telling us about your situation, Brian. You have given us so much juice for this conversation.

Brian: I am so ready for our next big meeting!

Roger: I too appreciate you bringing this and being open about it. It's helpful to apply this gift thing to something that's meaningful—to see if it really works. You can't bend it around to make the theory fit it. It's real.

Chris: Cath, the minute you said the first benefit was about acting with courage, what went through my mind was, "Why would we limit it to classrooms?" How do you use your core gift to act with courage in your life? In your marriage, your school, your church—all parts of your life.

Cath: I'm really aware of an opportunity I had to bring my gift, and I was too scared to do it. There was a big meeting in our community about a sex offender who was going to move here. There was a hot and emotional and angry field in the room. I had actually met the guy, and I came to the meeting to support him in making a new life. But, as soon as I got in the room, I was so internally conflicted. All of a sudden I started to think, "What if he does re-offend? How am I going to live with that?" It was the most painful thing I've ever sat through in my whole life. I think of myself as a courageous person, and I couldn't get up the guts to speak. So I think there is a challenge in this. Part of giving your gift is dealing with the fear of what might come. I can still feel it and taste it. That's the other side—the failure to give your gift and the pain around that.

Roger: I can hear it in your voice, knowing that your gift is a lot about integrity. I hear difficulty between integrity and danger. Where do they overlap?

Cath: In that moment, they were exactly overlapping. But I want to make a different point. Even though I failed to give my gift that night, in the long run, the compassion I was called to develop for myself actually strengthened my gift overall. I think it was a necessary developmental moment for me to be able to continue to give and stand behind my gift.

Bruce: For me, one of the beautiful ideas about the gift is that when you are following your gift path, you find exactly the trouble you are meant to find. It strengthens you.

Cath: Initially, when I failed to give my gift, I felt a lot of shame and disappointment in myself. But in the process of working that through, I found a new level of self-compassion that I think has strengthened my ability to be compassionate with others and also given me more courage to give my gift.

Roger: That links it directly to Benefit Two—giving your gift to help with your own healing. That's good. It strengthened your gift.

Chris: You found that not giving your gift in a scary situation was worse than whatever you imagined might have happened had you given your gift. That's way further down the path than the person who is still weighing "Is this difficulty and pain worth it?" And now, since you've gone through that, you've confirmed, "Yes, it is." You are much more likely to give it in the future.

Cath: I won't know that till I come to it. But I do have a strong sense that it was a necessary step on the path.

Roger: It points back to the importance of knowing your gift and giving it. It's part of a long journey. It's like, on your deathbed, if you can look back and say, "Over the last few years, I don't think I've missed a chance to give my gift." That's the goal.

Renae: Yesterday, I watched Bruce's son carving on a stick of wood. As I remember that image of him carving, it reminds me that your gift is also an image, and you are carving away at it for your whole life.

Chris: And each slice with the knife hurts.

Renae: Yes it does, a bit. But, once you have a vision of what the image is going to be, then there is purpose. The purpose is to get to the shape you imagine.

Roger: You also have to make the cuts intentionally each time.

Chris: I'd like to believe our lives are just long enough for us to get to the point of saying, "Good enough."

Brian: In the gift interviewing process, one of the questions is "What's something you haven't had the courage to do?" My answer was that I couldn't think of anything. Cath, in telling that story, you just jogged my memory. One of the really good things I have done in the last five years has been to be courageous. But I do have a courage issue. That story, and the tone of your voice, brought mine up. I want to thank you for that. It's funny how only real truth telling, which is my gift, acts like a serum— it can bring up other truths. Thank you.

End.

11. BENEFIT TWO: HEALING YOURSELF AND HAVING COMPASSION FOR OTHERS

I want to look, but I don't want to see.

Most of us are attracted towards suffering, whether it is our own or someone else's. The traffic slows down at the car accident, and our curiosity to look conflicts with the part of us that does not want to see. In the same way, we have a push and pull with ourselves connected to our attraction towards, and at the same time our fear of, seeing deep within ourselves. What will I find? For myself, I am quite certain I have discovered the answer to that question, and it both frightens and consoles me. That which has the possibility for the most harm and torment is located in exactly the same location as that which has the possibility for me to find healing and joy. So the push and pull begins.

The attraction towards suffering can be seen most easily in our diligence at running away from it. If only we could! Every moment we spend developing and using a strategy for avoiding suffering is time spent exactly focused on our suffering. How could we miss the obvious? The running guarantees that we will end up back on the same doorstep, for in the running we will not have found the answers that enable us to knock on a different door—the door where healing is possible.

It's convenient that humans have an attraction towards suffering, because suffering has every intention of following us until we pay attention. Try as we might to avoid it, the effects of it influence our thoughts, feelings, and actions throughout each day. Why is it, if it hurts so much, that the discomfort has to reach a level of peak intensity before we act to eliminate the pain? We postpone our healing because we believe that the act of healing will hurt more than the current suffering we are experiencing. We know that the truths we will be required to face will undo the false truths which are precariously propping up our life in ways that benefit us in the moment by helping us to avoid suffering. These false truths, which allow us permission for destructive feelings, beliefs, and actions, are a disservice to both others and us in the long run. When we turn to genuinely face our true selves, the false truths are no longer there to prop us up and we begin to feel the shaky foundations of our life crumble away. The healing path is risky business because, for the period of time while a new foundation is being built, we are not certain who we really are.

Joseph Goldstein, founder of the Insight Meditation Society in Massachusetts, and writer of books on meditation and spirituality, reminds us that the search for healing is a descent rather than an ascent. We go down into our souls in a search for the cracks in our armor that allow us to see into the darkness. In the book *Transforming Suffering*, he comments:

> "Carl Jung said, 'One does not become enlightened by imagining figures of light, but by making the darkness conscious. The latter procedure, however, is disagreeable and therefore not popular.' It is disagreeable at first. What has been so amazing after all these years is that I think we come to a point where our commitment to the truth is so strong that actually there's a feeling of delight in seeing the flaws, in seeing defilements. Now, when I watch my mind, I'm so happy to see them because in seeing them is the possibility of being free to make choices that are guided more by loving kindness and compassion."[27]

When we define our core gift, it means we have gone through the process of recognizing that this gift is the opposing force to however our psyche has framed the largest suffering we have known during our life. At least during the gift discovery period, we have decided not to run from

---

27. Mitchell, Donald W. and Wiseman, James O.S.B. eds. *Transforming Suffering*. Page 101.

the suffering, but to intentionally act towards its recognition and our own healing. We also know when we give our core gift we are acting in opposition to that suffering. Each giving of the gift is one more notch in the signpost that marks our progress on a healing path.

Where does healing happen?

The modern approach asks us to believe that healing happens within each person. We may visit a therapist or talk with friends and loved ones, but the healing process is happening as a result of our internal thoughts and feelings. The essential task is to create an understanding of our hurt—both the root actions done to us by others and the resulting suffering we are experiencing. This understanding is created through a reflective process of questioning and resulting discovery of the true nature of our story. Through understanding our story, we develop compassion and an accompanying ability to forgive others and ourselves. Within this context for healing, the path is interior. Healing results from our own efforts to think, feel, and forgive our way through the process.

Does any part of the healing process occur outside of us? Are we required to act differently in the outside world as a necessary step for healing? While it is true that knowing your story, developing a compassionate understanding, and forgiveness are essential steps to healing, these three steps alone do not complete the process. If you stop at this point, it is likely you will stay stuck in this part of your story for a long, long, time. One of the other necessary steps to healing is to go out into the world again and consciously give your core gift. Because it is the specific opposing force to your suffering, it acts as an antidote for your healing. More than an escape from what has been difficult or a surface-level attempt to "be positive," this step in healing reconfirms that you have identified your suffering and have named the action you can take which will both heal you and, at the same time, serve the world.

In the giving of your gift, you are reaffirming that you will not be stopped by your suffering. In fact, you have an increased capacity you are willing to offer the world that was groomed and prepared out of your most difficult experiences. Giving your gift affirms you are not wandering aimlessly. There is a direction you are traveling, and giving your core gift declares to others the path you have chosen.

The process of healing requires you to be in the past and future at the very same moment—responding to the desire to give your core gift and move forward while casting a tender, compassionate, and wiser eye backward towards the difficulties you have known. No longer stuck in your story, you are once again moving towards the next joyful moment and the next difficulty you will face. It is in the moments when we are able to stand exactly in between our sorrow and joy—the light and darkness within us—that the genuine sweetness of life can be found. Neither taste drowning our senses, we can feel the fullness of the gift and wound as we engage in the world.

If healing is not solely reserved for the therapy couch or the privacy of our living room while we search for understanding in the middle of a self-help book—if healing requires acting differently out in the world—then where can we make these healing actions? Sobonfu Somé, in her book *Falling Out Of Grace*, reminds us that "in the modern world, people devote so much of themselves to their work that it often becomes the most important space in their life in which to heal and grow."[28]

Teachers can find healing while teaching

What opportunities are there for healing within our gift-giving life as a teacher? There are many possibilities.

Being aware of where you are currently giving your gift.

What are situations in which you are currently giving your gift? Many times, we are giving our gift in multiple ways already, and are pleasantly surprised when we recognize how full our gift-giving life is. This awareness provides a boost to us because we are affirmed for the path we are on. By intentionally deciding to be more aware of and to continue these opportunities, we place ourselves consciously in a gift-giving state more often. This brings us an appreciation of who we are, a respect for our intentions, and provides us with specific proof that in these gift-giving moments we have risen above our suffering.

Identify places in your teaching life where you could offer or expand the giving of your gift.

Paul is an English teacher who has a core gift of "helping others see the beauty in opposing ideas." Thinking through where he currently gives his

---

28. Somé, Sobonfu, *Falling Out Of Grace*. Page 71

gift, Paul realized he spends a considerable amount of time in the classroom focusing with students on the different ways to interpret the meaning of the readings he assigns. He also realized that he goes the extra mile in making sure that the quiet students get ample encouragement to speak up and share their viewpoints. What could he do to give his gift in other ways during the school day? He determines that he has been frustrated for a few years by the stagnant curriculum he is required to teach. He decides to approach other teachers and organize a committee to review more innovative curriculums and different ways to achieve similar student outcomes using more innovative approaches to the current curriculum. Far from feeling like this is a burden to take on, Paul is excited because his gift is in this area and he gets the opportunity to exercise his gift muscle. Also, Paul has decided that he will take on mentoring responsibility for one of his students who is struggling on the debate team. Both of these additional duties give him the opportunity to further give his gift during his teaching life.

Be seen for giving your gift.

Each time you are seen and then acknowledged by another person for giving your gift, it provides a healing moment in your life. Each acknowledgment is another conscious realization you have risen above your troubles, at least for this moment. By taking stock of all the situations in your life where you have the opportunity to give your gift, and then consciously contributing it whenever you can, you up the chances of being seen and acknowledged for this gift.

How is this different from the insistent call from your ego to be noticed? It is different because your ego will take any kind of gratification it can find. It doesn't care about the source, the kind of acknowledgment, or the intensity of the acknowledgment. It just wants to be stroked and pleased. Your gift, on the other hand, is looking for a very specific kind of acknowledgment—the verification that you have been seen or recognized for acting in direct opposition to what has hurt you in the past. When another person notices you in that precise act, your psyche cranks up the flag and sends out the marching band to notice. "You did it again!" it tells you. The emotional response to gift acknowledgment is most always more intense than acknowledgment for other kinds of good work and efforts you may be involved in.

Recognizing, each time you give your gift, you are acting in direct opposition to your wound.

We can act powerfully when we give our gift. Our actions have a grounding, intention, and assertiveness that cause us and others to note that something more than a casual interlude is taking place. The source of this powerfulness is intensified when we are aware that we are acting out our passion to break the cycle of our suffering by demonstrating to the world the action that would have stopped the hurt we experienced. When you are aware of your intentions, and acting out of a conscious powerfulness, a healing moment occurs within you.

Being aware of how your suffering is following you into your life as a teacher, and choosing to act out of both your gift and your wound.

Being aware of your gift means you are aware of your wound. Because healing is a continual process—most of us will not get a spontaneous eruption of permanent healing—we are faced with situations each day that trigger memories of our wounds. Oftentimes, the triggers occur through our relationships with others when their actions remind us of the person who hurt us. We witness another person criticizing a child, a person ignoring the suffering of another, a young woman not respecting the ideas of her friends, or an old man not taking the time to help a young boy to understand why his friends are ignoring him. In each case, we are witnessing what our psyche is sensing as a return to our own ordeal—we are once again in the moment of our suffering, living out the pain we have carried unhealed into our adult lives.

At other times, the trigger occurs when we witness another person not taking an action to save themselves from their hurt. Like us, we see that they are not enough in the moment to fend off what is hurting them. Whether it is not being strong enough, smart enough, or brave enough, we watch them succumb to their suffering and are triggered into our own memories of how we were not enough during our ordeals. In both situations, our wounds are triggered and we have the opportunity to act.

How will we respond? Healing action on our part occurs when we act out of a balance of our gift and our wound. The gift part of our action is using the alternative to the destruction we are witnessing to be helpful in the moment. We bring our capacity to the current situation by offering our gift. The wound part of our action is the source for our passion and our commitment to enter a situation where there most likely is danger involved. Having the courage to rise up against others who are causing hurt in others or acting in unhealthy ways towards themselves, requires us to withstand the likely backlash resulting from our intervention. We may become the new target for their hurt. Our determination to continue is rooted in the memory of our own suffering and the resulting desire for others not to experience the suffering we know so well.

Recognize recurring struggles in your life as rooted in gift trouble, not simply encountering difficult people or unlucky moments.

When we first encounter trouble, we are likely to act in ways that attempt to get rid of it. Whether our strategies are to face it or run from it, we want the issue resolved so the discomfort goes away. If we take a step back and postpone action for a moment, as we catch our breath we may realize that this trouble is familiar. Maybe not the exact circumstances, but the kind of trouble we are in feels like an old coat we are wearing. Perhaps it is a certain quality in another person that rubs us the wrong way whenever we see it. Maybe it is a behavior of ours that frustrates us. Maybe we find ourselves not being able to influence a group in the way we want to. Whatever the situation, it is another in a long string of similar events in our life. Coming back to us over and over again, it beckons us to use this opportunity to further understand our suffering and give our gift.

By slowing down and naming the circumstance as familiar, we open the possibility for healing. A quick fix is no longer the most important criterion for resolution. We now have a desire to understand the event in the larger context of our life. Benefit Four describes four common kinds of trouble a person encounters related to gifts. During these moments when we stop in our tracks and consider whether we are in "gift trouble," these four conditions are helpful to remember: 1) Is this trouble occurring because I am not giving my gift when I should be? 2) Have I encountered difficulty because another person is trying to block me from giving my gift? 3) Have I found trouble by using my gift in a way that is driving others away from me? 4) Am I suffering because I have been thrown into my wound and am therefore acting in ways that are hurtful to others or myself?

In these times of gift trouble, the opportunity presenting itself is for us to offer a larger possibility of ourselves to the world. As we question the roots of our circumstances and the threads of our life are further revealed, we reaffirm the path we are on and regain our commitment and our courage to continue. Tentativeness has difficulty surviving under these conditions.

Using your knowledge of the gift/wound idea as a source of compassion and forgiveness for others.

As I further understand how my gift and wound interact to bring both joy and suffering into my life, I become more willing to consider how this dynamic may be driving other people's interactions with me. When another person brings difficulty into our relationship, I consider how the person's actions may be rooted in their gift and suffering and am given the opportunity to choose the route of compassion rather than quickly lashing back or sulking away. The gift/wound idea brings the possibility of pause into our actions. It gives us a reason to slow down and consider the roots of our own and others' action.

The adage that carpenters live in shacks has solid ground to stand on within the gift/wound paradigm. What I see as my own wounds will most certainly rub me when I witness them in others. What I see as my own gift will most certainly cause a turbulent combination of joy and envy when I witness it being given by others. I am looking in the mirror and what I see will cause a strong reaction because it is a face other than my own. It is up to me to plant my reaction within a framework of regard, compassion, and forgiveness rather than anger and hostility.

I can also muster compassion and forgiveness for others when I recognize it is our gifts and wounds rising up to face each other in the moment. We have not meant to bring harm. Rather, it is our gifts and wounds trying to be seen and regarded that has caused the current difficulty in our relationship. The opposing forces of gifts create conflict, and this trouble will most certainly be taken personally by the involved parties unless it is framed as gift trouble.

For instance, a person with a gift for logic and order will be put off by a person with a gift for creativity and continuous consideration of ideas. One wants to make the plan for action and get on with it. The other wants to consider two more ideas before any decision is made. Trouble is the result. In another case, a person with a gift for standing by others is driven to anger by another person who has a gift for telling the truth. They are in a situation where a young person has lied, and the truth-gifted person wants to abandon the young person who has lied. The person with a gift of standing-by-others wants, at all cost, not to abandon the young person simply because of their current inability to tell the truth.

In situation after situation in our lives, we encounter humans with gifts and wounds which, on first appearance, conflict with our own gifts and wounds. If we take the time to frame the conflict within the gift/wound paradigm, we take a step towards the possibility of compassion and forgiveness because we see the trouble they have brought into our life is rooted in a struggle which is similar to ours—both of us are trying to live our life with purpose and integrity. As we develop our own gift further, we begin to see that we need the gifts of others to counteract and round out the limitations of our own gift. In this way, we need other humans. Standing alone, we are often not enough.

Benefit Two
Questions for Teachers:
1. In what teaching situations are you currently giving your gift?
2. Think of two new situations, in your life as a teacher, in which you would be excited and motivated to give your gift. These situations could be in a relationship with another person, as a project related to your work, or in furthering your education about your gift.
3. Which of the four recurring kinds of gift trouble is most common for you? What is the most recent example?
4. When you act out of your wound, what is your typical behavior?
5. What are trigger behaviors in others that set you off? How are those behaviors in others similar to or opposite of your own gift or wound?
6. Who do you know that has a similar gift to yours? What quality(s) in them do you most regard? What specifically do you want to learn more about from them?

Teacher's Dialogue
Benefit Two: Contributing to Your Own Healing and Being More Compassionate with Others

---

Roger: As I was reading this benefit, it took me to the relationship between the gift and the wound. I want to read a couple sentences from the book that were most striking to me. "While it is true that knowing your story, developing a compassionate understanding, and forgiveness are essential steps to healing, these three steps alone do not complete the process. If you stop at this point, it is likely you will remain stuck in this part of your story for a long, long, time." I had the sense, Bruce, that when you wrote this you limited yourself to just two "longs". *(Laughter)*

Bruce: I wanted to put six of those "longs" in.

Roger: Bruce is saying that one of the other necessary steps to healing is to go out into the world again and consciously give your core gift. To me, this is the contribution his book is making—the idea of the conscious giving of the gift. He goes on to say that you give your core gift "because it is the specific opposing force to your suffering and acts as the antidote for your healing. In the giving of your gift you are reaffirming that you will not be stopped by your suffering." What I was thinking about was the difference between the frame of knowing my strengths and using them, and knowing my gift and giving my gift. That distinction is huge. The difference between my strengths and my gift is that my gift is directly connected to my wounds.

Chris: You are talking about the difference between strengths and gifts, and the capacity to merge all these activities. A lot of what I consider to be my strong suits—what people say I'm good at—are things that were developed out of my wound. In the past, I didn't give those strengths as a way to heal my wound or acknowledge my gift, but to run away from my wound. In doing that I was also running away from my gift.

Roger: To become conscious of the gift you have to work through that. Part of the grief process is denial, and I remember learning from a guy named Ken Graves a while ago that denial has a very important function. It provides resistance. The function of denial is to create the space in time for the person to develop the inner and outer resources to be able to handle the grief and loss. I think there is a natural force in us to avoid challenge and pain. I remember the old Outward Bound slogan, "If you can't get out of it, you'll get into it." For a long time, I thought I could get out of it. During that time, I said to myself, "Well, I don't want to get out of this, I want to face it." But I really didn't. Later, there was a moment where I realized, "I actually can't get out of this." That realization brought a whole different level of gravity with it.

Chris: One of the ways I continued to get out of it was by being seduced by the rewards I got from giving my strong suits. But it kept me from really, truly, giving my gift. I started to get led down an in-authentic path that said my strong suits are the contribution I am making. That actually took me off course from what my soul yearns for, which is to bring the gift and wound more closely into my consciousness.

Renae: When you get on the path, you realize it will be a journey and it's going to require a flashlight. When I was twenty, thirty, and forty, I wanted so much to fix it. I got to a point when I was fifty that I just said, "To heck with it." Then when I was sixty, I began to think, "This fixing is going to take a while." (*Laughter*)

Roger: For me, twenty was "I want to fix it", thirty was "I've got it all fixed", and fifty was realizing that I had lied when I was thirty. Now, I not only still have to fix it, but I've also got to deal with the lying. (*Laughter*)

Renae: My daughter is thirty and she's telling me now, "I've got it all fixed, Mom. Let me tell you how it is, Mom."

Cath: Robert Kegan's book, *In Over Our Heads*, has a premise that most of us have not yet developed a level of consciousness to meet the complexities in life today. Just like kids, eventually, get the fact that they are not the center of the world—there is a continual journey that requires understanding deeper and deeper layers of complexity. One of the examples in the book is about how, as parents, we are so excited as our children get more and more mature, and we want to watch them exercising more responsibility and authority. And then they take the car and they are supposed to be home at midnight and they don't show up. Then we get upset because they haven't considered the impact on us. In terms of levels of consciousness, young people don't yet carry the awareness of their impact on us. I'm thinking that one possibility is that the idea of gifts might be a way to bridge the different levels of consciousness that people have in a given situation—"How do you see the world right now, and how are you going to give your gift?"

Chris: I think you're right. Underneath all the complexity and chaos is a very simple symmetry. An almost unspeakable beauty. The gift brings us back to that. The complexity causes us to get lost in the wounds of, "I'm not smart enough, I'm not good enough, I can't handle all this information…" I believe the complexity is important to understand, but if we get caught up in it, then we begin to believe we have to keep up the pace. That gets us to a kind of urgency that can only end in despair. The gift allows us to come back to what's really powerful and really true.

Cath: I'm thinking that gifts can be a handrail for students to navigate ambiguity. It's often times the ones who need all the handrails who can look like they are troublemakers. They ask so much of the rest of us. But they may be doing the best they can at the level of their consciousness, and they may be giving their gift.

Renae: It could also be that their gift is contributing to the necessity for handrails. That's part of how you hold the gift and balance the polarities.

Chris: What brings the polarities together is knowing my purpose—this is what I am and this is what I am not. That's the contribution of the gift and wound stuff. We are seduced into getting distracted by all the other complexities because we don't want to feel the pain of our path. For me, I'm trying to avoid the hard work of confronting the pain and sometimes taking on responsibility. I have a notion about grief—it is an opportunity for a wide-open broken heart that holds the possibility for developing more compassion. There is also a burden with that. Sometimes I'm just too lazy. I can get seduced into getting caught up in the pace and complexity and urgency. But it all begins to shift at the point when I have an intention of getting back to what's genuine. When I do that, the other stuff becomes less urgent and less confusing and less complex.

Renae: I really liked you talking about a "broken wide-open heart", because that metaphor also goes to "If I'm not willing to have my heart broken wide-open, then it's closed up." And the closed metaphor related to my heart is extremely painful to me. I could not go the rest of my life with a closed up heart.

Chris: Knowing you, I don't think you have to worry about that! (*Laughter*)

Renae: Your gift is attached to what you hurt about, and there are lots of ways to run away from that. Frankly, the concept that we've got to keep trying to be more and more and more, I believe, is the biggest distraction.

Cath: I currently know of a situation where two people are in a conflict with one another. I see how each one of them is stuck in the meaning that they are attributing to the actions of the other—they are attributing malice to those meanings. I care very much for both of the people, and they are really in a tough situation. One is a student, and the other is a faculty member. The student believes the faculty member is out to get her, and the faculty member believes the student is out to get her. It's awful, and it's awful to witness. I am aware of the amount of suffering that I feel, just in witnessing this and feeling somewhat helpless to influence it. I think that the levels of consciousness being asked for from these two people—they are either not activating it or can't hold it. Chris, when you talk about getting back to the simplicity it was very helpful to me. I can see that might be a way that I can stay in relationship with both of them through this and perhaps help them see that with each other if they are open to it. It is personally painful to watch people move into those locked situations with one another. To me it seems so clear how it's co-created.

Chris: There are people who have an antenna that can reach out far enough from themselves to pick up the pain of others.

Renae: Catherine, aren't you talking exactly about your core gift—to ease suffering? So that's what you see. When you know your gift, and you are contributing to your own healing, then, according to this benefit, you are going to be more compassionate towards others.

Roger: I have a question I want to ask: What has your experience been in terms of being healed by the act of giving your gift. Have you noticed a direct link to being able to be stronger? I think I've noticed it sometimes in the moment, but more often I've noticed it in hindsight.

Brian: I think, if you work through the process of healing your wound, eventually you are going to get to the place where the wound is the gift. It's not just that you are touching the wound and everyone can feel the tenderness there, but I think it actually can become a strength. The wound is no longer the primary issue. You are actually giving the gift out of it. For me, I think that's where I am. Most of the time, I don't feel very wounded. Actually, I feel real empowered most of the time. So I think I am giving my gift out of that place.

Chris: For me, real simply, it's having more clarity around what I intend to do. My gift gives me the power and the push. I'm not going to avoid this—I'm going to go out and seek this.

Renae: Sometimes moments of suffering come when I'm giving my gift. The suffering causes me to recognize, "Oh, that's what that's been about! That's why all this is going on." That clarity is so freeing that it takes me to a more real place. For me, that's healing. It helps me understand that doing it and toughing out the pain is worth it. Sometimes, in the moment, I think, "Well, that certainly was illuminating."

Roger: It's hard to talk about this without talking about the wound. Why my gift—holding the whole and recognizing the polarities—is so much a part of me is that I have been one of the polarities and I didn't get held. The people in power at the time could only hold one part of the polarity. So I have gotten very perceptive about unheld polarities because I've got such a big antenna for it. Because of that, the form that the giving of my gift takes is often to interrupt a process to make more space for the unspoken voice or polarity. I'm trying to go against the people in the room who are thinking, "We can figure this out if we just don't include that perspective over there." But I know it won't really get figured out and it will just keep repeating itself unless all the polarities are included. I have had this feeling, sometimes in the moment but usually afterwards, that by making more space for others I have also made more space for myself inside myself. The result is that I am less under the power of that pain.

Bruce: How do you make the space for polarities?

Roger: One of the things I've learned is not to get caught up in the frantic stuff. I try and create a space for reflection, because that's where you hear the polarities. One of my jobs is to make sure leaders understand how important it is to make time to do that.

Chris: I see it as creating a space where the gifts can emerge, whether it's theirs or mine. If you can slow it down, the gifts will appear.

Renae: That's one of the challenges of gifts. To have people believe there is the time to consider gifts.

Brian: Where I'm coming from in this discussion is, "What would it mean for a teacher to be in the later stages of their healing?" For me, as a literature teacher, the later stages of healing have to do with composing a world. Yes, we're reading a book, but let's put the book aside. What we are reading should teach us that we are always reading from the book of life. That's one of the things I've gotten from Wallace Stevens, the poet—it's all about the over layer of language that's covering everything.

Chris: Do you also challenge them to go to the next step of, "Pick up the pen and make your contribution?" Do you encourage them to author their own version?

Brian: I tell students that you are always doing that, whether you know it or not. If you don't know it, you are doing it weakly, so you might as well do it consciously.

Chris: You are saying to them, "What point is there in scribbling in the margins of your life?"

Roger: That's great, Brian, because that's the attitude that got me to face my wound. Here are your choices: You can either be unconscious of your wound and it's going to act out without you being aware, or you can be conscious of it and interact with it and tend to it. Those are the choices. My earlier consciousness was, "Oh, I can live in a way where I can avoid my wound and it won't get in the way." You are taking students to a new level of consciousness by offering that choice to them. It's sort of like when the dentist says, "I don't really care whether you want to floss or not. Just floss the teeth you want to keep." *(Laughter)* Most people start flossing a lot more.

Cath: You really respond to the practical and dire consequences!

Roger: It's just raising people's consciousness to the pain of their own choices. You decide, but don't be asleep.

Brian: My guess is that, early in one's teaching career, a person would be in a more wounded place and would gradually begin to be stronger and give their gift more. I believe that, with attention, wounds do heal. You learn things along the way. You do actually get wisdom, and teachers can model that process too. My teaching has evolved over time and I am a very different teacher now than when I started. The only consistent thing that I have done in teaching is to keep it real. That's the words I would use. A lot of times, I will just say to myself, "If I'm going to be real with myself, what would I say?" Whatever comes out is probably going to have a little bit of strangeness to it, it's going to be a little uncanny, and it can break things open. It can make people uncomfortable—but usually good things come out of it.

End.

12. BENEFIT THREE: RESTORING AND MAINTAINING HOPE

Knowing and using your core gift can be a powerful antidote to the deadening effects of working within an institutional environment.

I continually have opportunities to hear how punishing it can be to work within educational and social service bureaucracies of all kinds. Core gifts, when reinvigorated within an institutional environment, are one substantial way to function in a healthy way within an unhealthy system. By institution, I mean any community service structure, set up to help people, which is part of a larger system of accountability—usually due to governmental funding, laws, and policies.

Most all schools and social service agencies fall into this institutional framework. The size of the buildings or number of staff is irrelevant. I have seen local social service offices with five or ten employees that have a culture that operates under the same rules and practices of organizations with hundreds of employees. What becomes oppressing and disorienting to authenticity is the intrusion of the representative system's rules and mandates within what is frequently a group of caring community members who are trying to be personable and intimately connected. Whether it is a school or social service setting, the employees have no trouble making a long list of the rules and operating practices that have the effect of deadening creativity, increasing the walls between teacher and learner, and taking time away from the "real work."

As a result of these institutional pressures, there is often a feeling amongst the employees of a lack of respect for who they are and the tasks they are trying to accomplish. This lack of regard, in many cases, is seen as coming from "the administration." In my experience, administrators carry the same level of frustration about what "comes from above" as direct service employees. They are carrying messages and mandates which, oftentimes, they don't personally support but have to carry out in order to meet the agencies' rules. Did the school administrator get up in the morning and say to him- or herself, "I think I'll go to work today and create some obstacles for teachers that will make their life miserable"? Did the director of the social service agency take a management seminar entitled, "The Ten Energy Killers for Employees, and how you can implement them tomorrow?" Even the most suspicious employee would consider these two possibilities unlikely. As teachers, social service workers, and administrators, we are asked to pledge our allegiance to systemic rules that usually originate in people who are far removed—physically, emotionally, and intellectually—from either understanding or remembering how learning and change occur in individuals.

One way to think about staying healthy while serving others is to use breathing, both literally and figuratively, as a useful tool. Of course we breathe to stay alive, but breathing is also useful as a metaphor for how much we give, breathing out, and how much we receive, breathing in. When we are giving, giving, giving all day, we become short of the breath of life, losing the very energy and vitality that sustains our hope and our energy for serving others. Our willingness to breathe out more than we breathe in can come from two sources.

First, most institutional environments demand a constant breathing out. The pace of the work, the overcrowding in classrooms and social service offices, and the very idea of service itself, come with the underlying assumption that there is very little time to focus on yourself.

Second, this feeling of obligation to serve others is further intensified by the hidden killer of making time to breathe in—the limping voice inside the teacher saying that, if you really cared, you would be able to get more done by just trying a little harder, leaving even less time for taking care of yourself. This interior voice begins to stumble and stutter when we counter with different questions: At what expense to my own health am I obligated to serve others? Where does this internal message come from? Who did not care enough, or try hard enough, for me? What parts of myself will I be more able to accept if I sacrifice myself by working harder? Who was not there for me when I needed them? Whose approval am I trying to get by working harder? And perhaps the largest illusion of sacrificial service: that I can save myself from drowning in my own suffering by sacrificing my life for someone else. How are gifts helpful in rising up against these unhealthy urges and mandates?

Gifts are directly tied to hope.

One of the mind-twisting notions I have had to work at to better understand both motivation and hope is that there is no such thing as either an unmotivated or hopeless person. Every one of us is motivated by something in every action we take, and every person is hopeful that something they have pre-imagined will happen as a result of every action they take. In order to understand and help another person, I must separate out my judgments and desires about and for the other person's life from their own seeds of desire and motivation. I may not believe that the decision a person makes is a "good one," but that is quite different from whether or not the person has both motivation and hope in the situation. A person sitting on a couch, doing drugs, and watching television day after day is just as motivated as the schoolteacher who gets up at six in the morning, puts in a full day, and grades papers into the wee hours of the night. Apparently, motivation does not have an attribute of fairness to it, and requires an understanding beyond the usual self-serving mechanisms of gauging who is motivated and who is not.

Hope is based on two intertwined thinking processes. First, the person has a specific picture of a future they have named as "desirable" to move towards in their life. Second, the person believes there is some possibility, however small, that this vision is achievable. When a person has named a vision and believes there is a possibility they will get there, hope is seeded. When there is no specific vision, or the person believes there is no chance they will ever get closer to the vision, hope is unavailable.

When a person has articulated and gives their core gift, they have a source of hope and energy at their side. This is because they have articulated a vision of their future that includes their gift. They believe further understanding and giving their gift is an important part of their life's path. Second, the person believes it will be possible for them to use their gift, simply because they have been giving it their entire life. Both conditions for hope have been met—a vision and the belief it will be possible to get there. How can a teacher use this source of hope in their daily life?

Defining and using your core gift while teaching reminds you that teaching is more than a job. For you, it is also a calling.

The economics of sustaining life in an industrialized economy require a level of monetary income that reduces most people's ability to reject the idea of monetary work. The only question remaining is: What kind of work will we do? James Hollis reminds us:

> "It is a requisite part of our individuation to feel that we are productive, and not responding to one's calling can damage the soul. We do not really choose a vocation; rather it chooses us. Our only choice is how we respond."[29]

Vocation, literally from the Latin root of "calling," is more than simply a job. The desire to respond to a calling is deeper than the desire to respond to some of life's other pressures. When we ignore the attention our calling is asking of us, damage can result.

Gift giving originates from a calling within us. We give our gift because we believe it keeps us on our path for serving the world and healing ourselves. The continual giving of the gift reaffirms we have shifted our commitment from "taking a teaching job" towards the "vocation and calling to teach." It calls us to remember, as the poet and teacher Brian Anderson says:

That work is not a chore
But a completion
Which lifts a granite life
Above the grave.[30]

Naming teaching as a vocation brings a vitality that inspires and enlivens. We want to teach, not so much because we are good at it, but because

---

29. Hollis, James. *The Middle Passage: From Misery to Meaning in Midlife.* Inner City Books. Toronto, Canada. 1973. Page 72.

30. Anderson, Brian. *Allegory.* 2002. Unpublished.

we are committed to discovering more of who we are. Once you see your core gift as connected to the purpose of your life, you are actively looking for and engaged in opportunities to learn more about it and give it. Knowing that your core gift is related to teaching is a constant reminder to keep at it—both at times when things are difficult and also when things are going very well. If you believe you are on the path you are supposed to be on, getting in the car and driving to the school is more than transporting yourself to work. You are driving towards the purpose of your life.

Gifts are tied to your hope that you belong.

Because your core gift is connected to how you have framed the purpose of your life, when someone acknowledges you for giving it you feel a deep sense of belonging and satisfaction. After all, someone has seen you for who you really are. One of the conditions for feeling welcome amongst others is that you are seen and valued for your true nature. When your gift is acknowledged, part of the deepest recesses of your psyche feel welcomed because both your suffering and your gift have been acknowledged. Although others may not know the specific story of your life, you could not be sitting in this spot giving this gift without having had the story that is your story. You feel a sense of validation that is often more intense than the individuals around you may recognize or understand. In moments like this you feel alive in ways that you want to be alive. Hope thrives and prospers under these conditions.

Gifts confirm there is hope for a healthier future.

By learning about and giving your core gift, you have evidence you are changing and growing in healthy ways. There is hope for a better future. Knowing your core gift gives you both a primary reflective and prospective point for building your craft as a teacher. When you believe you have a core gift, you are inspired to learn about how your past was influenced by your gift, and also how your gift can benefit or cause trouble in the future.

Since many of the opportunities for "craft-building" we encounter as teachers come at points when we are in some way not successful or in trouble, it is helpful to know that the sources of trouble in your life can often be traced back to either giving your core gift too much or not enough. This is the reflective part. There is a tendency for people, whether they are consciously aware of their core gift or not, to give it freely in all areas of their life. When you give your core gift too much, your life can get out of balance. You may feel highly motivated and inspired, but the other areas of your life are suffering and not getting the attention they should. How many of us feel consumed by our teaching careers? How many teachers make jokes about "getting a life?"

On the other side, if you are not giving your core gift because you are consumed by the mundane aspects of teaching, or are giving it in ways that are not healthy for you or others, you can experience feelings of frustration, anger, and anxiousness. Oftentimes, these feelings are placed as blame on yourself or others, not realizing that it is really just turbulence in your life created by your inability to give your core gift in a way that benefits yourself and others. Your core gift has an urgent nature to it. It is a powerful attribute of who you are, and wants to be seen and used. Your core gift also offers a prospective point of reflection. Because it is coming out of you, consciously or not, your awareness and intention determine whether it is used in a way that supports a purposeful path or simply results in an unfocused release of energy and activity.

As you continue to build your craft, you find new areas of interest within your gift, new ways to give it, and new reasons to be excited and motivated. The person's core gift does not change, but their understanding of it and ability to use it can change dramatically. This is particularly true for those of us who take the time to identify our core gift and seek to bring it more fully into our life.

For instance, if your core gift is "to motivate others," then your core gift will always be "to motivate others." However, you will continue to learn skills throughout your life that will increase your ability to motivate others. By remembering experiences from your own life when others did not provide help by motivating or encouraging, you might also increase your understanding of why it is so important to give this core gift to others. You also will begin to notice other people who are good at motivation, and will have a desire to spend time with those individuals so you can learn from each other.

Giving gifts puts you into the spiritual pipeline.

Where do gifts originate? Many people believe that their innate gifts and talents are gifts from however they define spirit. Because of this connection, it is possible to consider gift-giving moments as having a spiritual connectivity that ties us to powers greater than ourselves. Going to the source of the glue that we believe holds both the world and our imagination together can be rejuvenating and enlivening—although not always entertaining and enjoyable.

In thinking about the quality of the teaching that we provide, it is possible to define levels of craft that go from "providing data and facts to others" to "creating conditions which cause humans to reflect upon and connect with the great mysteries." Milton Glaser, artist and teacher, makes a connection between art and work that caused me to re-affirm that teaching is an art and often has a quality to it that goes beyond simple learning and into the realm of great work, mystery, and art. Look what he has to say:

> "I have a recommendation. We eliminate the word art and replace it with work and develop the following descriptions:
> 1. Work that goes beyond its functional intention and moves us in deep and mysterious ways we call great work.
> 2. Work that is conceived and executed with elegance and rigor we call good work.
> 3. Work that meets its intended need honestly and without pretense we simply call work.
> 4. Everything else, the sad and shoddy stuff of daily life, can come under the heading of bad work."[31]

When we are giving our gift and are connected with spirit, there is an opportunity to do great work. We are not acting solely out of our own ego and learning needs—we are in touch with wisdom and forces beyond simple human capacity. By giving a gift that was given to us by spirit, we are acting out of a greatness that propels our actions into the realm of purposeful connection with the great mysteries. My attraction towards Glaser's definition of great work is that it is the only definition within the four he describes that includes being connected with mystery. What is larger than me that I cannot fully understand?

Is it possible to think of a teacher in a third-grade classroom, pounding out math facts with a rowdy bunch of distracted eight-year-olds, as doing great work? Not only is it possible to think of that teacher in that regard, it

---

31. Glaser, Milton. *Art is Work*. The Overlook Press. Woodstock, NY. 2000. Page 7

is necessary for my hope to thrive. In my estimation, a healthy future for the world rests in the possibility of children being in touch with the great mysteries within all the contexts for learning within their growing minds and spirits. Certainly mathematics, with its attachment to symbols that require a leap of faith to understand, is full of opportunity for a teacher to encourage a child's fascination with mystery.

Benefit Three
Questions for Teachers:
1. How do you describe your work life related to breathing in and breathing out? How is your oxygen supply? How can your gift be a source of oxygen?
2. What hopes do you have for learning more about and giving your gift? How can teaching be an avenue for those desires?
3. Tell a story about a recent teaching situation in which you learned something about your gift.
4. What kinds of approaches and activities on your part help shift learning in your students from work to great work?
5. What is your response when someone says something about your gift that you perceive as critical or unsupportive? Describe the feelings and thoughts you have when someone notices you giving your gift and affirms you for it.
6. What is your understanding about how gifts and spirit are connected and useful to each other in your life?

Teachers Dialogue
Benefit Three: Continually Restoring Your Energy and Maintaining Hope

Renae: The most difficult part of teaching is not teaching. It's the surrounding environment, and all the demands placed on us that take time away from teaching. It's so incredibly frustrating and produces a kind of division between everyone involved. It's really noticeable when we get a new Administrator. They come in and they make changes, and, at the same time, we have parents we are trying to connect with who are getting lost in all those changes. I'm not putting any judgments on the people involved, but it just happens again and again and again.

Roger: The requirements for change just stack up.

Renae: Not only is there a requirement for change, but there is a requirement for you to embrace that change. For the teachers who don't know their gift or have that kind of insight, it must be really awful. My immediate colleagues and I knew that giving our gift with the kids was more valuable than the changes we were being asked to make. I don't want to go into this any more. I just want to say that my courage to continue teaching came from being with the children and giving my gift.

Cath: That was the antidote that kept you from becoming completely dispirited?

Renae: Yes, and I worked with colleagues—and I'm sure you have too—who are completely discouraged. That's why my response to this gift thing is so strong. Perhaps this can help deal with some of the pain in the educational system.

Brian: In my work environment, in the last year, we have been asked to learn a brand new computerized attendance system, learn a virtual education system where we enter six school scores on a rubric for each student for three different papers, enter the records and all the test scores for every student, learn a brand new culminating project program that is just as complex as "Word" or anything like that. All of our staff meetings have been about how to enter that data. We can barely get all this done. So there is no chance for any discussion about your whole purpose—all the reasons you really want to teach. That's the real politic about what's going on in the school.

Roger: Everything gets shoved down.

Brian: Your job description requires you to attend to these things. With the little bit of other time you have, you try to keep the spark burning about why you are really there. I guess that's the courage part—to actually keep your priorities in the face of that.

Chris: We are fundamentally here to teach. If you aren't allowed adequate time because of all the peripheral demands—and if you aren't allowed to have conversations about and work towards being a more effective teacher—then no child will be left behind because no child can move forward. Why are we teaching? Isn't teaching about helping a student to discover their life's work?

Renae: I never heard that phrase, "We're here to help you with your life's work", being raised in a true sense in our school. And, no matter how wonderful these other new mandates are couched, after a while, the cynicism just takes over. Teachers begin to think that this new curriculum, even if it is perfect, is just someone else's opportunity to shine on our backs.

Cath: My job is so easy compared to yours. The one similarity I can see is, in our group, the work that administrative people do often seems so incongruent with how we want to do our jobs as teachers. Much of their purpose is about efficiency and effectiveness—they want eight weeks of lead-time. That's so different from the immediacy of teaching. Sometimes it's hard to get aligned around our original purpose. Why are we all here together?

Chris: Again, it's coming up. Why are we here? What is going to keep us stuck and what is going to carry us forward?

Renae: Some of the division between administration and teachers has to do with us having different gifts. You can also see the same kind of division between math and language arts teachers. If we could just be together and find out what each other's life work really is, then maybe there could be some coming together. Are we beyond that? If a secretary's life work is keeping the records organized and straight, then maybe they are looking at me like I'm not supporting their life's work! According to them, I'm not doing my job. If we talked about each other's gifts, maybe we could work something out between us.

Roger: I'm realizing it's a similar thing for me in my job working with businesses—my clients feel that pull and pressure to function in an environment where it is not set up to succeed. There is so little time to stop and think that it doesn't occur to people to remember, "Oh, we don't have to play by all the rules." Your nose is about this far from the grindstone and you've got someone breathing down your neck. It's all going so fast there is no time to yell, "Stop!" So the biggest difficulty is getting people to feel free enough to say stop. We did a little remodel at our house. The guy putting the furnace in shows up in a big truck, and I can hear all this swearing going on while he is looking for his stuff in the truck. I go out and say "Good morning, how's it going?", and he says, "Oh boy, you don't want to know". And I say, "Well, actually, before you go in my house, I'm curious about what's going on." He says, "I have this big, huge beautiful truck—they just gave it to me today—but it is completely unorganized. I can't use it to work on your job because I don't know where anything is, and they didn't give me any time to figure out and organize things in a way that I know how to use it. You are paying for that." It was just such a classic example. There's no time to plan and get your head above the bubble—to use all your intelligence. All the intelligence is being used to race around and solve intractable problems. And everyone is thinking, "I'm not doing the job I could be doing. We could be doing this a lot better." That's the difficulty I see all the time in organizations.

Chris: And all his boss is thinking is, "What's his problem? He's got the best damn truck that money can buy."

Roger: This goes to larger societal issues for me. Our culture just keeps moving down this path where accumulation of power and money is the most important and sacred thing. There is less validation for meaningful things. That's why I think the idea of gifts is so interesting—because a core gift is the kind of thing that can get people's attention in the face of this kind of pressure. It's like one of the questions I heard that Brian asks his students, "Let's think a little bit about what you want your experience to be like on your deathbed." That gets people's attention. It's a more powerful question than all the pressure. But it takes that level now for people to pay attention. When people get out of the rapids, and hang out in the eddy together, they can figure out strategies and ways to operate that will solve the problem. It creates a sense of empowerment. We've got to get out of the rapids.

Chris: It takes courage to be the one to say, whether there is permission or not, "We've got to stop. We've got to change the course."

Roger: I have a colleague who wrote a thing about the "tyranny of the urgent". About how urgency tyrannizes us and moves us away from what is essential. If you've got something to remind you of the essential in the face of the urgent, you've really got something. The idea of a core gift can do that.

Cath: I've been asking myself and other people, "How come the movie, *Lord of the Rings*, is so popular? As people start to talk to me about that, I am seeing that there is a deep hunger in the psyche of the culture being captured by the movie. It seems to be about, "Who can I rely on in my trials and tribulations, and will I have what it takes?" Gifts are one way of knowing what each of us is going to contribute on the journey.

Renae: It takes real leadership—and I don't mean just administrators—to bring together a group like that who is collapsing. For instance, I have seen teachers who had a real gift for making communication work and bringing people together. When that teacher left, the void was noticeable, and there was a shock to the system because no one else took that role.

Roger: The term leader, in this context, is someone who is holding the whole. They are thinking about what's best for the whole, rather than what's best for their own faction. It's easy to say a good leader holds the whole, but we all know some are doing that well and some aren't. You know, it's a "get up on the balcony" kind of thing. Start to look at the whole of it and encourage the group to start to talk at that level.

Renae: I think that's a core gift. To see the whole and be able to communicate that to people with other kinds of gifts—to help them see they are part of a whole.

Cath: I was thinking that being aware of your core gift also helps you to get a balcony view—to get above things. When you really believe your gift is only part of what is necessary, you begin to value other people's gifts because you need them to be successful. I'm thinking that we need more conversations about what's keeping us from giving our gifts to the students and the community. The sense of loss in that discussion would, I think, be huge.

Brian: My view of our staff is that we have too many critical people. But what I'm thinking about now is that those critical people are bringing their gift. If I look at it that way, then the real problem is that the others with different gifts have been silent. They lack the courage to give their gifts. The only courageous teachers on our staff are the critical ones.

Roger: That's what gets tolerated and validated by whoever is holding the container.

Brian: Part of the culture of my school is that those gift-givers, the critical ones, are dominant and most powerful. But that is because we have a huge silent majority who so hate the negative kind of climate that they become silenced and don't want any part of the interaction.

Roger: I would also say it's because no one is standing up and saying, "What's going on here? We can do better."

Brian: This is another way to look at it. That the other teachers are not demanding equal time to give their gifts and make positive contributions and trying to lead with their gifts.

Roger: It's so common for a group to get organized around a vocal minority, and meanwhile the silent majority goes from motivated to apathetic. "This train is going nowhere because nobody is shutting those people up or dealing with that."

Chris: That becomes their truth. Their vision of the world.

Roger: Leadership loses a lot of credibility in situations where the vocal minority is tolerated and all other resources go wasted.

Chris: There is a piece of research about Rhesus monkeys and bonding from the University of Wisconsin. They built a pyramid of steps in a room and put five monkeys in there. They starved the monkeys and then hung a bunch of bananas at the top of the pyramid. All the monkeys had to do was walk up the pyramid and they could get fed. The minute one monkey started up, the researchers hosed all the monkeys down with cold water. All of them. Then they took one of the monkeys out, and put a fresh one in with the ones who had been hosed down. The minute that new monkey started to climb the pyramid, it was attacked by the other monkeys and dragged back down. They didn't want to get hosed down. The next day they put another new monkey in the cage, and that monkey was attacked by one who had been attacked the day before, even though that monkey had not been hosed down. Over a period of time, they had replaced all the monkeys. Now there were five monkeys in the cage who had never been hosed, but would not let each other go up the pyramid to eat. The finding of the research was that the monkeys learned, "Why aren't we doing this? That's just the way things are around here."

Roger: I think gifts is a real contribution to the energy, "Guess what, there is no cold water."

Chris: Related to this discussion, it takes tremendous courage to say you are going to give your gift and not going to be a part of the way things are.

End.

THE TEACHER-STUDENT RELATIONSHIP: BENEFITS FOUR, FIVE, AND SIX

13. BENEFIT FOUR: WELCOMING STUDENTS AND REDUCING NON-DESIRABLE BEHAVIORS

What is the basis you use for welcoming students into the life of your classroom? What would they say you regard and reward them for? Being on time? Not being trouble? Getting good grades or successfully carrying out the requests you have of them? These questions raise fear in me that, for myself, students' answers may not be what I hope. My actions and how I have designed the learning environment send very specific messages about the basis for welcoming, and those messages may serve to promote my own success rather than create a meaningful foundation for welcoming students. Rather than relying on my hopes and resulting assumptions about the truth, it may be interesting for me to ask students: "How do you know you are welcome in this learning situation?"

Several years ago, there was heightened concern for school safety in my hometown after the Columbine high school shooting incident in the midwestern United States. Recognizing that students who kill other students are most often framed as "loners" and also as young people who feel misunderstood and mistreated, we (a small group of students, a school administrator, and I) decided to ask students a few simple questions in order to get a reading on how students saw themselves and how safe they felt within the school environment. We came up with a short list of questions, and positioned volunteer students at the doorway to each school to gather data from students in the sixth to twelfth grades. I vividly remember the results. One of the questions asked the student if he or she knew their gifts. About three-quarters of the students said they could identify their gifts. Another question asked the student if he or she had been identified and acknowledged for those gifts. Only about one-third of the students felt they had been seen and acknowledged for their gifts.

What information does this give us, as adults involved in the lives of young people? What is the likely behavior of a young person who does not feel seen and valued for the essence of who they are? It may be possible for a suspicious adult to attribute these students' responses to the angst of youth—just another example of the unrelenting complaints from young people about how hard life is and how misunderstood they are. My guess is that this desire in some adults serves to further their real desire—to blame young people for their condition. "If they would just try a little harder, like I had to do, things would be better for them."

At what point did young people begin to bear the burden of discovering and being seen for who they are without the arduous support of adults? I know the answer to that question for myself. It was seeded at the points during my youth when I realized I was not going to get meaningful help in figuring out who I was or what I should be doing. By meaningful help, I am speaking of something beyond the encouragement to be successful in the outside world by going to college, getting a good job, and avoiding trouble. Help with unraveling and understanding the world inside myself was noticeably absent during my youth, as I suspect it also was for my peers. Who am I? This question helps determine your gift, your talents, and how you want to be welcomed in the world. If the older people in a community do not take the primary responsibility for this task, what does that say about how we value our own gifts? We are living, in our families, schools, and communities, with the devastating results of what happens when adults do not take a commanding and unrelenting role in helping young people feel seen and valued for who they really are.

In contrast, a few years ago I attended the classroom party celebrating my daughter's final day in fourth grade. In preparation for the party, the students had taken classroom time to carefully identify the primary contribution that each fellow student brought to the classroom. Out of all the ways you could describe this person, what is their strongest attribute? As the teacher read the essence statement created by the students for each other, you could see the pride in the student (and the tears in parents' eyes as their child's statement was read). This is the idea of the gift in it's most simple and elegant form. Nine-year-old children seeing the essence in each other and being able to declare, in simple but powerful words, that gift. What do you suppose each student will carry in his or her psyche out of that last day in school? It will likely be the memory of being seen clearly and feeling welcome amongst their peers.

As teachers, we have to make a strong and open statement, backed by our actions and the design of our activities within the learning environment, that we are welcoming students because *we need the essence of who they are as an essential part of the glue that holds the classroom together.* A student should be clear how the classroom is not complete when he or she is not present. Other students need to be clear what capacity and strength is not as available when another student is not present. Students and teachers must know each other's gifts in order for this understanding to occur. When the essence of each student is known, learners are able to understand and witness what "whole community" means, and carry the desire for wholeness forward as a distinct and available memory. Students deserve this opportunity as a foundational part of their education. If we, as adults, had known better when we were younger, perhaps we would have expected the same for ourselves. Or perhaps we did expect it, and did not receive what we knew in our bones was an essential ingredient for our growth. We, and the students in front of us, are part of a multi-generational pattern of disregarding the essential gifts of young people.

Remembering gifts strengthens and renews your commitment to the idea that teachers and students are worthy of each other's regard and attention.
One of the foundations for respecting another person is the belief that he or she has an important contribution to make to the world. One root of *respect*, "to look at again," reminds us that the first time we look we see the surface of who the person is—our judgments about their actions, their appearance, and our fear of the difficulties this stranger may bring into our life. Then, if we choose to respect the person, we look again. This time, we calm our inner voice of judgment and fear and make a genuine effort to see who the person really is. Where has this person been, why are they on my doorstep in this moment, and where are they going? Whatever the current condition of the person, they have essential capacities that are worth nurturing and bringing more fully into the world. This is also supported

by the popular reclamation of the Latin root of "education," *educare*, which translates to "bring out what is within."

Breaking down the limiting notion that education is all about stuffing facts inside a person and filling them up, both educare and core gifts are defined by the idea that there are essential seeds of wisdom in each of us that are worthy of bringing out and building upon. This is especially important to remember when a student acts in a way that brings difficulty into the classroom, because it is a reminder that the student is larger than their current behavior, even though this behavior may be consuming the learning environment.

Core gifts are also important to remember on days when you are not giving teaching your full attention. Whether it originates from being tired, not having the desire to carefully listen, just interested in getting to the moment when the day is over, being frustrated with the latest unhelpful policy or rule mandated from above, or wanting the students to do (for once) what you ask them to do—a lack of authentic, centered, and focused attention will surely lead towards trouble in the classroom. When teachers and students are aware of each other's core gifts, they are reminded that the person in front of them is on a worthy path and is deserving of attention. Students are asked what they can contribute; core gifts thus provide a specific way for both students and teachers to welcome each other into the learning environment. Giving your core gift is a powerful way to feel "at home" and welcome within yourself, and be welcomed by others, in any situation. When teachers and students begin to see each other's gifts as essential attributes of each other's unique style, regard and appreciation develop that can sustain connection through moments when a student or teacher acts in ways that push others away.

Often, what is broken inside a young person is the same thing that is broken in the community—the belief that all of us are worthy of love and all of us have a contribution to make. When a young person is in trouble, he or she needs a bridge to find their way back into community. Giving their gift can be that bridge. When a young person believes they have something valuable to contribute, and the community provides opportunity for that contribution to be made, hope is restored, desire comes to life, and both students and communities become whole again.

Gift-aware teachers see trouble in a student as the giftedness of the person trying to come out.

What is the root of an undesirable behavior, either in a learning situation or in other parts of the person's life? In fact, this undesirable behavior may be the frustrated core gift of the person, unseen for too long and trying desperately to be noticed by the only means left—by drawing attention to itself in a dramatic way.

I met a young person a while back who said to me, "I know what my gift is. It's the power of persuasion and motivation. I just have the power to make people believe that they can do something. I've done some bad things with that gift, let me tell you. But I want to do good. You know what I want? I want people to really ask me how I'm doing...not to wonder what I'm up to and trying to get away with. That's what I need. Everybody thinks I'm trying to con them. I don't want to be a deer in the headlights anymore."

We are faced with students throughout the course of our professional life who have a strong sense of identity, and yet create trouble within the environment we have set up for learning. If you have been teaching for a few years, it is likely you have encountered every one of these students:

- A student with a core gift for finding the truth who challenges every statement the teacher makes.
- A student with a core gift for leadership who gathers students in groups to tease or physically bully other students.
- A student with a core gift for logic and order who challenges each rule in the family, classroom, and the larger community.
- A student with a core gift for compassion and feeling who is overly dramatic and draws attention to him or herself by yelling and carrying on in the hallways.

When a student acts out, finding a way for them to give their core gift in a healthy, contributing way is one of the most powerful tools a teacher can use to draw the student back into the learning environment. The usual approach to reducing behavior,[32] which is to get the student

---

32. Gift identification and giving fit nicely within the framework of the current "positive behavioral support" (PBS) movement. PBS asks the teacher to name what the student is trying to get from the behavior, and then find a way for them to get that same result in

to do less of the offending action, is exactly the wrong strategy to use in a situation where the gift of the person is coming out in unhealthy ways. The gift-aware teacher strives to intensify and help the person go into their gift further as the method to bring the person back to using their gift in a healthy way.

Gifts acknowledge what is not going to go away.

The gift is not going to go away. You can't eliminate the person's desire to give their gift. It's like the bubble under the carpet— pushing it down in one spot will cause it to rise up in another. In the above situations, what could you do to provide a healthy and contributing way for each student to reengage in the environment? For instance, with the truth-finding student, you could:

- Ask the student to list all the alternative views of truth related to an idea being presented, with both positive and negative attributes of each.
- Ask the student to defend a position that he/she does not believe in.
- Ask the student to define the difference between "the truth" and what is true for him or her.
- Tell the student a story about a time when you knew the truth needed to be told and you didn't have the courage to tell it.
- Ask the student to tell a story about a time when they thought something was true but found out later it wasn't.
- Assign the student to investigate the root words related to truth, and how different cultures interpret truth.
- Have a sidebar discussion with the student and acknowledge their passion for the truth and why truth is so important in a learning environment.
- Gather this student and others who have a similar gift for truth finding to talk about how their gift has helped them.
- Ask this same group of students to tell stories to each other about how their gift has gotten them in trouble.

---

a positive way. When a teacher recognizes a student's gift, and then offers alternative ways for him or her to give it, the desired outcome of positive behavioral support is achieved.

- Ask this same group of students what they are most afraid of related to their gift.
- Ask the student to tell a story about a time when they told the truth and it was helpful in a situation.
- Ask the student to describe why secrets are bad.
- Ask the student to describe a situation where keeping a secret could be a good thing.

Gift-giving balances a person's behavior.

Gifts have a self-leveling quality to them. When they are acknowledged, they will adjust themselves to be seen and used with acceptable levels of both intensity and frequency. The task of the teacher is to find ways for the person's gift to be contributed in a healthy way. Rather than trying to reduce the giving of the gift, the teacher finds ways to reorient this powerful capacity in the person. Punishment, in cases where the gift is being given in ways that are not helpful, sends the message to the person's psyche that the most valuable part of who they are is not worthy of others' attention and gratitude. The likely result of this awareness is a building resentment, a purposeful lack of appreciation of others' gifts, and a continuing escalation of disrupting behavior.

Gifts highlight and help accurately define four kinds of disruptive behavior.

Teachers who orient themselves to using gift identification and giving strategies in a learning environment are on the lookout for four different sources of trouble that can stem from gifts:

1. *Not giving gift.* A student who forgets to, or chooses not to, give their gift will often be unmotivated to participate in learning environments. This is primarily due to the student not making a connection between the learning topic and the direction of their life. When a student begins to give their gift, the connection is remembered and the student becomes engaged and alive with the possibility that their engagement will serve their future.

2. *Somebody else restricting or not letting you give your gift.* A student who is restricted in giving their gift is likely to escalate their behavior in order to draw attention to the fact that their gift is not being received. Gifts want to be seen, and will resort to most any

mechanism to be recognized within a group.

3. *Giving your gift in a way that drives others away.* Oftentimes the person will give their gift in a way that is "too much" for the rest of the group. Being insistent on giving their gift when it's not the contribution that's really needed at that time, giving their gift at the expense of others making their contribution, giving their gift in such a forceful way that it becomes seen as an angry, aggressive, or hurtful gesture—all are forms of gift-giving trouble.

4. *Staying in the opposite, the wound. At times, a person will retreat into their suffering rather than give their gift.* This usually occurs at times when courage is required for gift giving, and the person gets thrown back into the feelings that accompanied the original suffering (the opposite of their gift). The effect of this is usually a behavior that is incongruent with the situation. For example, consider a person who has a gift for welcoming others, and who was severely not welcomed in their own life. When there is a new person in a group who needs welcoming, but who is seen as marginally acceptable to group members, the person with a gift for welcoming may suddenly become quiet or even contribute reasons why the new person should not be welcomed. The situation has triggered them to retreat into their old wounds and act out the conditions under which they did not feel welcome. In this moment, they are intent on not letting the newcomer receive the welcoming that they did not get.

Giving your gift in inappropriate ways and not giving your gift at all are both forms of hiding.

Both have the result of not being seen for who you really are. A student who acts in ways that drive the teacher and other students away receives a response of negative attention. The negative attention can come about in many forms; each type is attention received for the not-loving, not-caring, and not-compassionate part of the student. In the same way, the student who is silent and not giving their gift receives no attention for the loving and caring parts of who he or she is. Neither student gets acknowledgment or receives attention for the gift that greatly defines their character and their calling.

Over time, both of these students will begin to frame who they are in terms of their disrupting or hiding behavior, and begin to assume it as the fundamental descriptor of who they are. As the person begins to define him- or herself, more and more, as trouble, they will have an increasing desire to defend that part of themselves. As hope for being seen in other ways gradually dissipates, the person retreats into silence or escalates the disruptive behavior as a way to receive what is now seen as the only way they can get love and attention. Teachers who use gift identification and giving strategies provide students with a powerful and healing alternative—to be seen for who they really are.

The student's core gift can be the ticket into relationships.

For students who have life stories of feeling unwelcome, identifying and using their gift can provide specific strategies for increasing opportunities for being seen and valued. This can have the effect of reducing other kinds of behavior for which they receive attention. Our psyches want to be acknowledged. We will get that acknowledgement any way we can and, as our options diminish, our behavior becomes more and more outlandish until we finally are literally screaming for attention. Or, as noted previously, the screaming can take the form of silence and retreat. Both behaviors are efforts to be seen.

When a student is given the opportunity to give their gift, and is witnessed for it, there is an immediate response of feeling welcome. The more the student is acknowledged for giving his or her gift, the more welcome they feel. Students who are oriented towards feeling not welcome will respond to gift-giving opportunities when they are taught about their gift and provided the opening for giving it. This can become a natural way for a student to look for attention, and at the same time increase his or her skill in giving their gift.

The students receiving this person's gift also begin to frame the student as gift giving rather than either disruptive or too quiet. The giving of the gift is the mechanism that causes the person and the group to accurately perceive each other. The person sees the group as not out to get him or her, but rather as a group who values the person. The group sees the person as someone with a contribution to make. On both sides, there is an increased understanding of the worthiness of the other.

Benefit Four
Questions for Teachers:

1. How do you welcome students? What do you think students would say is not welcoming about your behavior? Is this connected to your gift in any way?

2. Describe a student who is disruptive to the learning environment. Given this behavior, can you guess what the person's gift might be?

3. How do you use your gift to protect yourself? How is your gift a defensive posture towards the world?

4. Which one of the strategies listed for engaging a truth-gifted student intrigues you? Why?

5. Out of the list of four kinds of trouble you can get into with your gift, which one is most common with you? Which one causes the largest emotional response in you?

6. Who helped you determine the purpose of your life? What did they do to help?

Teacher's Dialogue
Benefit Four: Welcoming Students and Reducing Non-Desirable Behaviors

Chris: Most of the work I do is around helping people who have what others call "undesirable behavior." But I'd like to preface that by saying it's not clear what undesirable behavior is in a classroom. For instance, as a teacher, I'm more worried about the kid who doesn't say anything than the kid who is in my face being disruptive. You can figure out a kid like that right away. They give themselves away. I'm more worried about the kid who hasn't given me anything—no clues to help me figure out where they are.

Renae: When you are talking to a parent of one of those children, and you help them to see the gift, or remind them of the gift, in their child, it can be very comforting to them. If a child is remarkable or unique—for whatever reason—sometimes that's worrisome to parents. It's my job as a teacher to tell the parents, "What's stirring in there is growth, and it's good."

Chris: You are able to help them see their child and tell them about the potential, rather than having them see what is going on as a problem. And your capacity to see that in a child is part of your gift?

Renae: Yes, that's true.

Chris: When a student is being resistant, or in some kind of trouble, aren't they really asking: "Why am I here? It's clear to me why you are all here, but what contribution am I bringing? That's not so clear to me." Resistance is often the wound side revealing itself. My interest is in learning how people can have a sense of belonging and figure out who loves them. That's what schools are about—they are places where relationships can begin and grow while people are learning. My particular interest is in the difficult behavior part that can erupt during that process.

Roger: A lot of the teaching and training work I do in businesses is around what is called "non-desirable" behavior. Whether you want to call it productivity or change or cohesion or effectiveness, at some level it involves dealing with resistance and resistant behavior, which many leaders immediately see as non-desirable. I have a frame for those situations, which is like this: If we knew enough about what the person who we see as "resistant" was experiencing internally, we would be brought to tears by the courage and effectiveness they are bringing to the show. But, if you look at it through the lens of your own world as a teacher or leader—by your own fears about what you are trying to pull off and are challenged by—you don't see or hear any of that. Everyone has a gift they are bringing towards the adaptive change, and resistance is really moving towards the change as opposed to moving away from it. Every resistant viewpoint is an expression of concern—it's all moving towards an attempt to adapt. The resistant contribution is a gift to the change process.

Chris: Are there any distinctions between adults and children? One of the distinctions I make for myself is that kids are, at the root, more deal-ing with a struggle around "I'm not enough" or "I don't belong." Adults are dealing more with the struggle of "I'm really on my own here—I have to figure this stuff out alone." Although these are related questions, adults have the added weight of realizing no one is going to bail them out. The positive side of this is that adults get to feel like they are in charge of it.

Brian: I feel like this is one of my weakest areas. I don't actually work with very many disruptive students. I don't think the techniques I use work very well with disruptive students.

Chris: The principles are the same, but the strategies are different. It's simple, but it's not easy. Interpreting it to a specific student is where it gets hard. For me, the beginning of that process is to just abide with the ten-sion and emotion that goes along with the feeling that "Oh, things are not going well!" As a teacher there is a certain amount of wanting students to find their own path and grow, but at the same time wanting the boundar-ies to be secure. For me, I don't mind little disagreements or clarifications, but I really don't want someone to vehemently reject or challenge what I have said. Boom, that really gets me at an emotional level. I see it as a non-desirable behavior because I've got this certain lens that I don't want interrupted. What are some of the things you rely on that that help you enter difficulty you are having with the student?

Cath: Before I had this language of a core gift to lean into, I did have a sense that being home with myself is important. When I am challenged in the classroom I recognize that, when I feel at home with myself, the chal-lenge from the student is oftentimes an opportunity for something really creative to happen. If I'm not feeling at home with myself—if I'm feeling insecure or not up to the task—then that challenge feels threatening to me and I want to manage, control, or push it down. Having language around the core gift now, it's fun for me to think about what "being home with myself" means in relationship to my core gift. It's another way of stay-ing grounded and centered in that moment when there is a disruption or something unplanned for is happening. I am certain that I have to be able to trust my own resources and the resources in the classroom as a whole to meet whatever is happening in some kind of creative way. When there is a challenge, it's usually an important voice coming through in that moment—people who often times don't get heard.

Chris: A man who has taught me a great deal says that the individuals who act out the most are really not problems, they are revolutionaries. They are the ones who are standing up and shouting, "This is not right and I won't stand for it anymore." If you can look at those students as the voice of change or reason, it creates opportunities.

Renae: To me, that is the point of the job of teaching. Right there. The student, by explaining to you how this environment doesn't work—or by withdrawing from the environment—is letting you know they are trying to learn. And my response is, "Let's get into it and figure it out." We have very structured homework we send home with children in the third grade. We do this so, when we are in class together, we can spend the time validating or invalidating the work that we do together. Most often, the issues that arise are personal. So I have to address them on a personal level. The children come in with wounds and baggage...

Chris: All of which comes right over to you...

Renae: Oh yes, in behaviors that come out right in your face. Many children have serious baggage that is really bringing them down and incapacitating them to learn and deal with the choices I am asking them to make in the classroom. Sometimes a child needs a break from their serious life and an opportunity to be a child for a few hours. In order to help this child release some of his or her struggles, I explain to them that the environment is a safe one. I tell them there is a classroom door, and there is a bag outside the door with their name on it. They can put all their troubles in the bag, and they can leave it outside the door. It's still outside, with their name on it, and they can haul it off because it is theirs to deal with. But while they are in my classroom today, they are children, and they can sit back with other children and breathe and relax. Often, for children with extreme loads, this is very effective. It takes reminding them sometimes, but generally they get that idea and they can be in the class without feeling trapped by the big load they are carrying.

Chris: Does the environment you create also include the permission to bring your bag into the classroom and dump it out so they can deal with it?

Renae: Oh, absolutely. You can talk about it anytime you want. Generally, that kind of thing comes out in conflicts between children. I believe totally in the wisdom of children, and in giving them opportunities to share their lives with each other. It is amazing how, when it becomes clear from one child to another why they are crying, they can organize themselves to help each other. They really can work it out. There are a lot of children who have major wounds, and they sometimes need a little more one on one from me. But the majority of kids can work it out amongst themselves.

Chris: A lot of my work in schools is with kids who are about to be booted out of classrooms for assaulting teachers or other students. I ask them, "Why is this such an awful place?"

Renae: One reason it's awful is that the student doesn't feel like they have any choices.

Chris: What I'm hearing from you is that you try to find, for each kid, the tension and the balance between security and autonomy. "I'm responsible for the safety in this classroom, and I'll assure you that I will be there."

Renae: I will be there, being who I am. And it's possible for you to be who you are.

Chris: And you do that so they can explore the autonomy part of it? Those two things are incompatible in a lot of ways. If you are safe, sound, and secure, you are compromising or jeopardizing your independence, because there is dependence that goes with security. On the other hand, if you are just out there doing your autonomous, independent thing, you are compromising and jeopardizing a certain amount of security.

Renae: In that sense, I am managing that balance. Children understand that there are social norms and there is a social order. Truly, I don't know any child who does not think that's eminently fair. For instance, I had a student with autism. Other children understood this kid who needs to be under that table and has to have quiet around him. As a teacher, all I had to do was say to the other students, "This is something he needs." And the other students respond with a simple, "Oh, that's o.k." And then they are off and running again. For that age child, it's really different than it is with adults. Adults get freaked out, but the children are fine with it.

Roger: As opposed to a teacher saying, "That's none of your business," which is the other way you could respond to one child's curiosity about the needs of another child. But that dishonors the kid asking the question.

Renae: Yes, and that also dishonors the whole environment. Because you can't say that this part is free for you to understand, but this part is none of your business. That's ridiculous.

Roger: That's what jacks up all the problems and makes it not work in the classroom—is to try and protect a child in that way by withholding information.

Renae: That doesn't work because you've now just made that kid so different that they will have a hard time being accepted.

Chris: Most adults went to school when there was even a worse response than "It's none of your business that the kid is under the table." For us, as students, it was none of our business why those kids were not even in our class—they were over there in that special classroom all alone by themselves.

Renae: My prime directive with students is to tell them the truth and be real with them to the extent that's reasonable to their development.

Cath: The cultivating of wisdom is knowing something has happened and then being able to ask questions that validate your knowingness. That entire wisdom process gets truncated by "you're not allowed to know."

Roger: When the truth is not told, the basic underlying message the student receives is "You can't handle it." So it not only truncates the learning process, it truncates resilience. Renae, I'm hearing in what you are saying a very clear desire to build resilience whenever possible, and you assume students can handle it and will let you know if they can't.

Renae: Yes. We have a child in our class who has a lot of behavior and learning development issues. He was in our face, driving us all crazy, and everyone was complaining about him. He was out of school one day, and I got the other students in a circle and said, "O.K. today we're going to talk about this child. I'm hearing a lot of complaints, and anything you say will be fine, there will be no judgment." The children went around the circle speaking, saying "he does this" and "he does that." I just kept affirming them by saying, "You are absolutely right, he does." And then, about the third time around the circle, a youngster stopped me and said, "Now, wait a minute. Remember when I was in first grade, how I behaved like that? And I'm a lot better now." And all the other students went, "Yea, we remember that and you are a lot better now." And then they started to develop strategies for how they could support this student. Those kinds of experiences, time and time again, have taught me that you can really trust children.

Chris: That's been my experience, too. Whenever I am in a classroom working with a behavior issue in a student, after listening to the kids I would just say, "Now, what are you all going to do about it?" And their first response is, "What do you mean? You are an adult, that's your job." But, as adults, that's a mistake I think we've been making for a long time…that we always know what a kid needs and what will work, and that it's our job. I think we are too far away from being kids ourselves to always know what will be helpful. You have to trust the brilliance of children. You have to let them know that they do have the answers, and you supply the permission and let them know that you are behind them and will help guide them through it. Because, no matter who decides what to do, in the end it's going to be about what the kids do with other kids.

Roger: A lot of these dynamics are not that different when we are talking about adults. There may be more of a mask that has been developed, so there is more to work through. For the leader, it's the same as for the teacher—the basic strategy is to get real. We're going to be really clear about power, both what I am authorized to do and what you are authorized to do. I think that's one of the main tools for the leader, and it's often times very confused. So many leaders think they have to make everybody comfortable. That's the Achilles heel. But their primary job is to listen and acknowledge. There is also a part around setting some boundaries for people who go beyond the usual norms. That's the place where leaders have to be clear about their authority.

Cath: I think it's best if people have a chance to influence the boundaries for what is acceptable in the classroom.

Roger: Yes, but oftentimes the group doesn't want the work of taking accountability for their own stuff…to face the challenges around their own resilience. They'd just rather have somebody else deal with it. The leader is responsible for saying it's going to happen, and then asking "how" to the group. The troublemakers will respond by saying, "If I can't decide whether it's going to happen, then I'm not going to say how it should happen." As a leader, you've got to let that comment go right by and get involved with the people who are interested in contributing. The resistant people will come around to helping with the "how" if they are not excluded. There is a bus that is going, and they are deciding to be on it or not. Most will decide to get on the bus.

Chris; I liked what you said earlier—that resistance is not really pushing against, it's just a different way to move toward it and there is potentially something of value within their resistance. I think this has something to do with core gifts. It may be that the person is trying to give their gift, but others see it as a criticism or resistance. Worse yet, the giving of their gift may not be valued because they are so clumsy in giving it...it drives people away from them. The teacher may be critical or even punitive in response to the way the person is giving their gift. If it comes across as clumsy, or because the wound screams louder than the gift, we see a potential contribution as abrasive, offensive, and non-desirable. But what they are really trying to do is say, "I have something to contribute."

Roger: In any working group, it's often the same people who challenge the change or challenge the leader. There is a way in which they repeatedly run for that office and get elected by the group to be in that role. Those people have a particular gift. Part of their gift is not to be railroaded by power. That may not be what's really going on, but somehow they take a stand in those situations. "We're not going to let you railroad this down our throats without talking about it." That's a very useful thing, although it's easy to perceive it as an attempt to stop all change. But, you know what, that's never been my experience. If their concerns get heard and acknowledged, those people often become the most committed when it comes time to change. But if they get blown off, it becomes about justice, and they never give up.

Renae: Do you think that, sometimes, there are major wounds in a person that overwhelm their ability to make a change?

Roger: When I find out that a person is known as being someone who always is resistant, it does help me to think, "Oh, this person may have wounds, but at the same time they are going to be a voice for justice." It really helps me to imagine that there is both a wound and a gift in what the person is bringing.

Cath: I thought you were going to go somewhere else with that. Let me see if I got what you just said—you are thinking that the resistance in a person may be part of their gift, and the situation brings out this gift.

Roger: Yes.

Cath: I was thinking that one way to use this core gift work would be that some of those resistant people could be unplugged from that role they usually play if we help them to be aware of their gift. We could redirect them to give their gift rather than just being resistant. That's the opposite of what you were saying.

Roger: That's possible too. What often happens is, when they are acknowledged and thanked for raising this resistance, all the distracting energy around doing it just falls away. They realize that the act is no longer a problem, but a service.

Brian: That's a different perspective. I think it would catch them off guard—to say to a person, "That's your gift and, no, we can't all do that. We're counting on you to bring up the resistance."

Chris: What is your experience when a person who is bringing undesirable behavior really feels acknowledged in some way for their contribution?

Renae: For the contribution to be seen and acknowledged by the teacher or the leader is one thing. But when peers acknowledge it, then a whole new dynamic opens up. That recognition really, for all of us, tends to open things up more.

Cath: To be acknowledged by who they see as their real community…

Renae: Related to wound versus gift, what I have noticed is that some people just keep revisiting their wound all the time. Their gift is less effective because they don't give it in a way that it can be seen and appreciated by others.

Chris: The closer a person is to their wound, the more likely they are to have their future be right behind them. They will continue to walk backwards right into their past, and the wound will be reopened, relived, and re-storied over and over again. There is no future in front of them.

Bruce: How do you help a student begin to look forwards instead of backwards—to become hopeful that there is something worth working towards?

Brian: How I talk about it with students is within the framework of "doing your life's work." That's about the future. I talk about the difference between work and your life's work. For many students, that is a shocking thing to consider. We read some of Annie Dillard's essays, and she talks about accomplishing your life's work before you die.

Chris: On the flip side, don't many kids respond, "Why does that matter? I'll never live to see twenty-five. Why are you having me talk about the future? None of my brothers or cousins have seen twenty-one. They're dead."

Brian: Yes. It can get that serious, and then their writing becomes meaningful for them. No one can really get around the concept of a meaningful life. It's a serious thing to consider what you need to do so that, when you die, you will feel like you've lived a full and meaningful life and are prepared to die. This is not just school stuff. Let's pretend we're not in school. This is real stuff that you need to figure out, or your life is not going to be very meaningful.

Chris: It sounds like your life's work as a teacher is to help students understand they've got a life's work. For all of us, I think the greatest gift we can have is that our work life is our life's work.

End.

14. BENEFIT FIVE: ESTABLISHING GENUINE, RATHER THAN POSITIONAL AUTHORITY

Benefit Four talked about welcoming students into a learning environment. What about the basis for you being welcomed and accepted within the same environment? What kind of welcoming does a teacher desire, and is that different from the welcoming a teacher deserves? How do you know when you have received that welcoming?

It may feel awkward, or even selfish and self-serving, for the teacher to take actions driven by a desire for a welcoming from the student. After all, who is in charge here, and who is supposed to be helping whom? When a teacher attends to his or her own welcoming desires, the fundamental rule of service in both modern education and social services—this is about the other person, not me—appears to be broken. If this is about the student learning, then what am I doing focusing on myself?

The idea that both students and teachers are a community of learners—we are all learning, at least partially, by sharing parts of our lives with each other—carries with it the obligation for relationship. This is true whether it is a one-to-one interaction on a street corner or social service cubicle, or in a classroom full of students. The learning environment asks more of students and teachers than simply digesting facts. It calls us to remember that we have just used the word *community* in the same sentence with the word *learners*. Once we introduce the desire for community within a learning environment, additional requirements appear. We now have more than students and teachers as designations of the people involved. Abiding by the language of community, there are also guests and hosts. A community of learners has the responsibility to show hospitality to each other in two contexts occurring at the same time—as learners and as guests and hosts in each other's lives.

What is hospitality, and how does it show itself in a learning environment? One clue comes from the fact that the words *guest* and *host* originate from the same roots. *Hospitality*, a generous and friendly reception of guests or strangers, also carries back to the same root. That *guest* and *host* spring from the same roots informs us that we can be both at the same time, and, in fact, teachers and students must take turns being the welcomers and the persons being welcomed. Reciprocity is built into the obligation on both sides. To know that you will be required to both give and receive a welcoming deepens the obligation to each other of both students and teachers in a learning community.

Henri Nouwen, in *The Wounded Healer*, approaches welcoming and hospitality from the perspective of a person who finds himself in the position of being a host:

> "But it has become very difficult for us today to fully understand the implications of hospitality. Like the Semitic nomads, we live in a desert with many lonely travelers who are looking for a moment of peace, for a fresh drink and for a sign of encouragement so that they can continue their mysterious search for freedom."[33]

What does it take for the stranger to be welcomed? After all, it is difficult for a person to focus on much of anything else until the condition of welcoming has been at least partially met. The longer we do not feel welcome, the more elevated our psyche senses and promotes this condition as a developing crisis.

Not feeling welcome occurs when our psyche senses that either we are not being seen accurately or are not being seen at all. Both have the same result—a feeling of loneliness and detachment from others that produces a sadness and anger that can have only two possible results. Either we re-

---

33. Nouwen, Henri, *The Wounded Healer*, Doubleday. New York, N.Y. 1972. Page 89.

treat further from the situation or respond with an action designed to draw attention to ourselves. Oftentimes this attention-getting action, because its roots stem from the anger and desperation of not feeling welcome, will drive others further away. Now even more anxious to get the welcoming we desire, we are left with nothing but further evidence of being unwelcome.

Finding the sources of welcoming.

There are three conditions that can result in a feeling of being welcomed by others. Any one of them is enough to create welcoming in a moment, but all three are essential for a feeling of sustained welcoming with another person or group. A learning community provides ample opportunity for all three to be understood, valued, and used by both teachers and students as welcoming glue.

The first opportunity for welcoming occurs during the moments when I sense that my relationship with another person is deepening. This deepening can come from increased feelings of emotion between us, an invitation to spend more time in each other's company, a sharing of personal stories, or an increase in the number of group members I feel connected to. The result of deepening relationships is a feeling of being more welcome and accepted.

The second opportunity for welcoming occurs as I deepen my interest in the learning topic. Although it may seem contrary that I can feel more welcome amongst others by developing a deeper interest in the learning topic, there is a logic embedded in this kind of welcoming. We feel a shared sense of history, values, and intentions with others who share similar interests. We imagine that this common ground will provide comfort and safety when we are amongst those group members. In the same way that auto mechanics feel aligned with others who repair cars, and typists are drawn to other typists, students and teachers can feel welcome amongst each other through sharing an interest in a learning topic. We believe our allies understand something of the struggle we are engaged in. This kind of welcoming requires the teacher to demonstrate an active interest in the topic by presenting him- or herself as a learner as well as a teacher. Teachers who believe the information and wisdom is only going one direction—rather than back and forth between teacher and learner—cannot receive this kind of welcoming.

The third opportunity for welcoming occurs when I am singled out from other group members and acknowledged for a contribution I have made. Whether small or large, the acknowledgment provides proof of my value to the group and furthers my feelings of being welcome.

These three kinds of welcoming are difficult for the teacher to receive until he or she distinguishes and uses the difference between positional power and genuine authority in the learning environment.

There are defined limits to positional power.

Positional power is a kind of authority bestowed on a person from out-side of him- or herself. It is given by another person or group to maintain order and carry forward the ritualized acts that sustain the activity that the positional power is responsible for. Social service workers are responsible for caring for those who are suffering. Parents are responsible for raising children. Company managers are responsible for monitoring employees and successful completion of the group's work. Spiritual leaders, for un-derstanding spirit-related matters and maintaining rituals for engagement with spirit.

Teachers, whether they are in a classroom, social service office, thera-py room, or street corner, are responsible for carrying forward the rituals for learning within the environment they are operating within. Teachers can use their positional authority as the source of permission to estab-lish rules for what kinds of interactions are acceptable between students and the teacher, and students with other students. Students get most of their questions about the environment answered through observation of the teacher's actions and the environment he or she has set up. Can I ask questions of the teacher? Under what conditions can I talk with another student? Can I make a joke?

Teachers may also use their positional authority to establish timing of events within the relationship. When are we to meet? How late can I be to a meeting and not get in trouble? When is our meeting over? When should we meet next?

Positional authority also can be used to arrange and maintain the physi-cal surroundings for the meeting between teacher and student. Where will we meet, and what will the surroundings be like? Social service workers can choose to meet within their offices or at their client's chosen location. Teachers meet within their classroom. Within those environments, teach-ers can most often control the elements in the physical location. What will be on the walls? How will the furniture be arranged? All of these decisions are within the positional authority domain of the teacher.

Most of all, however, the designation of positional power as "teacher" carries within it the symbolic and often literal capacity to declare who is, and who is not, welcome within the learning environment. This includes authorizing who is allowed to be physically present, but beyond that, when the student has said or done something which is acceptable or not acceptable within the learning environment. Positional power gives a teacher the power of judgment over the student. It is also true that the student is always in a position to judge the teacher, but there is not a presumed permission to make an overt claim of this to the teacher. Judgment of the teacher by the student can carry with it harsh penalties because it breaks the fundamental rule of positional power: The person with the positional power is in some way further up the hierarchical ladder. This higher position carries with it the idea that the teacher is somehow "more" than the student—whether that means having more power, being better than, smarter than, more capable, or simply more in some unexplainable but symbolic way. We know it is true, but we are not certain why. That we are to obey is the commanding expectation of positional power. This obligation comes from the assumption that we are in a position that is less than the leader.

Giving your gift is necessary to combat and resolve the loneliness and isolation that can result from positional power.

Authority based solely in positional power and status results in distance between humans. Neither inherently good nor evil, the distance simply is—until the person with the authority makes decisions about how to interact with those who do not hold the same authority. In those decisions about how to be in relationship, holders of positional power create the opening, or close the door, for their own welcoming. The student's perception of how you, as an authority figure, will interact with them has been determined before either of you meet. Other authority figures in their past have shaped their expectations of you, and your decision about how to confirm or alter those perceptions determines the level of isolation you will experience.

After fifteen years of public speaking, on stages and in classrooms, I still feel anxious whenever I stand in front of a group to speak. The anxiousness is not primarily rooted in wondering whether I understand the material, whether or not I will manage the time and get through all of the content, whether the dialogue will be lively and useful for the students and myself, or whether I will consider the day, on a larger scale, successful. My anxiousness is seeded in the simple wondering about whether or not I will receive a welcoming from the stranger this time. As soon as I get the smallest clue that my presence is welcome—by seeing someone's smile or a question about the material—my stance with the group shifts. The defensive posture I use as my initial protection relaxes, opening my heart and mind to explore more fully the possibilities present in the room.

Occasionally, I meet other teachers who make claims to having none of this uncertainty or anxiousness prior to standing up in front of a group. I do not trust them nor do I believe them. The desire for welcoming is an embedded and irrevocable desire in all humans approaching another human. They may indeed have mustered this level of confidence, but it has come at the expense of purposefully forgetting what it means to feel unwelcome. In this forgetting, they have lost their ability to tap the initial glue that exists between the teacher and student—the desire to be welcomed into the life of the other. Their confidence, not rooted in genuine authority but through the forced forgetting of their desire to feel welcome, has diminished their capacity for connection.

When students sense this kind of false confidence, they read it as a sign of false invulnerability. Any student worth his or her salt will begin to pick away at this pretense in the teacher. Until some sign of vulnerability is sensed in the teacher, the student's desire to learn is postponed and is replaced by an increasing urgency to discover a crack in the teacher's armor. Students want a welcoming from teachers who show a genuine side of who they are. When a teacher shows vulnerability, a student can begin to believe the welcoming they receive is truthful because it comes from that location of vulnerability within us. Soft underbellies have the desire to be seen by the soft underbelly in the other.

We are, all of us, wanting a welcoming from the other which erupts out of the memory of what it is like to feel unwelcome. In this way, the stranger knows their suffering can be carried, at least in part, by the host. The struggle for positional power between teachers and students interrupts the welcoming process and deforms learning in both student and teacher until the issue of welcoming is resolved.

The task of the teacher is to make clear the intention to welcome by introducing conditions of hospitality rather than punitive authority within the learning environment. Reducing the loneliness of positional power, and introducing the seeds of hospitality, are both possible through introducing genuine authority—the giving of the gift. Why is this? Loneliness and a lack of feeling welcome come from believing you are unseen and/or not valued by another. When positional power is relied on as the source of being seen, the psyche yearns for more. "When is someone going to acknowledge that I am more than what is on the surface? Yes, you have seen the power I have over you, but you have not seen the power that comes from within me."

Our psyche wants to deliver the message that what is inside has the possibility of carrying us forward together into the unknown greatness of our life together. Giving your gift presents the student with the opportunity to welcome you for your essential contribution to the world. Without giving your gift, the only welcome you can receive is for your positional power or your mere presence. Both are small acknowledgments, particularly since they will be drowned out by the moaning of your psyche in the background begging for something more.

Positional power carries with it an embedded predicament.

What is the student to do when he or she, and oftentimes the teacher, realize that the student is "more than" the teacher? This occurs in situations where the student contributes an idea or an action that is wiser, smarter, has better timing, or results in the group acknowledging the student as the leader. The student is put in a confused state during moments when it is clear that the teacher is not more than the student. How should I react when I am clearly wiser than the teacher? How does the teacher react?

In these moments when the rules of positional power are thrown up in the air, the teacher is at a fork in the road. He or she may choose to attempt to reclaim positional power by reestablishing that the teacher is, once again, "more" than the student. Strategies for reclaiming their "one up" on the student range from responding with a statement that they perceive is smarter than what the student has said or done, using punishment to reestablish the hierarchical balance, or saying something designed to make the student feel or appear small to other students. All of the beforementioned actions are driven by the desire for the teacher to be, once again, in an elevated status over the student.

In these moments, there is another fork in the road that offers the opportunity for the teacher to use another kind of authority. This kind of authority, which I am calling genuine authority, is different from positional power in one primary way. It is authority which springs from within the teacher rather than being bestowed from outside. Not fundamentally designed to receive its validation from outside sources, genuine authority is the result of actions that come from being on the path you are supposed to be on. Genuine authority is seeded in the gifts, wounds, and story of the teacher. The use of genuine authority in a situation does not come from being in a hierarchical position. It comes from the commitment to follow a thread of wisdom, and resulting actions determined by the desire to stay tuned and attached to this wisdom thread. The source for the teacher to receive a genuine welcoming from the student(s) comes from this second fork in the road—actions the teacher takes which stem from genuine authority.

Giving your gift opens the opportunity for you to receive three kinds of welcoming.

At the beginning of this section, I said there were three opportunities for welcoming, all of which are present within a learning environment. Giving your gift opens the possibility for all three.

The first opportunity for welcoming occurs during the moments when I sense that my relationship with another person is deepening.

By sharing your gift, both the describing of the gift and then the actual giving of your gift, you reveal a part of yourself that is more than your positional power. As students begin to see you more fully, they are opened to the possibility that you are a person that is open to genuine relationship beyond your positional power. Each day they walk into your life as a teacher, you have the opportunity to remind them of your fullness and offer them the opportunity to respond in kind to your generosity. As their desire for a welcoming becomes more outspoken and the students' gifts become known, both sides can provide the welcoming each of you is asking for.

The second opportunity for welcoming occurs as I deepen my interest in the learning topic.

This kind of welcoming requires the teacher to demonstrate an active interest in the topic by presenting him- or herself as a learner as well as a teacher. By revealing your unanswered questions about the topic, you show a genuine interest in learning more, as well as a revelation of what students perceive as a crack in your armor—you don't know it all. Furthermore, by acknowledging moments when a student has caused a further awakening in you related to the topic, you model yourself as a learner and teacher.

Another possibility within this second kind of welcoming is for the teacher to reveal how the topic is related to what has been difficult for him or her. This requires revealing part of your story, and within that story providing a glimpse of the suffering you have known. By revealing your emotional attachment to the learning topic—the connection between the topic and your own suffering—you reveal the source of your passion for learning. This encourages the student to explore his or her own passion for the topic and, through mutual acknowledgment, deepen the relationship.

The third opportunity for welcoming occurs when I am singled out from other group members and acknowledged for a contribution I have made.

Whether small or large, the acknowledgment of this contribution provides proof of my value to the group and furthers my feelings of being welcome. In a learning environment, when a teacher gives his or her gift, the opportunity for this kind of welcoming is opened. Any acknowledgment from the student that the teacher's gift has been given or seen is the source of this kind of welcoming. It is not enough for the teacher to be aware that he or she has given their gift. The student must acknowledge it.

We give our gifts as a conscious statement of our intention in the world, and someone outside us must see it in order for us to receive the welcome that we desire. A teacher with a gift for logic and order receives a welcoming when a student comments on how well the teacher has logically described a complicated topic. A teacher with a gift for compassion receives a welcoming when a student thanks the teacher for taking time to listen to a personal difficulty in the student's life. A teacher with a gift for standing by others, no matter what, receives a welcoming when they are thanked by a student for going with them to the principal's office when they are in trouble.

The courageous act of revealing your suffering to the student provides the most ample territory for receiving the kind of welcoming you most desire.

Indirectly, by receiving a welcoming when we have given our gift, our wound is acknowledged. Because the gift is the opposing force and antidote to our suffering, when our gift is seen, the kind of suffering we have experienced is revealed to the outside world. Through the giving of the gift, our psyche senses that our wound has been seen, and breathes a small sigh of relief.

What about a more direct route? When we speak directly of our suffering, acknowledge the resulting gift, and then are seen for giving that gift, we have established a mainline to receive the welcoming we most desire. There is no road more direct, and there are no conditions more powerful, for receiving a full welcoming. Is this path possible within a useful context for the student and as more than a self-serving gesture by the teacher? Not only possible, it provides one of the deepest learning opportunities for the student and is the primary source of healing within the learning environment for the teacher.

If we think of gifts and wounds as being two halves of the same whole, then recognition of each other's gifts is only half of the formula for receiving a full welcome. Revealing a hint of the source of the gift—the wound— is the other half. It might be that each half can act alone to produce a basis for welcoming, but the psyche still reads danger. What if the stranger focuses on my wound, and will not accept my gift? Or, what if the stranger will not accept my suffering, or uses my suffering to gain advantage over me? When the stranger believes that both their gift and their wound have been seen and welcomed, the feeling of genuine hospitality erupts. It is the obligation of the host, the teacher, to initiate this welcoming process and encourage both sides of revelation to occur.

I am not speaking of telling the long and detailed version of your life's difficulties. Being aware of whether or not you are telling your story primarily for the student's benefit or in service to your own healing is an ethical question which should be at the forefront of every teacher's consciousness before beginning to tell even the smallest part of their story. Is the teacher creating more weight for the student to carry by telling part of his or her story? The understanding and release of weight and suffering in the student is the goal of the teacher's story. When the student is given the weight of the teacher's suffering to carry, the teacher is the only one who has benefited from telling the story. The student is now a student no more. They have become the convenient target of a teacher who has placed their own interest above the student's and is willing to have the student suffer as a consequence. Teachers who feel an enormous sense of relief after telling their story have just created a burden for the student through an unethical use of their positional power.

Revealing suffering in a learning context does not usually require sharing stories of open, gaping wounds. When a teacher tells a story of suffering which is "larger"—either by being more intense or longer—the student feels a requirement to turn his or her attention away from themselves and attend to what they perceive as your need for compassion. The purpose of the teacher's story—to open the imagination and learning of the student—has just been undermined by the story. Instead, the context for a teacher revealing suffering is limited to describing how your own story is tied to roots of your passion for the learning topic. The careful sharing of parts of your life story reveals this passion, and triggers the student to consider the roots of their passion for the learning topic. This cycle creates the mainline, the most powerful welcoming possible, for the teacher and keeps the focus of the situation on the student's learning.

Margaret is a forty-year-old English teacher in a suburban high school. She has taught for fifteen years, and lives a comfortable life in a suburban neighborhood near the school. She is well liked by students and other faculty, and intends to live out her life as a teacher. On the surface, Margaret's life appears to be smooth sailing. It has not always been this way.

Growing up, Margaret's father was in the military. During her school years, she moved five different times, to different parts of the world, as her father's assignments changed. At first, going in and out of new neighborhoods and new schools, Margaret eagerly searched for and made new friendships. Being talkative, bright, and active, she found success in each new place.

The trouble for Margaret was not in going to new places. It was in leaving the old. Each last day in a town, as Margaret said her goodbyes, she felt a deep sense of loss. After the first few leavings she learned that, although they would write back and forth for a time, eventually those relationships would be lost as she and her friends grew up, changed interests, and grew apart. After several moves, Margaret became less interested in finding new friends at the new places, knowing it was all going to end soon and be forgotten.

She began, about age thirteen, to retreat into a world in which she believed she was her only true friend, the only friend who wouldn't eventually leave her. She became more and more isolated from her family, the schools she entered and then left, and the roots of her desire for friends. Spending most of her time in her bedroom, Margaret turned to books as a source of friendship. Her love for books and language carried her towards her decision to become an English teacher.

Margaret's psyche named this experience of repeated broken relationships as her greatest suffering. Triggered by this suffering, Margaret's gift—to stand by others, no matter what—surfaced and became active in her life. For Margaret, hope came in the form of her desire for lasting relationships and people she could depend on. What are some of the ways Margaret can, as a teacher, reveal her suffering and use her gift in the classroom?

- Margaret can choose to tell her story of moving when she was a child, and the loneliness it produced in her. In the same story, Margaret can talk about the solace that books provided her and that the roots of her career as a teacher were seeded in that loneliness. In that story, she has revealed her source of passion for the topic—the loneliness of not having friends—and seeded the student's desire to locate their source of passion. Is my story similar to the teacher's? How do I deal with loneliness? I can see that the teacher understands how lonely it can be to be a teenager. Could books be helpful to me? As the student begins to compare his or her life with the teacher's, Margaret's gift of creating enduring relationships and standing by others has opened possibilities for deeper connections.
- Margaret can use her gift to demonstrate her desire for enduring relationships in the learning environment by not giving up on the boy in the third row who seems disinterested and may not pass the class. She sees beyond the surface-level disinterest, and has a curiosity about why this young man has lost his attention.
- Another way she can use her gift, and share her suffering, is to talk about how books were her lifeline through tough times, when things seemed out of control or too lonely. By describing her use of books as a problem-solving tool, she offers a possible lifeline to lonely students.
- Margaret can describe books as something that last in a world that seems fragmented and full of change and loss. Books are visible evidence of a past, and offer hope for a future in which the past can be remembered. Like her hope for lasting relationships, books are enduring. Margaret's gift reminds students that books are something solid to hang on to.

- Margaret can use her story to awaken students' desire to welcome each other in the classroom. By telling her story of repeated loss of relationship, and the ensuing loneliness, Margaret reminds students that they have the desire and ability to welcome each other and create a community where no one feels left out.

Each time Margaret enters the terrain of her suffering by telling her story and using teaching strategies that focus on using books as a source of hope and genuine relationships, she provides a link to her own passion, offers her genuine authority to the learning environment, and finds another opportunity for healing in her life. All this is possible for Margaret and her students, in the middle of an otherwise ordinary week, while she is teaching English in a suburban high school in the middle of America. The rich mystery, elegant simplicity, and healing power of the gift makes itself available, once more, to citizens who find themselves standing on each other's doorstep.

Receiving your welcoming should not be a necessary condition for welcoming the student.

In closing this benefit, it is important to remember that the teacher is often in situations where they will not receive a welcoming until multiple meetings have occurred between the student and teacher. The teacher may never receive a welcome at all. In the meantime, the teacher relies on the welcoming they feel within themselves to carry them. Nouwen reminds us that hospitality requires, first of all, "that the host feel at home in his own house, and secondly that he create a free and fearless place for the unexpected visitor."[34]

Although it is difficult to welcome others when, at the same time, you are trying to get your own welcoming needs met, that is the condition which all hosts find themselves in. The courage of the host to welcome the stranger, in spite of not knowing whether he or she will receive a welcoming in return, is a demonstration of character that does not go unnoticed by the observant guest. That the host chooses to act at all is, in itself, a sign of welcoming. The integrity of the teacher is demonstrated within these moments for all learners to witness and return.

---

34. Nouwen, Henri, *The Wounded Healer*, Doubleday. New York, N.Y. 1972. Page 89.

Benefit Five
Questions for Teachers:

1. Where, in your life as a teacher, do you feel welcome? This can be with other individuals, a group, or a physical location. For each welcoming situation you identify, what specifically causes this feeling of being welcome?

2. Where, in your life as a teacher, would you like to feel more welcome? What specifically would it take for that to happen?

3. What is your typical behavior when you find yourself in a situation where you do not feel welcome?

4. What specific ways do you welcome students? This can include classroom activities, your teaching style, and the way you have organized physical surroundings.

5. How is your passion for the topics you teach tied to your suffering?

6. What story could you safely tell from your own life that could help students understand how your suffering is tied to your passion for the learning topic?

7. What is your typical reaction when a student is "more" than you are in a learning situation?

Teacher's Dialogue
Benefit Five: Being Welcomed and Establishing Genuine Rather than Positional
Authority with the Student

Brian: When I went into teaching, it was the positional authority I hated the most. Schools can be a lot like prisons. Students feel trapped and they don't know what's going to happen. I spent the first part of my teaching career making fun of all those kinds of authority in how I taught.

Chris: How are you different now?

Brian: I always try to teach by showing that I'm actually interested in the curriculum—by talking with interest and getting really excited about it. I do believe students respond to that. Even if they aren't interested in my topic, they often say, "Wow, he was really interested and excited about that." Sometimes they say it with a bizarre look on their face like, "Why would that have interested him so much?" But I do think that is my real authority. It doesn't come from my title. The only time I use the other kind of positional authority is as a last ditch go-to place when everything else hasn't worked. But, any time I do that, I know it's because the real reasons for being in school have fallen apart.

Bruce: What is the real reason to be in school?

Brian: The reason we hold school is to make sense out of our lives, and that's really quite a helpful thing. And, as my wife has said to me, we have a moral obligation to get smart. A moral obligation. I always tell students that your life doesn't mean anything unless you make it mean something, and it is true that you will remain stupid unless you make an effort to get smarter. I emphasize the seriousness of the situation. I ask students to explain to me the benefits of being stupid. Why is that appealing? *(laughter)* They seem to respond to the idea that, on a fundamental level, it's not such a great thing to be stupid.

Chris: It's true…if the teacher doesn't define the purpose, then how is the student going to know why they are there? I hear you calling the student to a higher purpose.

Brian: I try to keep the focus on meaningful work rather than the evaluation, although this runs counter to the standards movement which is running full force now in our schools. The moral obligation I feel is to help people get smarter. As a last ditch effort, I will say that you are going to have to take a standards test, and these skills will be a part of it, so that's the purpose. But when I say that, it's out of desperation. To me, that's not really a purpose. The test is going to be over, but they are still going to have to go on.

Chris: You also know that kids object to that kind of authority at a really visceral level. For some children, testing begins and ends the purpose of school. It sounds like you are encouraging them to set their sights higher.

Brian: There are a group of students who just want to do well on the tests. Their comfort level requires making sure it's primarily about the tests. But I don't think that's most students.

Roger: For me, it seems like what we are talking about is both the challenge and the bind. It's like Joseph Campbell talking about the left hand path and the right hand path. There's the thing that feeds our souls and there is also the practical, worldly part of life. We have to find a way to hold both. For me, as a teacher in business environments, I have to ask: "How do I support the interest in employee learning and, at the same time, be responsible for getting some results?" Those things seem like they work at cross-purposes so often. Part of the challenge is to teach in a way that holds both energies and links them—it's not like we have to go back and forth between inspiration and drudgery.

Chris: So the master teacher is one who makes it, not two paths, but one?

Renae: Developmentally, until about age eight, giving a child an evaluation is without any purpose. They have no understanding of it. But, come third grade or so, they start to get the idea that there are standards and expectations for performance.

Roger: They begin to get that there is this whole outside thing going on. People are watching them.

Renae: Yes. For some of the kids, it is a major shock the moment they recognize school is not all about them. It's often such a moment for them when I say, "You know, you really don't have a choice about this." I keep wanting to stress how developmental this is. If you talk to a six year old about these issues, they give you the message this really is not part of their agenda. But, about eight or nine, they start to understand. They are connecting more to peers and noticing how they line up with others. Up until that age, they are more playing along side each other, saying to themselves, "I appreciate there are other bodies in my universe, but I am the center." But as they develop, there is a growing awareness that comparisons are going to be a part of things.

Chris: The curious part of this for me is that, developmentally, children are moving away from the idea they are the center of the universe. Part of that self-centeredness comes from the belief that they think everyone else sees the world the same way they do. It's just like you're saying, Renae. A child's orientation is, "I am the center of the universe, and I'm pretty sure you think I'm the center of the universe, too." And that's when we get into conflict with children, when we tell them that's not true. But the larger idea of spirituality, for me, confirms that we are all the center of the universe. We are all God. The struggle is in helping a child learn that, yes, you are the center of the universe, but I am too. That's a very difficult thing for a person to understand. It sounds like two messages.

Roger: It's the Buddhist thing, "Not one, not two." It's the idea that there is a way of going through life where it's all about me. At the same time, I have to connect with and I am in relationship with the other. So it's not one or two. It's both.

Cath: I want to go back and connect this with the left hand path and the right hand path you were talking about earlier, Roger. So many people in middle age travel the right hand path and get to a point in their life where they start to realize, "What is this other path—what have I been missing?" It seems like one of the purposes of teaching is to keep the student connected to what is meaningful. "What do you want to do before you die?" Brian, it seems like you are very interested in connecting students with the left hand path, certainly at a much younger age than I was connected to it.

Chris: It's an issue of urgency. We are naturally inclined toward responding to emergencies. We can respond to the urgency of the left hand path or the urgency of the right hand path. I think we have to create the urgency for the left hand path. They are both demanding our time and attention. Part of the notion of the gift is that it is demanding our attention all the time. You can either learn how to pay attention to it, or you can fight it. And that's where I think we get locked in the wound as the wound, and not as its capacity to inform and guide our giving of the gift. I see the path stuff as very similar. You can get locked in the day-to-day demands and expectation and earning and keeping up with the neighbors, or you can respond to the urgency of the left hand path. What feeds your soul and gives you purpose and meaning on a much higher intention than the urgency to get my pension plan going. On the other hand, if we get so concerned about the gift, we lose some of the pragmatics. A person can get hungry if they just focus on their gift.

Renae: With children, the seed of the left hand path, the gift, is there already. But the pragmatics come along and are a shock because the child is living in their soul. If you spend any length of time genuinely connected with children, it connects you to your soul. That's probably the reason I went back to teaching in the middle of my life. To get reconnected with my soul though children.

Chris: A minister told me, "Your children know an awful lot more than you can right now, because it was just a very short time ago they were with God." He had this notion that in this temporal life, the first arc is a moving away from our understanding of God and the second arc is moving back towards God. In the beginning we have it all, we lose it, and them we go back to find it again to prepare ourselves to be ready to enter death.

Brian: Bruce talks about using your wound to share and make connections between students. I know I did that early in my teaching. I used a lot of my own experiences. But I don't think about it like that now. One young woman, who I had as a student fifteen years ago, just sent me an email. In it she said, "The thing about you as a teacher is that you were real with us. You didn't talk down to us. You talked straight across to us like it was a real concern for you." I know what she is talking about, and I do think that is one of the ways I get my authority. I was thinking how I have continued and grown with that over the years. Part of how I got that authority was talking about the part of myself that Bruce refers to as wounds. The way I do it now—and I don't know if it's right or not—is I'm always in my classroom talking to myself. I used to be trying to make connections with others by trying to say things to make the connection, but I've found the best way to make connections is to talk as if there is no one in the room. What I mean by that is that I am talking to myself in order to discover and understand my own urgent interest in the learning topic. I think students respond to that more than when you try to share with them something you have thought up to try and connect with them. I believe one of the things we have to do, as teachers, is to help students learn how to talk to themselves. We can model that. I don't think teachers do that very much, because they aren't comfortable doing it in front of students. When I'm not effective, what it looks like is me sitting in front of the room rambling like there is no one there. That's the bad version of what I am talking about. The good version is when you talk to yourself with an urgency that creates the opening for students to do that with themselves. As a teacher, you can create the possibility that everyone in the room, by talking to themselves, is deeply connecting with others. When students see this is happening, they go "Oh…" It's really quite a moment.

Bruce: Everyone's genuine authority is present and alive in those moments…

Brian: Yes. It's also possible to create that kind of connectedness, one-to-one, in the spaces between classes. I make an effort to notice those moments and use them. Usually, I make relationships with students by singling them out for a contribution they have made. I acknowledge their gifts. But sometimes that backfires. Last week, I told a student that she was the most talented writer that I had seen in twenty-six years of teaching. She looked at me like I was lying to her. Many times, the honor students—when you tell them they have gifts—deny it at first and become very uncomfortable. I have had students come in after class to tell me why their papers are much worse than what I have told them they are, and then begin to criticize their own work very intensely. I have one student who has a writing style like Franz Kafka. She is a visionary, and can compose these elaborate sentences with good flow in her writing. I was trying to explain that to her and she said, "No, this is horrible. You graded this way too high."

Chris: Why do you think so many of these students have problems having their gifts acknowledged?

Brian: What's interesting to me is that I find just the reverse with students who have a more difficult time writing. They often think their work is much better than it actually is. I think those two phenomena are related. When I first noticed it, I stopped praising the high-end students because the praise would cause them not to do well. They would actually get worse under praise.

Renae: It's almost like they are saying, "How can I find my gift if you are just going to praise me?"

Brian: I said to one student recently, "This is the best class I have ever had." And she said to me, "How come you never told us that?" I realized I had trained myself not to praise the gifted students! I get very confused and mixed about how to handle this area.

Chris: I have a personal reason for asking, because I reacted the same way when I was in school. I was considered a gifted student, and I saw any praise as a burden. It just increased the expectations and it felt like it was going to crush me. I did everything in my power to lower the bar. But it sounds like your students want you to raise the bar.

Roger: I want to change the subject a little. The central issue seems to be about how people handle the whole idea of power. Teachers and other kinds of leaders are authorized to have decision-making authority. They are appointed, they aren't elected. But how they hold that power—and where they think it comes from—seems to make the difference about how well they can hold the responsibility for results and also engage people and their contributions. The people who think all their power has been given to them by someone other than the people they are teaching or leading get sucked down the black hole of just telling people what to do all the time. There are also people with authority who understand that, even though the people that are sitting in front of them didn't elect them into that leadership position, their authority does come from those very same people.

Bruce: Can you give us an example of what you are talking about?

Roger: I'm thinking of a client whose cultural heritage, according to her, is one where she is very comfortable with authority above her. She has none of the sixties rebellious kind of stuff. She has to work hard to understand people having trouble with authority. For her, authority is comforting and it helps calm her down when expectations and consequences are really clear. But when she gives that to people she is supervising, they are totally distracted by this level of authority. I've watched her, and her gift is certainly about being clear about what's expected. She's not mean about it, but she's way more direct than most managers. Part of her learning has been to realize that people will make their contributions a lot more joyfully and easily if she can be a little more honoring of their left hand path. She's really had to learn how to balance that. Personally, it's been challenging for me to work with her. I'm a rebellious person, and I can get into a reactive stance with her, having a similar reaction that her employees have. Emotionally, I can feel it coming on. The other thing I struggle with is not telling her what to do. I know she would love that. I am trying to hold this space for her to think about authority a little differently, and she gets really frustrated with me when I don't just lay it out for her. So we have this constant meta conversation going on: "What do you think you are here to learn about in this life?" She has gotten in touch with her own interest and need to broaden how she thinks about authority. Without her having her own goals in this area, we'd just be in a fight about it. What I know is this: people value power, and where they think the power comes from is so central.

Chris: It also helps to distinguish between organizational power and relational power. One of the things that appears in organizations is that people who very often have the least formal power are the ones who make things happen. They do it through two other ways—their relationships and their tenure. The regular channels may take three months for a decision, but you ask the right person and it can happen in a day. Some people have unbelievable power, but no position.

Roger: This whole gift thing is so great because it opens up a way to talk about holding both kinds of power. You know, people have had such awful experiences with power. For me, it's all about how to enact your authorization with a sense of justice. How do we use power and justice in a way that encourages people to make their contributions?

Renae: So often, I hear about teachers being uncomfortable with power.

Roger: If there are problems with power, I would look to the leader first. He or she has to create the container so it can be dealt with in a respectful way.

Cath: There is a sacred trust when I authorize somebody. I will trust you to do the right thing on my behalf. I give you my power to write the whole of the story, and I'm hoping you will include me in the writing of it. One of the tragedies in this era is that the sacred trust has been really broken. You know, *Question Authority* was the bumper sticker of the sixties. Many people believe the people in authority betrayed the trust of the people who authorized it. So there is very little, or no, respect for authority now. My thing is: How can I restore a sacred trust in the classroom? How can I be respectful of what students actually allow me to do? Things which I could not do without that allowance. How can I continue to include them in writing more and more of their stories and not just give it all to them.

Roger: That's where I think the gift comes in. Many leaders and teachers are so threatened about being transparent about their own learning goals. They think they will lose credibility and respect if they talk about what they are trying to learn. But what is true is that exactly the opposite happens. It's a clear choice when the leader says, "We're going to focus on what you need to learn, but I'm out of this". The other choice is, "Yea, you've got some learning to do but I also have some things to learn. And I want you to nudge me as well." That's when it gets human and fundamental and beyond the roles we are assigned. We are all just learning together. That's where the gift thing is really useful.

Renae: Our new principal came with exactly that approach. She was clear about who she was and what she was trying to learn. It really calmed things down and relaxed everyone. But, over time, her authority was diminished by authorities over her who didn't have that same approach. What she had to offer was denied and then the trust was lost again. You're right…that is the basis for real authority.

Cath: I'm just realizing this conversation is going to help me at work next week. I'm in a conflict and I think I'm going to approach the conversation a little differently than I was thinking. I want to start by asking "How don't we see each others gifts?"

Bruce: Conflicts are a powerful venue for using gifts. When we have taken the time to acknowledge our gifts, we have acknowledged some of the greatness of who we are and now that's present in the room in the midst of the conflict. Your gift is sitting over there, and my gift is sitting here, and we can talk about our troubles with our gifts helping us along and buffering our desire to lash out at each other. In conflicted situations, I believe the presence of our gifts helps us to keep away from "you are a bad person." What's at the heart of this is the intention to love. If I see can your gift while I am feeling the rub between us, I can still see you as somebody worthy of respect.

End.

15. BENEFIT SIX: USING MENTORING/ SECOND-LEVEL LEARNING MOMENTS

Part Three of this book described the phenomenon of second-level learning and how teachers can encourage students into this kind of reflection and resulting change. Good teaching triggers understanding in the student that transcends mere memorization of facts. We want the learning to stick, and the stickiness comes as a result of the student answering the question: "How can this piece of data be useful to me? If I can count change correctly, I will be able to know what coins I need in order to purchase a candy bar at the store." Second-level learning results in a particular kind of stickiness, occurring at a deeper level than an awareness there could be a candy bar in my future. It occurs when a student integrates information into his/her life and alters current thinking or behavior in a way that furthers his/her life purpose.

Teachers, by understanding and using the gift idea, can instigate and promote second-level learning and mentor students in the following ways:

The gift paradigm encourages second-level learning by breaking down some of the modern assumptions about mentoring.

There is little disagreement in all the definitions I have found about what a mentor is. Two elements, someone you trust and who has experience in the area you are seeking help, appear in most of the descriptors. The word mentor stems from *The Odyssey* by Homer, and was the name of the man who advised Telemachus as he set out on the long and dangerous journey to find his father. We have, over the years, distorted the idea of mentoring far away from the original actions of Mentor in Homer's story. The influence of educational and social service institutions on mentoring, as they usurp the word and alter it for their own use, has been particularly devastating. Connecting mentoring with core gifts is one path back towards dispelling some of these modern, and limiting, beliefs.

First, gifts are not concerned with a person's age. Your gift is looking for trusted advisement from wherever it can find it. In my own life, I have been instructed about my gift from watching a fourteen-year-old boy with a similar gift to mine, acting within the context of his family. I also have been mentored by a fifty-year-old woman.

Modern mentoring, particularly in volunteer social service and school programs, typically sets up older people to mentor younger people. Beneath this design there lies the belief that, simply because I am older, I have something you need. That may or may not be true. Gifts scorn this assumption, knowing that what is valued is information about the gift, regardless of the source or age of the person. Some of the age-related confusion we have encountered is the result of an increasing blending of the words elder and mentor. Elder is a type of positional authority bestowed upon an older person by the group they are a part of. Most often in older culture, it came after completing a set of rituals designed to prepare the person for this status. Once designated, the person has the responsibility for guidance of the community and perpetuation of the rituals that sustain community life.

Being a mentor, on the other hand, means that you have been chosen to provide advisement related to your specific gift. Being a mentor does not give a person general positional authority over an entire community—it is individually oriented and issue specific. There is no age associated with the designation. While it is possible for an elder to also be a mentor to a particular person, this is not a given assumption. Teachers, by acknowledging and using their gift and providing opportunities for students to do the same, open the possibility for teachers and students of all ages to see each other as possible mentors.

Second, your gift will attract students with similar gifts. Within this attraction is an important distinction that profoundly affects the power of a mentoring interaction: The student must choose the mentor. Most mentoring programs search for volunteers, and then assign them to people requesting help.[35] Sometimes, the person is assigned a mentor without ever having met him or her. This breaks one of the fundamental rules of mentoring—the gift in a person detects something it desires from another person and chooses that person as a mentor. Within this choosing is the acknowledgment that the gift in a person wants something from the gift in the one who has been chosen. The condition of motivation has been met for learning, which provides the fuel for the student to pay attention.

When the mentor gets to choose the student, or the student is assigned to a mentor, there is no built-in motivation in the student, and the mentor is in a position of patronizing the student by believing he or she has something to offer the student, regardless of the student's desire. The student correctly senses this "I know more than you do, so I have a right to be in your life" approach, usually offered with a sincere desire to help, as controlling and dangerous. He or she may listen out of politeness or fear of retribution if they walked away, but does not pay attention to the information from a place of deep desire within.

Third, another limiting assumption within modern mentoring is the idea of attaching people who are seen as incapable with mentors who are seen as more capable. I am able to be your mentor because I have my life

---

35. To use mentoring in a more genuine and traditional sense, social service programs would offer both volunteers and people being served by the agency the opportunity to identify their gifts. In addition, they also would be able to clarify their dominant talents and skills. Once the gifts are known, social service recipients would be offered the opportunity to meet volunteers with similar gifts and decide whether to select them as mentors. The two distinguishing characteristics within this paradigm are the identification of gifts in both parties as a condition for the mentoring connection, and the student having the power to select the mentor. While many organizations understand the usefulness of this paradigm, there are powerful forces working against its adoption. First, many volunteers think in terms of helping a person who is "disadvantaged" rather than gifted. They do not believe it is likely they will receive reciprocal help from the client that is beyond feeling good about helping a person who is in trouble. Second, programs are oriented to providing service to the client. To offer gift identification service to the volunteer seems, on the surface, to contradict funding requirements and the mission of the organization. Third, when volunteers learn that identification of their gifts involves reflection upon their suffering, many will run the other way. It is more than they bargained for when they signed up to help—"I thought this was going to be about another person's suffering!"

put together more completely than you. I am a mentor because I am more successful than you. I am able to be your mentor because I have been through your troubles and know a lot more than you. Modern mentoring is set up under the condition of the mentor being "more" than the student in some way. The gifts within us know this is not always true, and is certainly not a condition for mentoring to occur.

Oftentimes, we are mentored by others who are in precarious and desperate circumstances. Our gift seeks out the trouble the mentor has known as the fundamental source of curiosity and information. The student finds comfort and delight and hope in discovering that the mentor is frightened, is struggling, and still has the courage to continue on. As Somé reminds us, teachers and mentors help us to satisfy our "...souls desire to deal with this burden."[36] When we see the mentor is carrying a burden, carrying our load does not feel so lonely. When a mentor presents him- or herself as having "made it," the student is easily swayed towards beginning to mimic the mentor so they, too, can be successful. The student drops their load on the path and tries to pick up the same load the mentor is carrying. Sooner or later, the student will have to return to pick up their own weight they have discarded on the path. When mentors present their struggles honestly to the student, the student is reminded that there is no easy way out. Each of us has our own difficulties. The courage the mentor shows becomes the primary yearning of the student rather than simply copying the path of the mentor.

Fourth, modern mentoring has within it the idea that the mentor has achieved the status of mentor as a result of having a "complete" understanding of the issue about which the student is trying to learn. There is an assumption that the mentor has explored all the nooks and crannies of the topic, and can provide an answer to most any question the student may ask. A walking encyclopedia of wisdom, the mentor sits comfortably and secure, waiting for the question to be asked so the answer can be given. In *Power in the Helping Professions*, Adolf Guggenbuhl-Craig describes the typical behavior of a therapist operating under these assumptions. His description touches a recognizable place within me as I evaluate my teaching

---

36. Somé, Sobonfu. *Falling Out Of Grace.* Page 96

approach during moments when I am not in right relationship with the student.

> "When the patient tells him of his troubles, the analyst lets it be seen that he already understands everything. Through the use of certain gestures, such as a sage nodding of the head, and pregnant remarks interjected among the patient's statements, the analyst creates an impression that, while he may not be prepared to communicate all his knowing and profound thoughts, he has already plumbed the very depths of his patient's soul."[37]

This "expert" model of mentoring, in which the person desiring the status of mentor tries to contain a batch of wisdom as a form of positional power, is offered at the expense of one of the most useful aspects of honest mentoring. There is reciprocity to the act of mentoring—the student is also making an offering to the mentor. The mentor will learn from the student.

The framework for reciprocity in mentoring is built on the foundation that, while gifts in individuals are often similar, each person has a distinct and different style of giving their gift. The style they use to give their gift causes a person to want to learn different aspects of the gift, so they can expand their style to further their gift-giving capacity. Take the example of John and Paula, who both have a gift for motivating others. John's style for giving his gift of motivation is to listen with compassion, acknowledge the person's suffering, and carefully develop solutions that will get the person moving. Paula, also with a gift for motivation, has a completely different style. In order to motivate others, she bluntly challenges the person and gives them a verbal, or literal, "kick in the butt" to get them on the road. Paula and John are both very good at motivating others, but their styles are dramatically different.

In this difference lies the possibility for mutual mentoring. Curious about expanding their own unique style, each will question the other about how they motivate others. This curiosity about how the other person gives their gift can result in learning about and adopting some of the other person's gift-giving style. Without the assumption of reciprocity in

---

37. Guggenbuhl-Craig, Adolf. *Power in the Helping Professions.* Spring Publications. Dallas, Texas. 1971. Page 39

mentoring, this exchange is not possible.

Fifth, both the mentor and the student are afraid. Modern mentoring comes with the assumption that, because the mentor has such complete knowledge, they are less afraid of the topic being explored by the student and mentor. This is not how fear works when gifts are involved. The mentor may indeed have grown beyond some of the fears the student is struggling with, but the mentor has most certainly grown towards new fears in other areas of their gift. Because gifts are attached to wounds, whenever gifts are being learned about and expanded, both student and mentor are vulnerable to new areas of healing. These new areas of exploration cause the psyche to become alert and wary—any return to the original suffering is a signal of danger.

Because students and mentors also might have completely different original kinds of suffering which produced their similar gifts, one person may have no fear in an area that causes the other to want to run the other way. It is the job of both student and mentor to explore areas of their gift that the other either has no interest in or is afraid to explore. In this way, gift wisdom is expanded through the natural attraction of a person's yearning to give their gift by expanding their style and exploring deeper levels of healing.

You increase your motivation and ability to distinguish between students who want friendship and students who have identified you as a mentor.

A person with positional power is constantly attracting and repelling other people, depending on how they are using their power and how others are interpreting those actions. Distinguishing the source of others' attraction towards you, or their moving away from you, can be difficult to discern. Why is a student moving towards you? It could be for any number of reasons including friendship, desiring approval, choosing you as a mentor, passion for the learning topic, wanting to create a relationship where learning is more personal, believing there is a link between grades and success in their relationship with you, sensing a desire for you to feel welcome or for them to feel welcome, respect for hierarchical position, or a simple curiosity about who you are. Oftentimes, the reasons for attraction are overlapping and unknown to both parties initially and at different crossroads in the evolution of the relationship. The paradigm of gifts provides another source of information to consider when evaluating your relationship with a student.

Gifts are drawn towards each other, both to bask in the comfort of each other's company and also to stir up trouble. Similarly gifted individuals want to spend time together because their gifts are trying to learn from each other. We sense in those with similar gifts an opening to learn more about our gift, make decisions about the next step on the path, get practical problem-solving help, and share stories of what has been difficult. People who have oppositional gifts are also attracted towards each other for at least two reasons. First, our psyche may sense that we need gifts other than our own to successfully navigate a situation we are facing. Second, there is an attraction towards the conflict that may occur with people who have gifts opposite to ours. In the conflict, we discover more about the value of our own gift, expand elements of our own style in giving our gift, and also are offered the possibility of respecting and including the gifts of others in our life. Common reasons for the root of the initial conflict can come from us wanting to increase the value of our gift by devaluing other gifts, not seeing another person's gift as necessary in the situation, or believing our gift will not be fully seen and used if there are other gifts receiving attention.

When you are clear about and intentionally use your core gift and the elements of your teaching style that are related to your gift, you will more readily attract students who have chosen you as a mentor. This attraction will take two forms in the student as they move towards you. Either they will appear welcoming and gracious, or they will be hostile and repelling. Oftentimes, both hostile and welcoming actions by the student are being driven by their gift's desire to be in relationship with your gift. When you accurately read this as gift-driven behavior, you are able to respond to the student less out of your own need to feel welcome and more out of a larger imagination of the purpose of the interaction. You become curious about the source of the hostility rather than feeling a need to immediately become defensive. You are aware that within this seed of hostility is the hope for further gift discovery on both sides. You also are focused on wanting to accurately name the element of your style that has caused the attraction to occur. This element of your style is the connection between your gift and the student's gift, and can become the focus of the mentoring activity between you. It is likely that you are poised to learn at least as much as the student from the resulting conversation.

By publicly naming your gift, you model being on a path.

Modern education and social services are formulated around the learning of distinct topics. We learn math. We are asked to modify specific behaviors with our parents. We learn to drive. We learn to stop stealing from the store. Whether the context is school, family life, or sitting in a social service office trying to get out of the trouble, the model for learning is to separate out the distinct learning topic and focus on it. This Cartesian model for understanding, the assumption that everything can be broken down into parts in order to be understood, is not a helpful paradigm for working with life purpose issues. By their very design, our lives are complex entanglements of flesh and blood, emotions, relationships, intellectual understanding, and spirit. To affect one area is most certainly going to affect the others. The path of our lives, to the extent that we can stay on it, involves integrating and understanding the whole of things within the individual situations we are facing.

Teachers who reveal how their gift and life purpose are being influenced in different situations model the idea of integrating life purpose and situational problem solving. They demonstrate what it takes to attend to a path. This kind of living example is rare in education today as teaching becomes more focused on preparation for standardized tests. It also is disappearing in both publicly funded social services and amongst private therapeutic professionals as funding is reduced and specific time-limited interventions become the mainstay for measuring success. People looking for learning and help deserve our confirmation that they are larger than their current circumstances and have a path worthy of our regard. We show respect for their path, in part, by acknowledging our own.

Benefit Six
Questions for Teachers:
1. Who has chosen you as a mentor? How do you know you have been chosen? What do you think this person is trying to learn from you? How is this connected to your gift? Have you considered asking them what they are trying to learn?
2. Can you discern something you have learned from a person who has chosen you as a mentor? Have you gotten an unexpected benefit from the relationship?
3. Name two mentors from your past, and identify the element of their style, more than anything else, that you have tried to incorporate into your own gift-giving style.
4. Who is a new and current mentor in your life? What is the most distinctive element of their style that attracts you? What are you trying to learn from him or her?
5. Is there a student or mentor who rubs you the wrong way? How is this rub connected to your gift? What are you trying to learn from him or her?
6. What are some of the dangers, in a learning environment, with approaching the student/teacher relationship from the perspective of mentoring? What can you do to reduce the danger?
7. What is an area of your gift, or your gift-giving style, that is increasingly trying to get your attention? Who could be a mentor for you in this area?

Teacher's Dialogue
Benefit Six: Effectively Using Mentoring/Secondl-Level Learning Moments.

Renae: I really like what Bruce says about how the modern world has changed the meaning of mentoring. We have a mentorship program at my school. Teenagers with some training are assigned to mentor younger kids in my classroom and I am supposed to mentor the mentor. What I noticed was that sometimes the most important mentoring relationship was between the mentor and the younger student, but other times it seemed to be mostly about my relationship with the mentor— they would hardly get to know the younger student they were assigned to. One of those student mentors was Bill, a basketball player at the high school. He was having a struggle in school but was very powerful on the basketball court, and there was a lot of discussion about his effectiveness as a mentor because of the levels of scholarship that would be required. Right now I have, in my heart, this view of him on laying on the floor with his legs stretched out all over, and the kid he was assigned to mentor coming over and sitting next to him and seeing in him this power he had as an athlete and the compassion he had as a person. It was amazing. It went so far as all the children in the class demanding that their families go and watch him on the basketball court. So when you went to his games, there would be young kids from the class there to watch him. What I learned is that mentorship is so much more than just having a skill. The students mentored him as much as he mentored the young students. Every time they would see him on the street, he would be lifted by that. So this was a two-way thing over which I had no control except to provide the space.

Brian: I'm always interested in the students who choose me as a mentor. So often, the ones I most want to help have absolutely no need for me and the ones who I often don't want to help come to me—I have absolutely no idea why they are choosing me. It's a very mysterious process, and I don't understand it very well. I think you are chosen by others to be a mentor—you don't really have a role in the choosing. That's been my experience.

Renae: That's been my experience, too. People show up in my life and expect things of me that I'm not sure how to provide. But they can be very persistent. I often don't understand what they get out of it.

Brian: Maybe that's part of the mystery of the gift giving. We have a tradition at my school where the teachers line up and the seniors walk out and we say goodbye to each one of them individually. I'm always surprised at the ones who come up to me and talk about how meaningful I've been to them. I'm thinking, "I hardly knew you were in my room." I'm just floored that I have had this influence. And then the ones that I was talking to in the classroom, thinking I am having this big influence, just walk by me and nod. We don't know who we are influencing. Because of this, I think it's important to give the gift you know you have and recognize it has influences that you often can't control.

Chris: So, the giving of the gift is intentional, but the choosing of recipient may not be.

Brian: The gift will find where it needs to go, and will be received in ways you can't know or understand.

Bruce: If there was a way for the student to have the opportunity to be explicit about the source of their attraction to you—whatever it was about your gift they were trying to learn about— then a conversation could happen back and forth which could strengthen both of your gifts. The gift in both Brian and the student has a chance to grow, whether the gift is the same or oppositional.

Brian: I would say that level of discussion would happen so much further down the line. In my work, it's probably not going to happen. The reception of the gift, in itself, is quite a feat.

Bruce: Maybe, but I don't think we know much about how to encourage those moments. It may be easier than we think. One of the old definitions of mentoring is that the gift in me is speaking to the gift in the other person. It's a gift-to-gift conversation. But the specific focus of the exchange, and why the student must choose the mentor, is that there is an element in the student's gift-giving style they are trying to strengthen, and they sense that same element in the mentor's style—hence the attraction. Initially, the mentor usually has no way to know what part of his/her style is attracting the student. This all sounds complex, but I don't think it's as mysterious as we make it. It requires the person being mentored to clarify what their attraction is to the mentor. This usually requires the mentor's help, through careful questioning and listening. If, as teachers, we got better at encouraging this kind of clarification, we could get to the level of gift-to-gift conversation.

Renae: So I have a question: With your gift in mind, what would you be inclined to look for in a mentor...an oppositional gift or a similar gift?"

Chris: For me, I would look for a person with a gift that is familiar, that makes it safe and comfortable, but enough difference to make it challenging and provocative. This would help me be clear about the reasons for being together. I wouldn't see the person as a mentor if there were too many similarities. If there were too many differences, I may not be able to let down my defenses and biases that protect me from feeling the wound.

Cath: It seems like I'm discovering the nuances of my gift. Initially, since so much of my own personal suffering was around not having people who saw me or mentored me, it was critical to attach to people who simply encouraged me. That was the first step. As I reflected more and saw how my gift was operating in the world, I began to realize there was an under-developed truth telling that needed to accompany my gift, and so then I started finding people coming into my life who were very rigorous with me about what I wasn't seeing about myself, and kicking my ass around developing the courage to tell my truth more strongly. I'm thinking it will continue to be a process with me where the mentors I need will come to me and help continue to develop my ability to give my gift. My answer to your question is that sometimes it could be people who have very similar gifts, and sometimes it could be people who have very oppositional gifts.

Renae: I'm always interested in other people's views, and I like being challenged, so I'm not generally threatened by people with oppositional gifts. I have a sense that my gift expands around those people.

Chris: Discovering nuances is also where I'm at—increasing the times and places and ways I can give my gift. One of the struggles of adolescence is that the gift is calling really loudly, but our tools and talents around giving it are pretty limited. Young people often drive others away from them with the intensity of their gift. As I get older, even though my tools are getting expanded, my gift also keeps growing and seems to get greyer and greyer. There are so many ways to understand it and give it.

Bruce: It may help to make a distinction between your gift and the style you use to give it. The gift is very specific, but there are a handful of elements in your style that can alter and expand, which increases the variety of ways you can give your gift. At certain points in your life, you become concerned with building up a particular element of your style. Like you just said, Cath, at one point the truth telling part of your gift style was important to learn about and grow.

Roger: Bruce, it would help me to get oriented to this mentoring benefit if you would say a sentence or two about second-level learning and mentoring.

Bruce: At some point in my life, I learned that five plus five is ten, and stored that data in my brain. At another point in my real life when I needed to know that—like when I'm buying a candy bar and counting the change—that piece of information has value and becomes learned within the context of my life. At that point, it's learned at a "second-level", and has a usability and urgency beyond simple memorization.

Roger: So second level learning is about application?

Bruce: Right, it's taking facts into your life in a way that they have real value and are useful.

Roger: So, how does that relate to mentoring?

Bruce: Because mentoring and being mentored, when it's working right, is fundamentally a reciprocal process for both parties to make meaning in their lives. Second level learning, like mentoring, is a label to describe the discernment process of placing a meaning on facts you have learned.

Renae: That's exactly what has happened to me so many times. People who, years later—I don't even remember their name—come up to me and say, "Remember when you told me", and then they tell me where we were actually sitting at the time and what I said. I can't remember what they are talking about. Then they go on to say, "I've thought about it over and over again, and I made these decisions based on what you said."

Roger: I've been on both sides of that one. Mostly, I have the experience of going to someone who I considered a mentor and saying, "Remember when you said…", and seeing this blank look come over their face. My response was, "God, I thought I was important to you." I was living in this whole relationship that I realized they weren't in.

Renae: Speaking as someone who this has happened to a lot, it isn't that it wasn't important, it's just that you realize that when your gift is expressed and someone else is picking up what they need from it—it's just hard to know what effect you are having. How can I know what part of my style they are attached to?

Brian: Again, that's part of the mystery. It is usually happening at an unconscious level.

Renae: Yes.

Roger: This is like choosing a mate! Our choice is very unconscious but very specific. The same thing is true with mentors. I like that way of saying it—the gift in one person choosing the gift in another. Also, I can get attracted to certain students or clients too, and see that it's all about my need. The attraction for me is wanting to enjoy them or be stimulated by their thinking. When I think about it that way, it makes total sense that they might not be tuned into it. They don't have that need.

Brian: I'm laughing right now, because I am thinking of the mania of everything that attracts us. It's like we think, "Well, that would be a good thing to lick!" (Makes licking motion with his tongue)

Roger: I'm starting to go through my list of mentors to understand whether they've been similar or oppositional.

Brian: As a writing teacher, most of my mentors are actually writers who are dead. One aspect of mentoring is realizing that the dead can be your mentors—their outrage can be more alive than those who are living. They can still speak to you—sometimes making you judge those around you as half-dead. One thing I try to show students is that books are powerful and alive ghosts that can haunt you, in a good way, and speak to you. In my own life right now, it is those people—the dead—who are most important to me and most alive. I rarely feel lonely when I have them close. Trying to convey that idea without being laughed at has been very difficult for me.

Renae: I know just what you mean. I can think of someone right now, who, even though he is dead, I am very attracted to learning from.

Brian: Another aspect of mentoring, especially coming from modern literature and Emerson, says that everything comes from the self—that you don't need to go outside yourself for answers to anything. One of the things we try to do in journal writing, when teaching Emerson, is to show students that you can be your own mentor. For me, ultimately, the concept of mentoring is to get you to be your own mentor to the extent you are out of touch with yourself. You need the Great Self within to talk to you and tell you the direction you need to be going. What mentoring means now, in my own life, is using the Great Self within and the great dead that talk to me. They've been much more helpful than others. It seems like the more I go to others the more I get lost, unless I am feeling a certain calling for those few people. You don't need to go looking for mentors. That would be a bad decision. Wait, and you'll know when you are in their presence.

Chris: I'm confused between the differences of a mentor who comes into my life in a one-way exchange—say a writer or singer who says something which "mentors" me, and a mentor who enters my life in a mutual relationship. Where there is an exchange. I see mentoring as something where I'm being influenced but also exerting influence. I guess I have limited my definition of mentoring to an ongoing exchange of ideas and values. We consider things back and forth, and it results in both of us having a deeper understanding of who we are.

Roger: Are you saying it's a mutual choice?

Chris: Not necessarily. Some are intentional and some unintentional.

Roger: But you are saying there is a two-way street going on as opposed to...

Chris: Yes. When I have been a mentor, it's always been very clear to me that I have as much to learn as the person who has chosen me to be their mentor.

Roger: I've had a very different definition. I haven't thought of it as a two-way thing. For me, a mentor is someone who values me and who sees who I am, and also sees something beyond what I am able to see. They have a perspective that is larger than mine, and they are interested in helping me to enlarge and deepen who I am.

Brian: But I don't even know if they need to know they are doing it. Over and over again, I haven't even known I was being a mentor. I just gave my gift and it was received. In fact, I can't think of a time I tried to be a mentor and give my gift intentionally and it worked.

Roger: I think there is a continuum of awareness about that.

Chris: The minute you name something, the minute you say to yourself you are going to engage in a mentoring relationship, the likelihood of that happening just got diminished. As opposed to thinking, "There is something in me that is seeking and yearning, and if I'm of good fortune I will find someone who has a gift who will guide me."

Roger: Bruce, aren't you talking about mentoring as a conscious and intentional act?

Bruce: One of the notions of mentoring is that, when it's conscious, you can't be a mentor without expanding your own gift. The gifts in each of us are learning from each other. If Brian is the teacher and I am the student, and I go to him and say "We've got a similar gift going on here..."

Roger: But Bruce, few people can say that...

Bruce: Yes, that's exactly the problem. People aren't conscious of their gift, and also aren't clear about why they are attracted to the mentor. Because of that, much of the advantage—for both the student and mentor—is lost. When you know your gift, you can't give your gift to me without your gift getting stronger. The dynamic of reciprocity adds so much richness to the exchange.

Roger: For me to be mentored, it's been important that the person has had some kind of spiritual or core gift level of interest in me. I have put a light on them because of that. It's been a personal thing, and it has been one way.

Renae: For me, a mentor is someone who addresses both my gift and my suffering. That is what lifts my gift. Whatever method is used, I want my gift enhanced and my suffering to be reduced, or at least integrated in a better way.

Roger: I like the idea that the mentor is someone who is engaging me with my gift. That's the difference between a mentor and a teacher. I don't know if it's levels of consciousness, but there is some kind of boundary between a mentor and person being mentored. It's not a power kind of thing, but there is some sort of generational or elder thing going on.

Chris: But some of the most profound things I've been taught have been from kids.

Roger: I can accommodate that easily, because I have the same experience. I would just say that, at the level of consciousness I am striving for, they are somewhere where I want to be. It could be a six year old or an eighty year old.

Renae: Exactly.

Chris: I made the mistake of thinking of it as hierarchical, like age, and thinking it was up and down.

Roger: Well, I do mean it that way, but age and physicality and worldly stuff is irrelevant. The hierarchy exists in the level of consciousness. There's another thing: It seems to me that what the mentor is getting out of the exchange is at a different level. Whenever I've tried to go for intimacy across that boundary, it's exploded. I think that comes with the territory of mentoring.

Cath: I wonder if that's part of how the blow-up thing happens between mentors and students. How you are experiencing it is not how the other person is experiencing it. They may be caught in the up and down part of it. I certainly know about striving for intimacy with a mentor and having it backfire. "Nope, not going to happen here!" I have this desire to be at an intimate level with the one I aspire to be like and learn from.

Roger: There is a big difference between a mentoring moment and an on-going mentor. I think the blowups happen when you get more into the personal dynamics rather than the gift dynamics. If you stay in the gift dynamics, there is nothing to blow up. That's the problem—human beings accompany the gift-to-gift exchange! *(Laughter)*

Brian: There was a girl who, after she left my class, sent me a paper she wrote in graduate school. She said she just wanted me to know how much her writing has improved. She asked me to read her paper. Well, I had no interest in reading her paper and, after having read it, it was nothing I cared to acknowledge because I had no interest in it. I wrote her back a highly engaged letter telling her how wonderful her writing was. She apparently needed it.

Chris: What happened to your gift of truth telling? *(Laughter)*

Brian: I think that I had given my gift while she was in my class. I couldn't have intentionally crafted it at the time, and she took something out of it that I couldn't know. But when I got her letter, I think anything I would have consciously attempted to do, related to gift giving, would have been very destructive. If I had used my gift of truth telling, it probably would have been to critique her religious views and spark some kind of antagonistic discussion…

Chris: I would argue that you did her a disservice by not giving your gift.

Brian: But that's now how I give my gift! I would not even begin to approach it like you are describing. I was not trying to give her my gift.

Chris: That's what I said, you ran away from giving your gift.

Cath: I don't think this was about gifts at all. She was seeking your acknowledgment as a teacher, not your gift.

Roger: The trouble in all of this, I hear, is trying to hold two polarities. It's about trying to hold the human relationship and the gift exchange at the same time. I know when a student wants acknowledgement from me. The gift-to-gift exchange doesn't have any of those distractions.

Brian: Yes, you're right. What this student was asking for was, "Please pat me on the head." But that's not my gift. I will willingly pat anybody on the head—why wouldn't I? But it wasn't about gifts.

Roger: When there is a gift exchange that has gone on already, and you get a personal request like that lobbed over the net, can you hit back a gift response? That's what I think this is about. As opposed to getting caught in a personal dynamic.

Chris: If I want you to tell me it's great, and its not, and you tell me it's great, you aren't helping me.

Renae: What if there is no capacity for the student to handle it? It sounds to me like the student just wanted Brian to see the work and acknowledge it. "Look, see what I have done."

Bruce: Chris, is your gift—creating welcoming places where people can belong—wrapped up in your response? In this situation, it sounds like the student wanted to be welcomed and accepted by the teacher.

Chris: Alright. It's my own personal stuff getting in the way. When I've asked people I respect for their opinion, I was counting on them to tell me the truth. Brian's gift is truth telling, and I'm hearing that he wasn't telling her the truth. That's hard for me not to react to.

End.

V. YOUR TURN: FINDING YOUR CORE GIFT

16. PREPARING FOR THE PROCESS

How do you determine your core gift? How do you distinguish it from all your other gifts, talents and skills? Rather than just focusing on those times when you are teaching, the process of core gift identification works best when you use your whole life as the basis for gathering information. If you are a teacher, you can be sure that your core gift is being used by you daily in your work. But it is also true that you are using your core gift when you get home at night, in your relationships with friends over the span of your lifetime, when you were younger, in all the jobs you have ever had, and in your hobbies and other interests.

Many of the youth initiation practices from around the world were intended to help a young community member begin to establish their primary orientation to the world, which was named as their "gift." Once named, this then formed the fundamental relationship between the young person and the community. The community could depend on the person for effort and contributions made in this direction. Since most, if not all, of us in industrialized nations have not had the opportunity to go through a community-designed and sponsored initiation, we are left with the task of finding our purpose through self-reflection on our own or in the company of others interested in the idea of gifts and life purpose.

There is a reason why so many cultures from around the world included gift identification as a fundamental rite of passage for youth. In our bones, we know there is something we are supposed to be doing and, if only we could figure out what it is, we sense that we could act more intentionally and be seen for "who we really are." Perhaps we believe we would know what the "right" job is for us, how to find more happiness, who the best life partners would be, how to best spend our time, or how to help our children to know their own path. The truth is, when we know our core gift, it can help us to make decisions in all of those life areas. Although it is important to be careful not to hold your core gift accountable for all of your decisions, or to see it as the solution to all your problems or opportunities, it is true that most situations can benefit from reflecting on how your core gift can both help and detract from the action you are considering.

The false promise of awareness

Any process for self-discovery carries the possibility of a false promise. "There, I got it!" I exclaim, and then wander forward believing I have wrapped up, neat and tidy, that part of my life. Fully understood, I now can get on with other things. This wrap-it-up-neat-and-tidy approach to life, so explicit in the media's attraction to sound bites as a way of understanding complex issues, produces "answers" which are devoid of deeper understanding. Sooner or later, any serious process of self-discovery runs into the unmistakable and jarring realization that, no matter how much I understand this, I will never understand it all. After the initial disappointment that comes from knowing the journey will never be complete, we reach a larger condition of delight as we understand we have found something so immense, so full of possibility, that it is worthy of a life's work.

This awareness is particularly important to remember in gift identification. To remove the most essential quality of beauty about our gift—the mystery which propels the search—would be to remove the wanting to return, over and over again, to the well-point of understanding that is available. Rumi, the Sufi mystic and poet, has written extensively on the idea of gifts and the yearning for truth. Of the search he says, "I'd gladly spend years getting word of him, even third or fourth hand."[38]

---

38. From the Rumi poem *Has Anyone Seen the Boy?* Translated by Coleman Barks and John Moyne. *These Branching Moments.* Copper Beech Press. Providence, R.I. 1989.

There are many warnings in spiritual writings cautioning the reader to remember that the largest mysteries in life are reduced simply by the use of language to describe them. The first lines of the *Tao* say, "The Tao that can be told is not the eternal Tao. The name that can be named is not the eternal name." Michael Sells, in *The Mystical Languages of Unsaying*, cautions that language is not a complete enough vehicle to understand the forces larger than ourselves. He says, "in order to claim that the transcendent is beyond names, however, I must give it a name; the transcendent."[39] I heard Luis Rodriguez say, "There are deeper names we carry that we don't know or understand."[40] If it cannot be completely named and understood, can it be understood at all? Why should I bother to try to understand if it is beyond my reach? Sells goes on to say, "Yet as elusive as it is, mystery is in principle accessible to all." The hope for humans is that we can get a slice of it, just enough to whet our appetite and put us on a path which continues to open the mystery to our understanding. Each glimpse into the canyon offers us understanding about what our life has been and what it may be. That we cannot understand it completely may be the biggest gift of all since, near as I can tell, being the creator of all things is considerably more difficult than being human.

The process you are about to engage in is another step of understanding the expansive and mysterious nature of who you are. Rather than a final solution, it opens more layers of understanding which, when put into the medicine bag containing what you already know, reveals the next steps on the path. I know many people who have done the Core Gift Identification process multiple times. Each time it is done, they get a deeper understanding of their core gift and the suffering they have known. The process, as I have come to appreciate it, reveals the beauty within us that cannot be fully revealed.

Creating the optimum gift-finding environment

You can be assisted in identifying your core gift by setting up your

---

39. The references to the Tao and the Sells article are from the monograph *Rites of passage in our times*, by Josette Luvmour. Available through the EnCompass website www.EnCompass-nlr.org

40. Rodriguez, author of *Hearts and Hands: Creating Community in Violent Times*, works extensively with young and old who have found trouble. His work is inclusive of the principles of initiation and gifts.

environment in a way that contributes to an ability for reflection.[41] Although I have heard stories from people who recognized their core gift
while driving their car to work, most of us will find this task much easier
when we intentionally design our surroundings in a way that supports and
promotes reflective activity.

First, consider whether or not to do this task alone or with another
person. The first pathway for thread identification, which has you discover
what others say you have been bringing to situations, obviously requires
the company of others to do the task. But the other three methods can
be done either alone or with others. What is your preference? I would
encourage you to consider the benefits of core gift identification in the
company of another person when it makes sense to you. Having another
person there to ask you questions, and for you to reflect your answers to,
often helps with clarity. Because your core gift is simple on the surface,
and actively trying to be seen, oftentimes another person will have clarity
about your core gift before you do. After all, you are busy giving your core
gift, but others are busy seeing it and receiving it.

When we get mired down in deep reflection about our life, it can be
helpful to have another person there to remind us that what is obvious
may be more useful in core gift identification than our ability to be analytical and delve into the deep crevasses of our psyche. The final benefit
of doing this in the company of another person has to do with the idea
of the witness—at the moment when you discover your core gift, it is ex-
hilarating and deeply rewarding to have another person there to say, "I see
you for who you are." Your psyche is appreciative of any opportunity to
be seen accurately, and the feeling that results can, in itself, contribute to
your healing. One person has seen you for how you want to be seen, more
than any other way, in the world. In this moment, wherever you are in the
world, you are at home.

If you decide to invite another person into this process with you, how
do you decide who it will be? It may be helpful for you to think of the most

---

41. My understanding about the importance of environment in self-discovery processes came, in large part, from Orland Bishop—an internationally known healer and
Founder of the ShadeTree Mentoring Project in Los Angeles, California. Part of his approach to helping a person tap into their genuine authority—who they are and what the
world is calling them to be—is to help the person create a sanctuary in which they can
engage in this kind of serious reflection. He outlined the elements of sanctuary described
in this section.

important qualities you are looking for in the person you choose, rather than "how close" you feel to the person. Friendship is not a condition for assistance in gift discovery.

Within the framework of gift discovery, I believe it is generally not a good idea to choose your parents or other members of your immediate family. Because of the possibility of your suffering being tied to a member of your family, gift identification can get confusing when the very people who you believe caused your suffering are the same individuals helping you name your gift. My strong advice is to not engage in that potentially confusing and emotional environment while pursuing the naming of your gift.

Who else could you choose? Is there a person who you know would be the right one for you? One of the old ideas of mentoring is that it involves the gift in a person speaking to the gift in another person. It is worth considering who in the world may have a similar gift to you and whether or not they would be useful in this endeavor. You might also consider the style of the conversation that works best for you. Do you like a slow-paced conversation or a fast-paced one? Do you like humor? What about being asked lots of questions? Do you want to have the person mostly listen, or do you prefer them offering stories for you to reflect on?

Another consideration is the place you choose to do this reflective activity. We all have environments that we feel are more helpful than others when we reflect on our life. Some of us want to be in the woods, by a fire, in our living room, in a church, by the beach or a river. Consider what kind of place would be helpful to you in this activity, and go there. Your processes of understanding can be remarkably clearer when you attend to this need.

Next, consider the time of day. Do not squeeze this activity into the most convenient part of your day. All of us have times of day when we are most alert and able to reflect. For some it is the early morning; for others it is at midnight. Be intentional in setting up the time you will do this activity, and plan it at a time when interruptions can be controlled. For many of us, this will require asking others not to interrupt us, or finding a place where interruptions are unlikely.

Finally, it may be helpful to remember two qualities about core gifts that are often overlooked because they are so obvious. While not "environmental," they are part of the set-up necessary to facilitate a clear pathway as you begin the core gift identification process. The first is to remember that your core gift is supposed to be large. It may sound too big to be any-thing you could ever master, and that is exactly the point. Your core gift is worthy of you attending to it your whole life, so it is supposed to have enough scope that you cannot exhaust its possibilities.

The second is to remember that your gift is obvious. It is the tendency in most of us to connect our success with understanding ourselves to our level of "thinking ability." Because of this, we often make our thinking pro-cesses complex and multi-layered. Your core gift will be difficult to discern if you get invested in complicated thinking processes. Stay on the surface, and look for the obvious connections rather than probing the depths of situations. What is trying to be seen? Remember, core gifts were discern-able long before there was a therapeutic profession. Your core gift can be seen and used by you and others in the context of your ordinary life.

What are the steps in the Core Gift Identification process?

The process of finding your gift using the *Four Paths* method has a simple structure. It is in the answers you give and the resulting gift state-ment that the beauty of the process emerges. It works like this: there are four different methods, called *paths*, to identify what are called the *threads* of your life. *Threads* is just another way of saying *themes*, but the word threads is used because it implies that the themes are interwoven through-out all age periods and all activities of your life. Your core gift is one of these primary life threads. Step One has you complete as many of the thread identification paths as you choose, and within each path choose the primary, or most important, threads. Step Two has you consolidate the threads from the paths you have completed into one list, and then pro-vides instruction for how to narrow this list down to the four to six most important threads. Step Three provides instruction for how to choose your core gift from your list of four to six most important threads. Step Four outlines a simple process for making a "Core Gift Statement," which names your core gift and also identifies the primary talents you use to give that gift. Step Five, the last step, asks you to stop in your tracks and take some time to reflect on the experience and slowly re-enter your usual daily life. The following paragraphs provide a brief description of the four thread identification paths and why each produces clarity about your core gift. Following this description, the process begins!

Path Number One produces clarity about your core gift from asking the people in your life what you have brought to the relationship you have with them.

What is common about your contributions with your friends, family, and coworkers over the span of your entire life? In the midst of our daily lives, we are living and going from task to task, often unaware of how our gift and our suffering are affecting us. The question most of us have in our daily life is, "What do I need to do now to finish this task and what will the next task be?"

The people around us, however, as they continue to develop their relationship with us, have a different question about us. Instead of having questions about what we are doing, their question is, "Who is this person and what is our relationship like?" They ask this question in order to determine their level of safety and trust in our relationship, and also to determine how we might exchange our skills, talents, and gifts in service of each other and the activities we are mutually engaged in. Because the person in front of us is trying to define who we are, they are actively looking for information to answer that question. This puts them in a position, when they are looking without presupposed answers and judgments, to see both the small details of who we are and also the larger essence that we present to the world. If you ask enough people, you will see that there are easily identifiable and repeated patterns that keep showing up. One of these larger patterns will likely be your core gift.

Using Path Number Two, you identify the themes that keep reoccurring throughout your life that fall into the category of "what is similar about what I contribute to different situations I have been in?" In core gift language, these are called the threads because they are behaviors, events, and actions that are woven through and similar throughout your life. When you recall a wide variety of situations, and identify what you have brought to those situations, patterns will begin to emerge. Since we know that our core gift and our suffering are primary motivators for us, if we list the major threads in our life it is likely we will be listing our core gift as one of those threads.

Using Path Number Three, you can identify your core gift through understanding your suffering. As I said in an earlier chapter, your core gift is the opposing force to however your psyche has framed your largest suffering. By naming the part of your suffering which was most difficult for you, and then clearly describing what you believed would have stopped the suffering, your core gift can be further illuminated.

And in Path Number Four, you can gain clarity on your core gift through your connection with your spiritual practice. Through prayer, meditation, or other kinds of connection with spirit you can access messages, images, and other kinds of focus, which point in the direction of your core gift. Since our core gift is a gift from spirit, when we engage in our spiritual practice it is possible to gain clarity about our core gift through both a gift and a wound pathway.

Naming your core gift gets very focused when you use most or all of these approaches and blend the common threads between them to reveal your core gift. For each of us, there are individualized, precise, and common patterns that connect between all four of these thread identification paths. Once you have completed one or more of the methods, the next steps are designed to help organize the information you collect with each of the methods, name your primary threads, name your core gift, and develop a powerful core gift statement which you can use in many ways.

17. FINDING YOUR CORE GIFT

Are you ready to begin? To provide clarity and focus, here is a reminder of the steps you will go through to complete the process:

Step One: Using the Four Paths to Identify Your Threads
Step Two: Naming Your Primary Threads
Step Three: Identifying Your Core Gift
Step Four: Developing Your Core Gift Statement
Step Five: Leaving the Process

STEP ONE: Using the Four Paths to Identify Your Threads.

In this step, you will complete as many of the four thread identification paths as you choose. The purpose of each thread path is to identify the primary themes in your life that relate to your Core Gift. The more paths you complete, the more information you will have to accurately identify your gift. You may complete the paths in any order you choose, and do them over any length of time. There is, however, an energy that builds up once you engage in the process, and this energy is difficult to keep reclaiming if you drag the process out over a period of months. My suggestion is to complete the process over a few days or weeks.

Path Number One: Identifying your core gift through others' eyes.

I am suggesting the use of this thread identification first, because it reconfirms two important notions within core gift discovery. First, your core gift is actively a part of your life, but may be difficult for you to see because you are looking for something deep and mysterious. Second, our core gift is often more obvious to others than it is to us. It has been true for me that what I want to bring to situations is oftentimes different than what others tell me I do bring. By asking other people about your gift, you can get an accurate appraisal of the generous nature of your spirit as seen by others. You will undoubtedly get similar answers from many people, which confirms the direction of your gift.

How do you go about completing this method?

1. First, make a list of the important people from all parts of your life. This includes representatives from your past and current life, and from different sectors including work, play, community service, spiritual, schools, family, friends...the key here is wide variety. Out of this list, pick a handful (5-10), representing a cross section of your life, that you feel comfortable talking with about your gift.

2. Second, prior to asking each person to talk with you, think about how you will explain the reason(s) for asking. Generally, it helps to set the tone by telling the person that you are attempting to more closely define "who I am," and that you believe there are similarities in how you act in various situations. Seeing these similarities may be helpful to you.

3. Third, approach each person on your list. Ask him or her to think about your relationship with them from the day you met until the current moment, and ask them to name their ideas about your strongest qualities and/or the strongest contributions that you make to the mutual situations that you are in. For instance, you could ask them what you bring, more than anything, to the place you work. Or you could ask them what, more than anything else; you bring to your friendship. Notice that "more than anything else" is the key—you want the person to pick the highlights and the strongest contributions. It is helpful to get the person to limit their list to two or three different things. *Tip: It is common for people answering these questions to lump your skills, talents, and core gift into*

a general category, so you often will have to prompt them to be specific. Do not settle for an answer like, "Oh, you are a good helper." Ask the person to tell you how you are a good helper. Similarly, if the person says, "You are always so friendly," ask them what they mean by friendly. Your core gift is very specific, so you want the person to be as specific as possible.

4. Fourth, after you have asked everyone on your list, pick out the themes. What contributions are most frequently named? Are some of them the same, but with different slants or different wording? There may be many different answers, and your task is to see if you can notice the major themes sticking their head out above the rest. What is clearer than anything else? It may be helpful to organize the responses you got into different clusters that seem similar to you. Out of all the answers you have received, there will usually be three or four clusters. Be cautious about the difference between picking out the themes that you want to be there and the themes that actually are there. Using actual language from the people who have given you information, out of each cluster pick one phrase or a combination of phrases that represent that cluster accurately. List the three or four primary themes you have chosen on a separate sheet of paper.

5. Last, see if you can pick out the most dominant theme amongst the three or four phrases you have ended up with. Put a circle around it. One way to do this is to ask yourself, "If I went out and did most of the things on that list of phrases, is there one remaining item on the list that would be the result?" For example, in a recent workshop, a woman came up with these six themes:

Not afraid to face fearful situations
Good at lifting people's spirits
Stands by others
Comes up with creative ideas
Never gives up
Not judgmental

Looking at that list, she was able to see that the dominant theme for her was "Standing by others." By this, she meant that when she was willing to face fearful situations that other people were in, focused on helping to lift their spirits, tried to come up with good ideas to help the person get through their dilemma, never gave up on them, and was able to be non-judgmental, all those behaviors would result in her "standing by others." Remember, a different person with the same themes might have chosen a different dominant theme. The theme you pick out is in the area of your core gift.

If there is not one obvious dominant theme, look for patterns. Some-times, there will be three or four things that, when combined, name a specific core gift. For instance, if you get threads of "can see how it all fits together;" "always comes up with good ideas;" "listens to others;" and "isn't afraid of failing," it may be that your core gift is bringing creativity, or helping others through difficult times, or seeing structures and organizing solutions. If you get a cluster of items that you believe represents a pattern, you can also identify your core gift by looking at the cluster of items and naming what they are "fighting against." Another way of saying this is "If I wasn't doing these things, what would likely happen?" This perspective goes back to your suffering. You are doing a set of actions which, when it works, is the antidote to the primary suffering you have known. Often-times, in this moment, you will get both the naming of your core gift and increased clarity about how your psyche framed your suffering.

If you are not yet certain which thread to circle as your core gift from using this approach, don't worry. You have an important piece of the puz-zle, and you will continue to reveal more about your core gift by pursuing the other methods of core gift discovery.

Path Number Two: Identifying your core gift through the threads of your life.

William Stafford, in his poem *The Way It Is*, says, "There's a thread you follow. It goes among things that change. But it doesn't change."[42] This second approach to core gift identification comes from the belief that we use our core gift in all areas of our life. If we consider what we bring to our different life arenas, we may notice what Stafford calls the threads. The threads are the common attributes, approaches, or methods we use to bring understanding and take action across various areas of our life.

For instance, a person with a core gift in the area of creativity would rely on their creative capacity as the primary method to approach their

---

42. Stafford, Willaim. *The Way It Is*. Page 42.

life. They would look for relationships with people who are creative. Conversely, they would be attracted to helping others who were stuck because of a lack of creativity. In a dangerous situation, they would not look for the easiest way out—it is likely they would want to think of a way out of the situation that was new and creative. Instead of running away, they would ask themselves, "How can I solve this in a way that others would never think of?" They would be able to trace many of the difficulties they have faced in their life as rooted in being too creative, or in being unwilling to stick with one solution...they may see a pattern of wanting to keep using their creative powers and not be forced to make a choice. They may be resistant to working within rigid structures and following rules, and probably have a history of being seen as a troublemaker. All of the above things will be seen throughout all aspects of their life, and all tie back to the thread of being creative.

Seeing this thread can provide a deep relief for a person. All of a sudden, it all makes sense! How could I have not seen this before? This singular driving force is controlling my life. One of the fundamental benefits of recognizing this primary thread is that it instructs us that we need to at times depend on our other capacities, or other people, in order to move effectively through a situation. Our core gift wants to be used and seen, and doesn't care if we use any of our other talents or not. A life which is balanced and healthy depends on us using a wide variety of skills, talents, and external relationships. James Hollis, in *Creating A Life*, says, "One should never make a major decision on the basis of a single dream, or a single event, or a single voice. If it is Hermes, he will call upon us again and again, in dreams, in affect, in body, and in the situations which vouchsafe for a moment a vision of the whole."[43]

What is your major thread? What is the dominant talent (remember, your dominant talent is your core gift) you bring to many different situations in your life? The list of questions below can help you to discern the threads in your life by identifying the similarities between your answers.

Do the following steps:

1.   Read the questions, and for each one develop and write down a phrase or sentence that most accurately provides an answer. No-

---

43. Hollis, James. *Creating a Life: Finding Your Individual Path*. Page 111.

tice, I am asking for a phrase or sentence. The longer and more rambling your answers, the murkier and more difficult your core gift will be to identify. Keep asking yourself, for each question, "What is it, more than anything else?" Depend on the idea of common threads for your success in this core gift identification method rather than feeling the need to provide lengthy answers. Here are the questions:

a. What have you brought to many different situations throughout the course of your life? Consider when you were young, with friends, in your family, in your job, etc. List two or three attributes, skills, or talents that are common for you to bring to these settings.

b. What do you feel compelled to give when you encounter a person who is in trouble? Be specific about the kind of help you most often want to give. Is it problem solving, is it listening, is it giving the person encouragement, is it sitting in the midst of their suffering and just being there, is it telling stories? Be specific about the kind of help you most often want to give. List the one or two most important contributions you feel compelled to make.

c. What tasks are you doing when you become so engaged that you lose track of time? List moments when you lose track of time and then identify what is the common thread between those tasks...how are they similar?

d. Think of several situations where you have been in a disagreement or conflict with another person. What was your way of resolving those disagreements? See if you can identify a common thread in the way you approach and resolve conflict. Do you want to logically think your way through it, do you want to get strong emotions out, do you get really interested in the root of the other person's anger? The idea here is that we have a preferred method for moving through conflict, and this preferred method is rooted in our gift.

e. Think of several situations where you feel extremely full, alive, and grounded. What is it about those situations, or what you are doing in those situations, that is similar?

f. Think of four situations you were involved in that provoked strong emotions in you. What is the common link between those situations? (This thread may be a core gift thread or a wound thread, depending on whether or not you state it in positive or negative terms.)

g. Think of situations in your life where you have been in some kind of danger. What is common about how you have approached or problem-solved those situations?

h. Think about all the jobs, hobbies, and volunteer tasks you have been engaged in. What are similar talents you have brought to all of those?

i. How have you approached formal learning situations in your life? See if you can identify a common way you are attracted towards learning. Do you like to break things down into little pieces in order to understand? Do you like to think in big, broad, visionary terms? Are you driven by the feelings you have while you are learning? Do you like the company of others in a learning environment? What is the strongest thread for you related to formal learning situations?

j. What is a job that, if you could get it, would keep you up from excitement the night before your first day at work? What is it, more than anything else, about that job that would cause that level of excitement?

2. You have completed the questions. Next, circle the phrases or sentences that capture the primary threads you noticed between the ten questions. You are looking for three to five threads. To do this, go back and review your answers. Which stand out as the most repeated and common threads? What have you said, over and over again? The words may not be exactly the same in each answer, but you can see how they are connected. If you have several answers that are similar, but have different wording, circle the phrase you like the best. The other way to identify an important thread is to notice which answers provoke the strongest emotion in you. When you are in the area of your core gift, there will be both strong emotions and repeated answers.

3. Next, out of the threads you circled, pick the dominant one. You can do this in two different ways. One way is to ask, "What is the theme on this list that all the other themes I have chosen are serving?" Another way of asking this same question is, "If I went out and did most of the themes I have chosen, would one of the

themes on the list be the outcome or result?" Put a check mark next to this thread.

4. Once you have the three to five major threads written down in list form, and have put a check mark next to the dominant thread, you are done with this thread identification method. Save it along with the information you gathered from the first thread identification method.

Path Number Three: Identifying your core gift through your suffering.

This third method, identifying your core gift through your suffering, is not the most fun and entertaining way to discover your core gift. Using this pathway, however, can be quick, clear, and decisive. As I have said, the primary distinguishing characteristic that separates your core gift from all your other gifts is that it is the opposing force, or antidote, to however your psyche has framed your most serious suffering. Remember the stories of Mary and Tom in the previous chapter. Mary has a *core gift of peacemaking*, while Tom has a *core gift of standing by others, no matter what.* Their core gifts are different and yet they result from similar life situations. In each case, his or her psyche read the suffering situation and said, "If I could do this, or get someone else to do this, my suffering would stop."

It is difficult to overstate the desire of a person who has suffered in some significant way to bring the opposite experience to others. For instance, a person who was rejected by their family or significant people in their life may have a core gift for bringing unconditional love to others. A person who was discouraged from using their imagination may bring the core gift of ideas and creative thinking to others. A person who was part of a chaotic family may bring a core gift of structure and organization to others. A person whose family held the secret of abuse or alcoholism may bring the core gift of telling the truth. Through understanding the significant suffering you have experienced, it is possible to identify your core gift and further understand why it is so important for you to bring this core gift to others.

If you choose to use this method of core gift discovery, be gentle with yourself. If you are currently in a fragile state, consider not using this method, or use it with the assistance of a trusted ally or helping professional. However, just because you are considering your suffering does not mean you will need to excessively interrogate yourself or ramble without direction through the darkest periods of your life. Remember, your core gift is sitting on the surface actively trying to be seen. In the same way, your suffering is also sitting on the surface, trying to be seen and named.

Most readers will find deep satisfaction and revelation in using this method when it is used in combination with the other approaches outlined in this chapter. The reason for the satisfaction is that the core gift and the wound are in a dance together. When we are fully alive and aware, as my wife Gina so often reminds me, we have one foot in our gift and the other foot in our wound. In a gift discovery process, what would be the joy in focusing solely on suffering? For myself, I have a willingness to talk about my suffering if it is in the context of the capacities and contribution I intend to bring to the world. There have been times in my life when focusing on my suffering has created tremendous opportunity for healing, but the gift discovery process is asking for more than wound exploration—it is asking you to decipher the greatest contribution that you intend to make in this world. Given this context, considering both your gift and your wounds will result in the deepest satisfaction.

How can you go about discerning your gift through your suffering? Each person will have to find their own pathway into this discovery, but typical steps can be suggested.

1. The first step is to reflect on different periods in your life and what has been difficult for you during those times. Those of you who have, prior to reading this book, been engaged in self-discovery about difficult times in your life, might be able to easily identify the major event(s) that has been most difficult. If this kind of reflection is new for you, I would encourage you to use your felt senses as a way to determine your answer. What causes the largest uprising of feeling in you when you reflect on your life? Whether the feelings you have are anger, embarrassment, guilt, exposure, blame, or shame, the intensity of the emotion is the key clue to watch for. Another possibility is that there is a common kind of difficulty that you have encountered repeatedly in your life that you can name.

2. Once you have defined the event(s) that you believe has caused you the largest amount of suffering, the next step is to think back to that event and define what would have stopped the hurt. For instance, if you were not listened to, what would have stopped the

hurt is for someone to have taken the time to really listen to you. If you were part of a chaotic household because of alcoholism, someone to be dependable and take time to be with you might have stopped the hurt. If you were verbally abused when you did something wrong, it may be that what would have stopped the hurt would have been someone to give you unconditional love. Keep in mind that "what would have stopped the hurt" can be something another person could have done or something you could have done. You will be attracted one way or the other to a certain kind of answer. The only person who knows what would have stopped the hurt is you. This is not a deeply secreted conclusion—whatever your instinct tells you would have stopped the hurt is probably right on the mark. The more you use your brain in this discernment, the more you are apt to create an intellectual response which may be more pointed at what you think you should say than what the truth really is.

3. Once you have decided what would have stopped the hurt, you have identified the area of your gift—what you desire to help yourself and others attain. The words may not yet be quite as precise as they could be, but this thread is in the domain of your gift. Write your answer down, in a phrase or sentence, and put it with the other information you have gathered from the previous methods of gift discovery. Tip: Rather than using a one-word answer, see if you can add some other descriptive words to it. For instance, if you want to write down the word listen, see if there are any other words you could add to the phrase to make it more exact. One person might choose to say, "Listen without judgment," while another person might say, "Listen with respect," while still another person might respond with "Listen with a deep desire to understand what I am hearing." These descriptive words, when added to the other information you have gathered, will help you to be more precise when it comes time to name and describe your gift.

Again, this thread identification method is usually more effective, and more rewarding, when it is done in conjunction with other thread identification methods. When you have finished this method, you may want to take time to acknowledge the courage you mustered to face what has been difficult and acknowledge the truth of your story. Remember, out of this suffering has come your greatest strength. As Michael Meade says, once we understand this we can begin to think of our difficult experiences as purposeful suffering rather than purposeless suffering. It has not been for nothing that you have experienced this difficulty in your life. Much deeper than making lemonade out of lemons, your suffering and your gift are woven together to create a powerful capacity that is available to serve you and your community, should you choose to tap the immense power within.

Path Number Four: Identifying your core gift through your spiritual practice.

The final method of gift discovery is tailored to the codes, rituals, and practices of a person's faith tradition or spiritual practice. Because there are many different variations of practice, I am going to leave it to each person to determine how best to approach gift discovery within this context. There are, however, a couple of ideas that may be worth considering if you choose to use this method as part of your gift discovery process.

First, you can make a choice whether or not to use this method prior to the other methods, thereby allowing you to approach spirit with a mind that is not full of opinions—a blank slate. Or, you could do the other three methods first and bring this information to your spiritual source and ask for guidance and discernment of the different threads. Your choice in this matter is merely a personal preference—spirit already knows the answers to the questions you will be asking!

Second, this path may be particularly appealing if you believe that prayerful reflection or meditation has the capacity to make visible and to heal unconscious suffering. It is easy for me to fool myself and think I am operating out of the moment in my true and whole self, when I am really operating out of an unhealed unconscious desire seeded in my suffering. When we heal what is unconscious, we are less invested in protecting our suffering by covering our true self with unhealthy behaviors, addictions, and false truths. Can you receive assistance from spirit in bringing what is unconscious into your conscious being?

Third, it is likely that engaging in discernment of your gift through your spiritual practice will result in deeper understanding of both your gift and your suffering. It is in the unraveling of both, in a dance together, that healing occurs and our gifts can be fully understood and given.

As a last step for this method, write down what you have discovered, in whatever form makes sense to you, and put it with the information you have collected from the other methods. You may have several themes that have emerged, a story, some reflective writing, or simply an increased openness to the gift discovery process. This is the only path method in which there is not a structured requirement for the way you document what you have discovered.

STEP TWO: Naming Your Primary Threads.

How many of the thread paths did you complete? The more information you have, the easier it is to name your gift. This is because your gift, in each of the methods, is showing up from a different vantage point in your life. The more you are able to confirm your gift from different perspectives, the more accurate it becomes. If you have had difficulty with any of the methods, you may find comfort in the fact that many people struggle with some of the methods and move almost effortlessly through other methods. If you have fully engaged in the task, it is likely that you have more than enough information to name your primary threads and identify your Core Gift.

This step asks you to choose, from amongst the different threads you have discovered, the primary threads which are related to your Core Gift. Here are the instructions:

1. First, arrange the information from the last step from each of the four methods in a way you can see all of it in front of you. You may want to write the information you gathered from the four methods onto a new sheet of paper, in a list form. Take a minute to look at the information and notice what you are intrigued by—what is as you expected and what is different than you might have guessed?

2. Second, combine the information from all the last steps into clusters of similarity. To do this, I usually write each item from one of my last step lists down in a separate spot on a new piece of paper – spaced all over the page. Then I take the last step information from another path I completed, and see which items on this next path list fit with items I have already written on the new sheet. If they fit, I add them underneath the similar item I have already written. For those new items that don't fit with anything already on the paper, I put them in a new spot on the same paper – the start of another cluster. Note: When you are clustering effectively, you will end up with a range of three to six unique clusters as a

result of this step. If you have fewer than that, it is likely you are creating categories that are too expansive. Go back and make finer distinctions. If you have more than six clusters, it is likely you are not seeing the connecting links between the threads you have gathered. Sometimes this process takes some jockeying around. It may be that, when you get done, you will decide to take things out of one cluster and put them in another.

3. Third, look at each new cluster and choose a single, summing phrase from each. Now you have the clusters on a page in front of you. (Note: It is almost always true that the person's gift is represented by one of the clusters. Many people find comfort in this fact—now all that's left is the choosing.) In order to be precise about your gift, this step asks you to look at each cluster and pick one of the items in the cluster, or a combination of several items, that represents your most accurate description of what that cluster is all about. Usually, a person can look at the items in a specific cluster and say, "That one phrase is what I mean, more than the other phrases," or "I think combining these two phrases together would make a good phrase for that cluster." Look through each cluster and pick a phrase that is most accurate and compelling to you. It is often helpful to notice which phrases you are most emotionally drawn towards, and also which phrases have the most gritty, beautiful, or compelling language. Use the language in the phrases that you have already written down—do not develop a completely new set of words. The end product for this step is to have a list of phrases, one from each cluster, written on a new list in front of you. You will have anywhere from three to six phrases on this final list.

STEP THREE: Identifying Your Core Gift.

The task in naming your core gift is similar to what I asked you to do in each of the individual thread identification paths—to consolidate information and choose dominant threads. You now have, as a result of Step Two, a list of about three to six primary threads sitting in front you. The next step is to look at these primary threads and choose your gift.

To do this, you will be asked to answer four questions by putting a checkmark next to the thread on your list which is most related to your answer to each question. What usually happens is that the person begins to repeatedly check one of the threads as his or her answer to each of the four questions. When this repetition begins to happen, it is very likely that the core gift is being named. Here are the steps:

1. Answer the following questions. After you read each question, put a mark next to the phrase from your final Step Two list that most accurately answers the question for you. You can mark the same item multiple times, which is what usually happens. In fact, often-times the person marks the same phrase as their answer to all four questions. This is good news! It means your gift is in plain sight. Here are the four questions:

    a. Right now, in this moment, check the one that you think is closest to describing your gift. (This question is asked from the vantage point of your gift wanting to be seen by you. You have been walking all around it in this process, and there is a part of you that knows exactly which item on your list is your gift.)

    b. If you went out and did most of the things on the list, which remaining item would be the result of all those activities? Check that thread. (This question asks about your gift from the vantage point of logic – these actions would produce that result. Which item is the major theme? Is there is a thread on your list that all the other threads are serving?)

    c. Which one of the items on your list would you like to have gotten more of when you were growing up? Check the thread that most accurately describes this from your list. (This question is asked from the vantage point of your suffering.) Anoth-er way of asking this is, "Which item comes closest to naming what would have stopped the primary suffering you experi-enced?"

    d. Show this list of final threads to a few people in your life. Ask them to pick out the thing that they believe is most important to you on the list. Ask a minimum of three people; five is bet-ter. (This question is asked from the vantage point of other people often seeing your gift more clearly than you—after all, you are busy giving it and they are busy receiving it. What do they receive from you, more than anything else?)

2. Decide on your gift. There are a few ways to do this, and you can use them all and see how they compare.

   a. First, you may be certain of your gift at this point. Many people are. The four questions are designed to point you directly at your gift from different directions. If you know your gift for certain, you will have a physical reaction when seeing it on the page. Many people get a tear in their eye, a feeling of heightened or acute awareness, or a feeling of flushness or tingling in their body. This is your body telling you that you have accurately focused on something important, and it is putting you on a heightened state of alert. If you are certain which phrase is your gift, but you are not getting any physical reaction, it is likely that the phrase is pointed in the correct direction but is not accurate enough to cause an emotional response. You may want to go to the next chapter, Common Blockages to Identifying Your Core Gift, and read the suggestions given for clarifying the language and getting more specific.

   b. Second, are there multiple checkmarks by one of the threads? Many times, the person will know their gift because they keep checking the same thread, over and over again. This confirms the gift from multiple perspectives.

   c. Third, notice which item you checked from question c above, which asked you which one of the items you would have liked to have gotten more of when you were growing up. It is almost always true that the person's gift is linked to whichever thread they chose as their answer to that question. Remember, your gift is the opposing force to your suffering. Can you see how your answer to question c could be your gift? Notice your emotions as you consider that possibility.

   d. Last, if you still can't decide, you may want to sleep on it and come back the next day for a fresh look. Sometimes at this point the person has done so much "thinking" that they are becoming more confused than clear. What is obvious can no longer be seen. Oftentimes, looking at the page the next day, people are astounded that they couldn't see the previous day what is so obvious to them now.

   e. If you still are not sure what your Core Gift is, go to the next chapter on common blockages to identifying your gift and see if you can discover what is standing in your way.

3. Whichever phrase you have chosen as your core gift thread, use it to complete the sentence, "My gift is…"

STEP FOUR: Developing Your Core Gift Statement.

In each of us, there are two attributes to our core gift, and both are necessary to develop a complete gift statement. Core Gift Statements are composed of two sentences. The first is the gift itself. How do you describe this most significant thread and talent in your life? As a result of the last step, you now have that first part of the Core Gift Statement completed—"My Core Gift is…"

The second sentence of your Core Gift Statement describes the style you use to give that core gift. What are the specific methods you use to give your gift? If we watched you when you said you were giving your gift, what would we actually see you do? What would be your specific behaviors, thinking styles, and beliefs? The style used in giving a core gift is what distinguishes individuals with similar gifts from each other.

For instance, a teacher with a core gift for motivating others may have a style of giving this core gift which is focused on careful listening, helping people find their genuine motivation, and helping with problem solving. Another teacher, also with a core gift for motivating others, may focus on giving their core gift by giving people a verbal "kick in the butt," aggressively following up on a regular basis, and telling their own story as a way to encourage others. Although both teachers have a core gift for motivation, their style of giving their core gift is very different. Each of us, in giving our core gift, has a distinct style that we have an inclination towards. What is your style? Like your core gift, your style has been showing itself during the course of your life. You have already collected adequate information from the thread to accurately describe this style. To develop your second sentence, do the following:

1. Pick the elements of the style you use to give your gift. Look at the remaining threads on the list from which you chose your gift. Identify which of those threads that you would use if you were to go out and give your core gift today. You will see that most, if not all, of the threads remaining on your list are the exact behaviors, beliefs, and/or talents that you currently use whenever you give

your core gift. Those threads are your gift-giving style. Remember, these elements of your style are what make you distinct from other people with similar gifts. Nobody gives your gift exactly like you.

2. Make one more sentence, right underneath your final gift sentence, which starts with, "I give my gift by..." Finish this sentence by simply inserting the applicable remaining threads, with commas between each of them and a period at the end. You may have to play with the grammar of your phrases slightly, in order for the phrases to fit into the sentence. To maintain the clarity and focus of your Core Gift Statement, I suggest that you not list more than three or four threads in your second sentence.

3. Occasionally, a person wants to go back to the original consolidated list of threads they produced in Step Two and add a favorite style or phrase that pertains to how they give their gift. They just don't want to give it up, even though it didn't end up on their final list. Of course, go ahead. Just be careful you don't add so many things that it begins to look more like a list than a sentence. Short and simple clarity, coupled with beautiful phrases, are the hallmark of accurate and meaningful gift statements.

You now have a complete gift statement.

STEP FIVE: Leaving the Process.

After finishing, don't get up and immediately begin to do the dishes or any other task. You may want to take a minute to both acknowledge the beauty of your gift statement and to reflect on the suffering and joy that brought you to the point where you have this gift to contribute. The core gift statement sitting in front of you reveals the powerfulness of your place in the world, and what you intend to contribute. It is solid ground to stand on. Frequently, individuals feel emotions welling up inside them that acknowledge the hard work they have done to get to this point in their life. Here are some suggestions of things you can do as you move out of the gift identification process and back into your daily life:

1. Think of times in your life when you have given your gift and it has made a powerful difference in a situation. These memories are proof of the powerful contributions you have made to the world by giving your gift.

2. Sit in silence.

3. Engage in a ritual that acknowledges both the process you have
    been in and the outcome. Suggestions others have offered include
    prayer, lighting a candle, taking a bath, walking, consciously
    breathing, or ceremoniously adding your gift statement to your
    collection of other important personal items. Some people put
    their gift statement within a frame and put it in a place where they
    frequently see it, as a reminder of their path and their powerful
    nature.

4. Find a person to talk with about the process you have been en-
    gaged in and what you have discovered. Find a quiet moment to
    share your gift statement with a partner, your family, or other close
    person in your life. Ask them to tell you a story about a time they
    have witnessed you giving this gift in their life.

5. Think of a time in your life when you have given your gift and
    found some kind of trouble. In this moment, can you be com-
    passionate with yourself? See if you can discern what you might
    have done differently, if anything, in that situation. What was the
    trouble designed to teach you? How have you found similar kinds
    of trouble in your life

6. Use your spiritual practice to help you move out of this process.

18. COMMON BLOCKAGES TO IDENTIFYING A CORE GIFT

If you encounter difficulty discerning your gift, you may begin to ask yourself questions. Am I certain I have identified what is truly my core gift? Why are my answers so unclear? Why am I having such a hard time seeing the threads? Why aren't I more attached to my core gift? Why isn't my core gift what I thought it would be? This uncertainty is worth paying attention to, because it is usually a message that you have more work to do. This is good news—you are invested in the process and actively asking yourself honest questions. You will only get clearer by pursuing this uncertainty.

You can be sure of this: When you have discovered your core gift, you will know. My experience, and the experience of many others who I have witnessed going through the core gift identification process, is that there is little doubt when you hit the target. The words you use may be a little off, but you know the direction is accurate. Your first indication will be in the response of your physical body. If you have correctly identified your gift, you will have a physical reaction—whether it's a tear in your eye, a feeling of deep joy or elation, the hair on your arms tingling, or a sense of heightened or acute awareness—your body will tell you that you are close to something very, very important. The reaction, whatever it is, comes from the awareness that you have tapped a central piece of information about who you are. Your body, sensing an opportunity for pleasure or danger depending on what you do with the information, is putting you on alert and is poised to act. Remember: at the moment of gift discovery you are dancing around your most serious capacity and your most serious suffering.

If you do not experience any physical reaction, or you believe that you have not been able to accurately identify your gift, I have specific suggestions of next steps for you. In our Core Gift Identification workshops, we have noticed several root causes that can result in a person being blocked in their effort to accurately identify their gift. Some of the more common blockages are described briefly in this chapter, with suggestions for getting unstuck that have worked for others.

"I know what my gift is, but the information I have collected doesn't end up with that gift."

What is happening when a person's prior decision about their gift contradicts the evidence produced in the gift identification process? Three possibilities are immediately apparent. First, the evidence is faulty, or the person does not understand the evidence. The second possibility is that the person is attached to a certain imagination about who they want to be, and this imagination is different from who they really are. The third possibility is that you can't readily see how you could use the gift you identified during the process, so you want to switch to another of your strong talents and adopt it as a more useful, acceptable, logical, and employment-oriented gift.

Let's consider the first possibility—faulty evidence. One solution would be to go back to the four methods and do them once again, to compare the answers. The answers would be similar, although possibly more precise since you have a second shot at considering what you think. In a very few cases, this may be helpful and result in a change in how you name your gift. Saying this, however, I can only remember a handful of people for whom the evidence was the culprit in gift discovery blockages.

More often, the reason for the difference between what you think your gift is and the gift, which resulted from the process, has to do with what could be called the "wished-for gift." The wished-for gift is the result of one or more conditions under which a person wants to be seen and appreciated for having a certain attribute. Perhaps it is the talent or skill for which you receive constant praise and attention. Maybe it is the talent you use in a profession to which you are dedicated and want to be recognized. Perhaps you struggled and suffered through some professional training or college and want to be seen for being competent in that area. Whatever the reason, the wished-for gift brings little deep satisfaction.

We may do many things to try and convince ourselves we have a certain core gift. Our ego can be involved, trying its best to sway our decision away from the evidence. Our suffering may be trying to hide the truth of our story. We may, in an effort to be accepted by others, be responding to the needs and expectations they have of us. We may even be good at fulfilling these other-directed desires. But no matter how much we give these abilities, and no matter how much acknowledgment we receive, we still feel the emptiness in our soul. We have only satisfied what is on the top, and have not attempted to feed the depths of our deeper calling and our deeper suffering. This giving of surface-level skills and talents genuinely feels good in the moment, like the familiar sensation of so many momentary pleasures. But it quickly fades. It is the sugar rush of the false gift trying to get us to look the other way. We give our wished-for gift some more, and then some more, hoping each time we will feel the longing of our soul being satisfied. All of this is, usually, to avoid the paradox of the core gift. What deeply satisfies will, sooner or later, also deeply hurt.

If you have a difference between what you believe your gift is and what the process of gift identification resulted in, you can go to the doorstep of your suffering in order to determine the truth. Which thread is closest to the opposite, or healing force, of your suffering? In the midst of your suffering, what would have stopped the hurt? What could you or the other person have done which would have stopped the pain? Trust your feelings, not your brain. Whenever there is a question about a gift, the answer can be found if you are willing to dance with one foot in the gift and one foot in the wound—each foot making the moves necessary to locate the ground of understanding.

The third possibility is that you are not able to easily determine how you would use the gift that resulted from the identification methods. Because of that, you discount the accuracy of the gift or the gift discovery process. Occasionally, a person will say their gift is "useless," which usually means they cannot see how they could get a job and earn money by giving their gift. We are so oriented to a cash economy that we are willing to discard the most essential feature about ourselves if we can't see how it could result in employment!

It is helpful to remember, if you are trying to determine a way to make "practical use" of your gift in a job or other community situation, that your gift will be a part of the tasks within that environment, and does not encompass the full range of talents and skills you will contribute. For instance, what if your gift is "sticking up for people" and you worked in a company that manufactures chairs? Your job is to sand and varnish the assembled chairs. How could your gift apply in that situation? On the surface, it's not very obvious. But there are many possibilities. Perhaps you are the union representative, and you see yourself as sticking up for other laborers in the salary negotiations. Perhaps there is an old-timer working in the factory who isn't getting any respect from the younger workers. You step in and encourage the young people to respect their elders, telling stories about contributions the older person brings to the workplace. Perhaps you make it a habit to take new employees under your wing and help them learn the ropes and make it successfully through the first week.

All of these behaviors are part of the gift of "sticking up for people." You will notice that, whenever you give your gift, you feel a deep satisfaction that can carry you through other parts of your job that are much less appealing to you. You will also notice, once you know your gift, opportunities continually appear in front of you that offer the invitation for you to give your gift.

I met a young man this year who I was asked to help with gift discernment. When we first met, I asked him if he knew what his core gift was. He said he wasn't exactly sure, but knew he had one gift which, unfortunately, was useless in modern times. I asked him what that gift was, and he laughed while he said it was "being a swordsman." He had decided, probably correctly, that it would be difficult to find a paying job as a swordsman in the suburbs of California.

Relying on the theory that our core gift is a specific talent (sharpening swords) within a larger category (swordsman), I asked him if he could identify what he liked more than anything else about being a swordsman. He responded quickly with the following answer: "The part I love the most is how you can take the energy from their attack and bring it around to them. You block and you use their force to come back at them. It feels right to me. It's not just about winning. It's about the movement and the feel of it." I was completely awed by his ease in precisely naming the part of swordsmanship he was most drawn towards. The tone and pace in his voice informed me that he was speaking from a place inside of himself much deeper than surface-level thinking.

I encouraged him to think not only of being a swordsman, but also of other kinds of vocations that relied on the talent he had just described to me. I said to him, "That talent you described of redirecting energy back towards the person is an essential part of being a good mediator or counselor, it's an essential principle in the Tai Chi form of meditation and martial arts, and it's a basic principle underlying many healing methods. Could you imagine yourself moving in one of those directions if you could give that gift within those vocations?" This was a new idea to him, and I could tell his mind was working at considering the possibilities. Oftentimes, we limit ourselves by thinking of our gift as a specific kind of job, when it is actually an attribute that we can bring to many different kinds of jobs and situations in our lives.

Michael Meade helped me to initially understand this idea by saying, "a person might have the gift of timing...the ability to accurately know when to do something. That person might be an oarsman, striking the oar in the water at exactly the right moment. He might also be good working on an assembly line, putting the part on at exactly the right moment. He might be good at photography, knowing just the right moment to capture the image." One of the beautiful aspects of the gift idea is that it opens the possibility for the person to give their gift in a wide variety of different situations, with different people, and for different reasons. The recognition and naming of the gift provides an immediate relief to the idea that a person is limited in their capacity to contribute to their community or their own life.

Are you blocked by the "wished-for gift?" If not, see if any of the other blockages listed are helpful to you. But if you think this kind of blockage may be standing in your way, you might want to ask yourself questions like: Which one of the examples above caused me to wince and try and look the other way once again? What is the genuine source of my yearning to have a core gift that is different from the one sitting in front of me? Is the gift I discerned in the process not smart enough, good enough, not complicated and deep enough, not useful enough? What for me is "not enough" about it?

Our core gifts are on the surface, actively trying to be seen, and it is up to us to recognize the untapped power within a capacity which we have always had access to. Our attempts to discard our core gift will, in the end, cause a turbulence within us that will not go away.

"I was raised in a very good home. I can't identify any really bad things that have happened to me. I can't relate to this suffering you keep saying is the opposite of my core gift."

In talking this through with people, three reasons commonly surface as the root of this blockage. But before I go into the three reasons, I feel compelled to say something: I have never witnessed a person who, after engaging further in this conversation and the gift identification process, was not able to identify a serious suffering event(s) in their life. Suffering, like gifts, come with being human.

Now, back to the three reasons. First, the person may not want to bring their suffering to the surface during the gift identification process. This blockage may be conscious or unconscious. It could be due to not feeling safe within the environment of the conversation—whether it's the people around them, their attitude that day, or feeling like it's not the right time. They may also not be ready to uncover this suffering because they are afraid of what might happen as a result—they may fear the resulting emotions, be afraid of having to face the person who caused them harm, or simply choose not to disrupt the current status of their life.

The second reason, in some ways attached to the first, is that they are hesitant to "blame the other person." They are referring to the person they believe was responsible for the suffering they have faced. This hesitation to say "bad things" is, in my experience of listening to people, usually rooted in a fear of conflict. What if I had to face this person again? Within this category are also the individuals who are holding themselves responsible for their suffering. They believe they, in some way, deserved it or were too weak to fend off the person who harmed them. And finally, a person in this category may also be afraid to face the feelings they know are underneath the surface if they genuinely named the person and the hurt they have caused.

The third reason I frequently encounter is that the person feels their suffering is small compared to the other people in the world "who have really suffered." Usually the person will compare himself or herself to someone who was severely abused in a catastrophic manner, or possibly died as a result of their suffering. The person is sure that others' suffering is worse than theirs and they feel like they are complaining by mentioning it. I have had individuals tell me that, to talk about their suffering, was "like whining." I have had other individuals tell me "I've got nothing to complain about." *The trap of believing others have suffered more than you goes against one of the basic truths about suffering. Our psyches are not interested in comparing our suffering to others – it reads our suffering as serious, no matter what the condition of others in the world. It is our thinking processes, not our psyche, which elevate our suffering to the status of "not real suffering" or "suffering that is not as bad as others have experienced."*

I believe most of us would agree some suffering is worse than other kinds of suffering, but "rating the suffering" does not eliminate the need for each person to heal their own wounds. At some level, involving ourselves in an argument about "who has suffered more" is simply a tactic to delay facing our own suffering. Frequently, people with this blockage will talk about the need to "be strong" which, in most cases, involves trying to shut off the persistent voice of our psyche telling us there is serious healing work for us to attend to.

"My gift feels too general…it's true about me, but I don't have a strong reaction to it."

Another common difficultly reported stems from a lack of precision in naming the core gift. When this happens, a person will feel like the statement is accurate, but doesn't result in strong feelings or attachment. This is usually because the person has named as their core gift a cluster of skills and talents which carries a general and large label like "helping people;" "being kind;" "being a teacher;" or, one of the most common and least helpful outcomes, "being a parent." Because their specific gift is indeed one of the talents in this larger cluster, they get some feeling of association with the cluster but not the strong feelings that occur when the gift has been separated from the cluster and specifically named. Their frustrated reaction, I believe, is the result of an internalized knowing that there is a more accurate possibility within the general category they have named.

Within each of the general gift categories just mentioned—helping, kindness, teacher, or parent—there are a variety of skills and talents which, when used in coherence with each other, result in being a good teacher, helper, or parent. The idea of the core gift instructs us that there is one talent within that collection of necessary talents to which you are more attracted than all the other necessary talents. That talent is your core gift. Because this book is oriented towards teachers, let's take the example of a person who comes up with a core gift of "being a teacher," and feels dissatisfied with this outcome. Here is a partial list of typical skills and talents within the craft of teaching:

> Identify the sources of your own passion for the topic.
> Organize and sequence information.
> Create a hospitable learning environment.
> Use non-abusive behavioral intervention strategies.
> Encourage students to take risks in learning.
> Integrate the rules of the supporting institution within the immediate learning environment.

Out of the above list, or one a little longer but similar to it, every person who comes up with a core gift of being a teacher can locate a more accurate core gift. This precision in naming the core gift can get very explicit, particularly when you are able to identify the source of your largest suffering. Your precise core gift is the item within the list of teaching attributes that is most similar to what you believe would have stopped the suffering. I can make clear how your suffering and your core gift can be found within the list of teaching attributes by giving examples of the kinds of connections that can be made. The following are just examples, and do not represent the wide variety of possibilities within each area. Let's go back to the list of teaching attributes listed in the previous paragraph, and see how both the gift and suffering could be identified.

Identify the sources of your own passion for the topic.
> Example of possible core gift: Helping others to find their passion and act on it.

> Examples of possible suffering: Was somehow stopped from identifying or acting on something they believed in strongly, was punished for being creative, lived in a restrictive environment, was involved in an accident and couldn't achieve a dream or continue to do something they were passionate about.

Organize and sequence information.
> Example of possible core gift: Helping others to organize and create logical patterns and structures.

> Examples of possible suffering: Grew up in a chaotic home, experienced a serious event which resulted in an inability to think clearly, experienced suffering as a result of someone who was not being logical

and/or telling the truth.

Create a hospitable learning environment for learners.

Example of possible core gift: Creating welcoming and hospitable places.

Examples of possible suffering: Experienced abuse of any kind, was not accepted for a certain part of who they were, did not receive outward expressions of love, was ignored within their family.

Use non-abusive behavioral intervention strategies.

Example of possible core gift: Guiding others with respect and integrity.

Examples of possible suffering: Experienced abuse of any kind, was forced to do things they didn't want to do, did not receive praise for accomplishments, was criticized in a way that made them question their value and worth in the world.

Encourage students to take risks in learning.

Example of possible core gift: Motivating and encouraging others.

Examples of possible suffering: Was punished for being creative and taking risks, lived with a parent who was severely depressed as a result of a dead-end job, witnessed a parent or sibling suffer from an unwillingness to stand up to an abusive family member.

Integrate the rules of the institution within the learning environment.

Example of possible core gift: Being a peacemaker or being in-between.

Example of possible suffering: Grew up in a home with parents who were in conflict much of the time, lived in a home where speaking about emotions was not encouraged, suffered trauma as the result of a divorce, lived within a family with one controlling or dominating member, witnessed or suffered abuse which involved outward expression of anger.

If this kind of blockage is happens, it usually occurs at the point where you are choosing the dominant threads or common themes as the last step in each of the four paths. Go back to your chosen threads for each path and see if you have actually used your original answers when picking out the most dominant thread, or whether you saw a cluster of things and re-named it as a more general thread. The key here is to use your actual first answers as the language for the threads you choose rather than creating new language.

Another possibility is that you have chosen and written down a "big word," like love, compassion, truth, humility, or justice, as the dominant thread in some or all of the methods. These large words have multiple meanings to many people, and don't really result in a focused answer. If you have a "big word" as one of your dominant themes, go back and define, in one phrase or sentence, what it means to you. This will be very useful to you, because it will tailor the meaning of the word to your own experience and point towards your gift and your suffering. For instance, one person who comes up with a definition for compassion might define it as "being a good listener." Another person might define compassion as "paying attention to how the other person feels," while still another person might define it as "standing by someone who is hurting."

Your psyche does not care how the dictionary defines the word—it has its own definition and, for each person, his or her answer is the right one. The definition each person makes will lead them towards their gift because it precisely identifies the element of compassion to which they are most drawn. This is often a large key to identifying their gift, because it will keep reappearing with the other threads. Go back to your list and, if you have "big words," take a moment to develop a phrase that defines for you the meaning of that word.

You may also want to make a list of all the attributes of teaching, in your own words, and see if you can pick out the attribute which is most opposite of, or the antidote to, the most serious suffering which you named. "What would have stopped the hurt?"

"I have thought so much about this, and I just can't figure it out."
First of all, if this blockage is happening to you, the blockage itself may be a big clue to what your gift is. I have noticed that individuals who say they have thought about this deeply and still can't name their gift often have a core gift of helping others get clarity, find the truth, or put things in logical order. Another possible gift for a person who feels blocked in this way is the gift of helping others be seen for who they really are. After all, the more you are confused and the more you ask others for help, the more you are seen and in the company of others. This stuckness, a difficulty doing for ourselves what we want to help others do, makes perfect sense within the paradigm of gifts. What we want to help others achieve is what we struggle with the most in our lives. In that way, a person with a gift for helping others "discover the truth," "think clearly," or "be seen and

welcomed by others" may have substantial difficulty in their own life with these attributes. Our personal struggle in "giving our gift to ourselves" provides the opportunity for us to develop compassion for people in a similar struggle and gain wisdom we can relay to others.

Our organization got a call a while back from a woman who was considering coming to one of our Core Gift Identification workshops. She described herself as well educated, having extensive experience with self-reflection, and as having attended many "purpose of your life" workshops. My partner told me he spent more than an hour with her on the phone, answering question after question about the workshop. In the middle of the conversation she asked, "I've been to so many of these workshops. I never get any answers. Are you sure that I will know my gift if I attend your workshop?" He hung up the phone curious to meet this person, and wondering why she was having so much difficulty discerning her gift.

During the workshop, I sat with her small working group as they were helping each other discover their gifts. I noticed that whenever she answered a question, the first answer was never good enough. She would spin it around and around, and each time she finally allowed an answer to be written down she made a pronouncement that she didn't think it was quite accurate. As she moved through the process of gift discernment, each step proved more insurmountable to her than the last. In desperation, I finally said to her, "We spent more than an hour on the phone with you prior to the workshop answering your questions. When I walked in the door today, you came up to talk to me about changing our meeting room so it met your needs. During the first break in the workshop, you came up to me and said you felt badly because I didn't publicly acknowledge you for a comment you made in the group. In your small group this afternoon, you are unsatisfied with other people's answers and, as a result, keep questioning them about whether or not they really mean what they are saying. Now you are doing the same with your own answers. What is all that about? Is there a common link between all those actions?"

She was silent for quite some time, looking down, and then I began to see tears running down her face. As she began to weep, she looked up at me and said, "I just want to be seen for who I really am. It's not so important for me just to be noticed or get attention, as you are saying…what I really want is to be seen for who I really am." Her uncertainty about her answers, and her attention-getting behaviors were tied to her suffering, and the resulting gift was a sincere desire to help others be clearly understood and seen. Her inability to get for herself what she wants so desperately for others to receive—being accurately seen—was the result of her inability to think clearly about herself and be decisive enough to be seen accurately.

My guess is that she is very competent at helping other people to understand who they are and be accurately seen. Such is the paradox of gifts. There is wisdom in this paradox that is difficult for us to see in the midst of our oftentimes-frustrating attempts at understanding and giving our core gift.

The second thing I notice frequently when people say they have thought about this a lot and still can't come up with their core gift is that they are using their thinking skills as a way to avoid facing the truth of their suffering. "The longer I think about this and use my logic to keep finding patterns and connections, the more likely it is that I will find my gift." A person in this condition often speaks about not being able to get to a deep enough level of thinking, or believe their answers are not accurate enough. Of course, they are headed for disaster in a gift identification process. The answers you give are the right answers. What is obvious about the answers—what is on the top wanting to be seen—is most often the greased path into identifying your gift. The fog, which can be produced by hammering away at thinking processes, produces an increased inability to name the gift. I suspect this is the intention of many who express this type of confusion.

The way out of this is to change your orientation from a thinking process to a feeling process. Answer your questions from a feeling center in your body rather than from your brain. This will re-orient you in the correct direction and get you back on track.

Closing Note.
In the end, if you are completely blocked and just cannot name your gift, perhaps you have done enough for now. The inability to name your gift may simply be a message that the end product is not the most important part of the effort for you right now. You have started down a road that may involve some starts and stops. Once the gift idea gets into your psyche and begins to work, it is likely that you will keep coming back to it—curious about how you can understand more about and be enlivened by this greatness you are bringing to the world. I would encourage you not to think of a failure to name your gift as a failure of either you or the process.

It would be an easy way out to blame both. It is more likely that what has occurred within you as a result of your effort is exactly what should have occurred at this time. You have opened the door, and the light from your gift is already shining through. Sometimes time is necessary—more than skills, processes, and investigations—to fully reveal the truth about parts of ourselves. When you are ready for the next level of understanding, the voice of healing within you will appear on your doorstep.

INDEX

Note: Footnotes are indicated with a "n" followed by the footnote number.

BOOK ORDER FORM

The Teacher's Gift

Questions?	1-800-594-8766
Fax Orders:	206-463-6311
Email:	bookorder@communityactivators.com
Telephone Orders:	1-800-594-8766
Postal Orders:	The Teacher's Gift
	P.O. Box 328
	Vashon, WA 98070

Please send____book(s) at $16.00 each plus $4.00 shipping.

Washington residents please add $1.41 sales tax for each book.
Shipping note: Books will be sent priority mail (3-day delivery guarantee).

Name

Address

City   State   Zip

Telephone   Email

Payment method:

☐ Check enclosed   ☐ Visa   ☐ Mastercard

Card number   Expiration date

Name as it appears on card

Billing address (if different from shipping address)

Books may be purchased at reduced rates in quantity (5 or more copies) by
emailing bookorder@communityactivators.com.

Printed in the United States
39129LVS00004B/13-114